FROM OHIO TO OKINAWA...

My Father's Stories of Life, Death and Survival on the Battlefields in the Pacific During World War II

Jeff Snook

No part of this publication may be reproduced in whole or in part, or stored in a retrieval system, or transmitted in any form or by any means, electronic, mechanical, photocopying, recording, or otherwise, without written permission of the author, except for the inclusion of brief quotations in a review.
For information regarding permission, please write to:
info@barringerpublishing.com

Copyright © 2025 JEFFREY A. SNOOK
All rights reserved.

Barringer Publishing, Naples, Florida
www.barringerpublishing.com
Design and layout by Linda S. Duider

ISBN: 978-1-954396-95-1

Library of Congress Cataloging-in-Publication Data
From Ohio to Okinawa . . .
By William E. Snook and Jeffrey A. Snook

Printed in U.S.A.

FROM OHIO TO OKINAWA . . .

DEDICATION

⁓

This book is dedicated to the 16 million men of the U.S. Army, Marines, Navy, Air Force and Coast Guard who sacrificed and accomplished what needed to be done to win World War II.

. . . Especially to the 407,316 who gave all and never made it home to this great country we call the United States of America.

May their legacies and ultimate sacrifice live forever in our memories and in our history books.

And may their stories, like the one I am about to tell, always be told unapologetically and truthfully with the utmost pride and reverence.

Finally, to my children, Savanna and Dillon, may you always remember and remain very proud that you are grandchildren of a World War II hero, who gave four years of his life to fight for a much greater cause than himself.

■ JEFF SNOOK

JEFF SNOOK

TABLE OF CONTENTS

DEDICATION iii

INTRODUCTION 1

CHAPTER ONE
    "Am I Dying Today?" 17

CHAPTER TWO
    The Snook Heritage 27

CHAPTER THREE
    When the World Changed One Sunday 41

CHAPTER FOUR
    From Camp Wolters to Fort Ord to Paradise 56

CHAPTER FIVE
    The Sights, Sounds and Horror of Saipan 69

CHAPTER SIX
    Boating and Fishing "Unfairly" on R&R 88

CHAPTER SEVEN
    Okinawa 95

CHAPTER EIGHT
    Meeting Ernie Pyle 106

CHAPTER NINE
    Uncle George and His Famous Commander 112

CHAPTER TEN
    The End of World War II............................ 127

CHAPTER ELEVEN
    Victory Accomplished, Returning Home............... 134

CHAPTER TWELVE
    They Were Made for Each Other 143

CHAPTER THIRTEEN
    We Were Baby Boomers.............................. 155

CHAPTER FOURTEEN
    The Wonderful Woman Dad Fell in Love With.......... 165

CHAPTER FIFTEEN
    Dad, Me and Our Love of Sports 179

CHAPTER SIXTEEN
    Like Dad, I Dodged a Few "Bullets".................. 199

CHAPTER SEVENTEEN
    Hawaii: Our Mutual Paradise......................... 218

CHAPTER EIGHTEEN
    Saying Goodbye: Their Final Years.................... 236

CHAPTER NINETEEN
    My Sister Becky 268

CHAPTER TWENTY
    Legacies: What We Leave Behind 279

AFTERWORD.. 293

JEFF SNOOK

FROM OHIO TO OKINAWA...

INTRODUCTION

"You got any draft beer here?" he would ask the bartender.

"Sure do!" would come the reply. "And this one is on me! Thank you for your service, sir!"

That was an interaction I witnessed dozens of times over the years.

You see, my father liked to drink a cold one.

Not just a cool beer that was canned or bottled, but an ice-cold, shivers-to-the-spine DRAFT BEER. In fact, I saw him often drop an ice cube or two into his suds if it wasn't the proper temperature.

"Well, we had access to beer during the war once in a while," he would explain. "We could buy it in Hawaii for a nickel a can, and we had it on R&R in the Pacific, but we didn't always have ice to keep it cold. And I never liked warm beer..."

For the final 25 years of his life or so, Dad often wore a black hat with the words "World War II Veteran" adorned on the front. On the right side of it, he had pinned a few of his medals, such as his Bronze Star.

That was his title, and those were the symbols which made him so proud. They were a large part of his legacy, and he fully realized it. When he put that hat on his head, it was like wearing a badge of honor to him.

Most servers and customers of restaurants and bars across the country appreciate our veterans, especially those from World War II. I saw first-hand how often he was treated so well, always with reverence, and it always warmed my heart.

I'll give you another example: Mom, Dad and I were sitting in a restaurant in West Palm Beach one night, when a young boy, no older than 10, approached Dad.

He nervously turned to look back at his parents. He was timid and shy, and after all, he was approaching a stranger, something I am sure he had been taught not to do.

"Go ahead!" his father told him. "You can do it! Tell him!"

He then extended his hand, which Dad shook.

"Thank you for your service, sir!" the little boy said.

Dad patted the boy on the head and said, "Why, thank you, son! I sure appreciate that!"

The little boy turned and ran back to his parents, his good deed accomplished. I could tell he was proud of himself for doing it.

I looked at Mom and she had tears in her eyes. So did I.

What I often witnessed being in Dad's presence as he progressed into his late 80s and then 90s was as if fellow citizens realized our World War II vets were dying by the hundreds every day, about to go the way of the dinosaurs. Their existence and accomplishments had largely faded into the history books.

Most people had just wanted to show their appreciation for what these elderly men had sacrificed so many decades earlier, years before most of them were even born.

And now that great man is gone, too, and I am left with the hundreds of pictures, a few videos and a lifetime of memories of him and the stories of what he did for us—his family, his community and his country.

Do you remember that generation that helped win World War II, the one they called the greatest?

"The Greatest Generation."

My father was part of that.

For that matter, so was my mother. Through my parents and their many friends and their stories of yesteryear, even as a kid, I was always drawn to those who were a part of it. From hearing

FROM OHIO TO OKINAWA . . .

about their Manhattan-sipping, draft-beer drinking, swing-dancing nights to the stories of their penny-pinching days and hardships surviving the Great Depression to winning the big war and saving the world, I loved hanging out with and talking to all of them.

I could relate to them as much, if not more, than anyone my own age. Plus, they had much better stories. They faced hardships and survived. They believed in the basics of happiness and living a meaningful life: Having a roof over their head, a church in which to worship, food on the table and a good family and friends to share their love and laughter.

As I grew up, along with my sister and brother, we were raised by two of the best sources who lived through it all.

They were part of "the good ol' days" that really weren't that good or prosperous at all, most of the time, that is. But they still had a world of fun along the way. They lived their lives to the fullest even when their bank account was somewhat empty.

I don't know how to fully explain it other than when I watch movies like *From Here to Eternity*, or *Casablanca*, or *It's a Wonderful Life*, I want to go back in time. Maybe I have romanticized the World War II era too much and too often in my mind, but there is no underestimating the effect that the big war and those who fought it had on the world as we know it today.

American soldiers, sailors and airmen and their sheer strength, resolve and patriotism, were the main reasons it was won by the good guys. They sacrificed and went to battle so freedom could ring throughout most of the world today.

Make no mistake, I fully realize—as most Americans should realize for many generations to come—that the war was mostly pure hell on earth for those who fought in it . . .

For men like my father: William Edgar Snook Sr.

William "Ed" Snook, making a toast with his favorite beverage, 2011, at the age of 92.

Although everyone who knew him just called him "Ed," he fit perfectly into it and was directly out of central casting.

When he was younger, he looked like a cross between Dean Martin and Tony Curtis, with dark black hair, a prominent nose and a clef in his chin. He was a handsome guy, possessed a great sense of humor and was as tough as a two-dollar steak.

Dad was born January 21, 1919, in the small town of Ashland, Ohio, a place he loved but knew he had to leave—as well as leaving his job, his parents and six siblings—in the summer of 1941 to train to fight for his country if America ever entered World War II.

It was already raging full throttle in Europe.

During that summer, before most Americans had ever heard of a faraway place called Pearl Harbor, most people figured war would soon be on the United States' doorstep.

Of course, it arrived on one Sunday morning 18 days before Christmas—the country, and the world for that matter, was shocked by what happened on December 7, 1941. And with it, that distant fear turned into an instant reality.

Soon after Pearl Harbor was attacked by Japan that morning, Dad and his 27th Infantry Division comrades were shipped from Camp Wolters in Mineral Wells, Texas, to Fort Ord in Monterey, California, and then to Sand Island, Hawaii to prepare to battle the Japanese military in the Pacific Theater.

For the following four years, he was a soldier on the battlefield, at times barely surviving all the brushes with death which an intense ground war offers. He was brave at times, scared to death at others, but he always gave it his all in combat.

When it was all over 47 months later, and the good guys had won, he returned home, met a 19-year-old girl named Ferne Darlene Biddinger, asked her out, then married her, and they eventually had three children.

Of which I am the youngest.

As I said, my father was proud of his service to his country. He was proud of his comrades and how they fought, and proud of the missions they faced, which they ultimately won. They finished undefeated in battles. But the ones who returned had lost friends and comrades along the way. They saw death up close, and the inches that came between it and survival.

This may seem strange, but Dad was proud he survived the war, because there were many days and nights in which he believed he wouldn't. He always told us how he felt so very lucky and fortunate to return home.

The reason was simple: He saw so many of his brothers-in-arms, close friends, die right next to him. For a few, the final words they ever heard on this earth came from my father's mouth. Dad realized that more than 405,000 others—the U.S. death toll during those fateful four years—did not make it home. He was proud of the end result and also proud he lived to tell about it—so proud that he talked about the war often.

I am well aware of what was more common: Many veterans don't speak about the wars in which they fought. They don't detail the horrors, the lasting nightmares, the gruesomeness of it, or the how's and why's of what they experienced.

But my father did.

Often.

At times, those memories consumed him, he admitted.

In fact, he talked about it so often that when he started with, "One time, during the war . . ." we, his children, as well as Mom would smile and look at each other. We knew what was coming. We were about to be entertained with another story from somewhere in time from 1941-45.

Make no mistake, we never really tired of hearing his stories and it was not that they bored us, we smiled only because we had heard many of them several times before. We knew some of them by heart. Still, we listened once again, only because we knew he was so proud to tell them. I like to think he was brave for reliving them all over again. The fact is, we all loved his stories.

But we loved him even more.

I like to think that my father just had that same effect on people which he had on all of us. I would categorize him as a genuine "people person" and I would be shocked to hear if anyone who knew him didn't like him. He was just a lovable guy. He also lived his life by Will Rogers' quote: "There are no strangers, only friends I have not yet met."

Dad had a big smile, a big laugh, a big personality and a big heart.

It was rare when he and I walked into a bar or restaurant when we didn't walk out without him making another friend. On top of that, Dad possessed supreme character and integrity.

He stood for all the right things.

To me, and to my family, he was a hero—our hero.

When he told an intense story of the battlefield, however, he usually added a self-deprecating line along the lines of, "But I was just one soldier, one of thousands . . ."

After experiencing the utter brutality and gruesomeness of combat, and that thin line—inches at times for him—which separated those who came home from those who did not, I know he realized he was given a second chance at life once the war ended.

Because he often said so.

"There were so many times I just didn't think I would make it to return home," he said.

Therefore, once he did, I am sure that he figured, "Why not make the most of it?"

I am also sure he believed that he owed his buddies who died next to him that much. I once watched the movie *Saving Private Ryan* with him and that final line uttered by Tom Hanks' character—"Earn this!"—rang true with my father.

I watched that movie for the first time with Dad, while on vacation on the Big Island of Hawaii, where he spent much of 1942, and when it was over, he became emotional. That movie took him right back to the war, because it was so accurate, so true to what he experienced.

The opening scene of American soldiers storming the beach at Normandy on June 6, 1944, was exactly what he experienced 10 days later, halfway around the world in Saipan. He saw buddies next to him drop over from a sniper's bullet. His fingers shook after shooting enemy soldiers. He saw bodies obliterated and mutilated.

My father earned it alright.

He earned every day, month and year that passed after October of 1945.

Most of all, he knew that his country, and this may sound corny, but it is so true—and his countrymen—were worth fighting and dying for. He was just that patriotic.

I remember one time while he was in his 80s, my parents attended a social gathering when a younger veteran from the Vietnam era, a man who was a friend of the family, happened to voice some complaints about benefits the Veteran's Administration had not covered for him. He made the mistake of turning to my father to ask him if he ever had the same complaints, given that Dad had lost almost all of his hearing in his right ear during the war after a shell exploded near him.

For lack of a better word, my father got downright pissed off at the guy's question.

"You know, the way I figure it, this country really doesn't owe me a damn thing," Dad said forcefully. "I am the one who owes my country . . . and I owe it everything I have."

The younger vet didn't say another word about the subject.

Yet, it was once a discussion between my parents at the dinner table and I overheard it. At times, Mom became exasperated with him over his less than perfect hearing. It was frustrating for her and she once demanded he press the issue with the VA about seeking coverage for his often-failing hearing aids.

He often would fumble with them or bang them against something to get them to work. I often heard them whistling from a room away.

"Ferne, let me say this one more time and this will be it!" he said to her. "I did not go fight for my country in order to receive free health insurance or to get money from the government. I did it because it was the right thing to do! And I would do it all over again for nothing in return. And if I had to sacrifice my hearing, while other guys sacrificed their lives, so be it!"

That summed up my father in a nutshell. And to my knowledge, at least in front of us, my mother never broached the subject again.

My father loved many things, besides that aforementioned cold draft beer. He loved either peanuts or popcorn to go along with it, the Cleveland Indians, Cavaliers and Browns, the Ohio State Buckeyes, playing basketball almost every day with his buddies at the local YMCA (until he was 85 years old), fishing for perch or walleye on Lake Erie, a good ham and Swiss sandwich with hot mustard, just about any soup, any Clint Eastwood movie . . . in fact any show or movie with horses, cowboys, or guns.

"I would have made a great cowboy in the 1800s," he once told me. "Those guys had to be tough just to survive. They rode horses, could shoot pistols and rifles, and beat up the bad guys . . . all the stuff I love."

But we all had no doubt he loved our mother the most.

When he returned from the war, his old job at A.L. Garber's Manufacturing in Ashland was waiting for him. It was there he met the secretary seven years younger.

They went on their first date November 30, 1945, and were married exactly seven months later, on June 30, 1946.

And they really were a match made in heaven.

They were married for 72 years, and it may seem strange, but I never remember them having many cross words between them, apart from that brief spat about his VA benefits.

Their marriage of almost three-quarters of a century symbolized what Dad stood for. He was a man defined by a simple number: One.

One wife.
One family.
One hometown.

One state.
One flag.
One country.
I like to believe he spent his life extremely loyal to them all.
In fact, he was devoted to those things to the very end.
And what's not to love about that?

Anyway, while spending my career as a sportswriter, I usually had a tape recorder close by for most of my adult life. And as Dad told one of his many war stories during his final years, whether it be from a barstool somewhere or from my dining table in Florida while he ate breakfast or played cards with Mom, I often turned it on and peppered him with questions.

Dad would talk and I would tape him. And along the way, I too slipped in a few good stories of my career. Dad was nothing if not a good listener, too, as much as he could anyway with his hearing impairment. In turn, he loved my sports stories as much as I loved his war stories.

I never thought much about what I would do with all those recordings, other than pass them down to my children to ensure they understood what their grandpa once did for his country. That is, until a spring morning in 2015 when I grabbed my coffee and walked into my dining room at our home in Atlantis, Florida. I sat down next to Mom and Dad as they played their usual morning game of gin.

That was the manner in which my parents started most days during the last 20 years or so of their lives. They would sip their coffee, and after Mom served Dad his cereal, toast and sometimes a grapefruit or a banana, one of them started dealing from the deck.

Their games were either hearts or gin. My father, among his other talents, was basically the unofficial card shark of the family, since he had an almost perfect memory of what cards had been played and what was left in the deck, and a lifetime of experience of playing virtually every card game there was. Along with other couples, they often played euchre or bridge, too.

I often joked that I wanted to plop him down at a blackjack table in Las Vegas and let him go to work, but his hearing loss would have prevented any money-making scheme I had concocted. Nobody can beat six-deck blackjack, anyway, no matter what was portrayed in the movie *Rain Man*.

Anyway, every winter after Dad had retired in 1985, my parents spent those months with me in South Florida, staying either in a nearby condo in Lantana, or later with me and my family, in a guest bedroom of our house when he became too frail for my mom to take care of by herself.

And their morning routine never altered, no matter where they were.

As the years wore on him, and Dad lived into his 90s, he always wore that hat I had mentioned or another with a red 27th Infantry logo. They both were a matter of pride for him. As I pushed him in his wheelchair, people everywhere would reach out to shake his hand with these words, "Thank you for your service!"

He would always smile and thank them back. And a free beer now and then was common.

"Dad, I really think you wear that hat just for the free beer," I joked to him more than once.

He always laughed at that one.

Anyway, one day in 2015, I told him, "Dad, you have told us your war stories forever . . . It's time for us to write a book about them."

I then laid down a yellow legal pad and started my tape recorder again.

"A book?" he asked. "About me? I don't know if I am worth writing about. I was just another soldier. But I can tell you my stories . . . if you want to hear them again. I think the younger generation needs to know about that war . . ."

There wasn't any question I asked which was off-limits to him, either. I wanted to know every detail of what combat was like, those times when bullets, bombs and body parts were flying, because Dad was right in the thick of it.

How did that feel to save a man's life? What was life on the battlefield like? Was it close to what the movies showed? Did he ever kill an enemy solider, and if so, how did it feel to take another man's life?

He would answer them all in great detail, and in great honesty. I want to add that his language was not always politically correct by today's standards, and he used terms in describing the Japanese army and its soldiers that were very common for his time, especially during a time of war. I will not change his words here, for accuracy's sake, nor will I apologize for him.

Even though I was born in 1960, somewhat late to be the son of a World War II vet, the more I read and understood over the years, I felt an obligation to tell their stories, specifically—his story.

Many World War II vets grew up somewhat poor, were raised by honest and strict parents with strong values, and worked like dogs to put food on the table; they were as honest as the day was long; they wanted no part of the government supporting them in any way, even during the Great Depression; and yet, they were damn patriotic; and they also seemed to love the simplest things in life—a good ballgame to watch, a card game to play, a good drink before or during dinner, the U.S. flag to honor and stand for, and a family to raise.

I sincerely believe they stood for the good things in life. The best things. The greatest things.

And I always wanted to write a book about it.

The problem was, I got bogged down with a few other writing projects which came with deadlines and time passed.

And passed . . . and passed some more.

And then Dad passed, too.

My father died about three and a half years after that day I told him of my intentions, on the evening of November 17, 2018, to be exact, and I was to blame for an unfinished book of his life.

But as I continued to write following his death, I started to realize something else. This book had a deeper meaning. This wasn't only about him and his sacrifice and his effort for those four years in service. It was about the legacy he left behind. My parents' legacy.

It was also about me, my brother, sister, the seven grandchildren and the 11 great-grandchildren who followed them. It also was about my relationship with him and the many stories and laughs we shared together.

We all not only loved, we widely worshipped my father for what he stood for, how he fought and almost died for his beloved country—but also for how he lived the next 73-plus years after he came home.

All of our lives now are intertwined with his legacy.

Our lives are due to his legacy—and Mom's too—and the fact he came home from the war when so many others did not. Maybe it was luck at times, as he said. And maybe it was divine intervention, an act of God perhaps.

I will tell you that he believed in both.

Anyway, when soldiers like him were fortunate to return home in 1945 and '46, they married and fathered children—and that is how the Baby Boomer Generation was created.

And I am a part of that.

Five years after Dad died, in 2023, my daughter Savanna came to me and also wanted to know more about my life. She wanted to know my stories—and her grandfather's—as well as our family background.

Of course, his were of much more significance. His were life-and-death. His service to his country provided a much greater cause.

Mine were of a sportswriter who was fortunate to write about great athletes and coaches, memorable games and events, and encounters and friendships with a few familiar names along the way.

I, too, ironically and for some odd reason, later lost the hearing in my right ear and have faced more than my share of near-death experiences, but none had to do with fighting for our country. None had to do with securing freedoms we often take for granted.

My dad was the real hero.

I am only the son of a war hero.

Our collective stories became part of the book you are now holding in your hands.

Of course, as I said, my biggest regret is that I didn't tell his before he died.

I do feel guilty in the irony that I never missed a deadline during my newspaper career. If a game ended at 11 p.m. and I had to have my story filed by 11:15 p.m., I sent it by 11:14. No problem. I made it. I always made it.

But not this time. This undoubtedly was the most important deadline of my life—to write a book about my father, our relationship, and his generation and to tell his story in time for him to read it— and I missed it.

That's one crucial lesson you learn as you grow older: Your friends and family will not be here forever. As the years pass, your losses mount and the number of funerals you attend grows.

Nevertheless, I still believe Dad's life is one worth telling, if only for a glimpse into one of the 16 million American heroes who served their country during World War II.

Their stories are worth being told and worth knowing, and I had unfiltered access to only one of them: The American soldier whom I knew best.

Oh, let me get back to that cold beer thing. My mother would be mortified I began a book about him in this manner. She was a woman who always purchased Dad's beer at a drive-through store, so nobody in town would witness her placing alcoholic beverages in her shopping cart.

But don't get the wrong idea. I will state right here and now that Dad was always responsible. He knew when to stop. They both did. At home or at dinner, he usually stopped at two or three beers, and I saw him have more than that only a handful of times in my entire life.

And in his defense, each of those were due to my influence.

Mom always claimed, "Jeff, he never drinks more than two . . . unless you are around him!"

She had me there. It now seems so ironic to think that in the beginning of my life, he would pick me up and prop me on a stool of a bar somewhere near Lake Erie, order a Pepsi or a Coke for me while he and his fishing buddies downed a few beers and laughed it up.

Then more than 50 years later, near the end of his, when he could not take but a step or two, I had to push him in his wheelchair if we ever wanted to go out for a cold one together. I then would help him up to a barstool, fold his wheelchair and stash it somewhere nearby.

That is life's natural course, I guess. It always comes full circle—if you are lucky.

The fact is, when I think back on all those great times we had together, it wasn't that I wanted to entice him with one more cold one, it is just that I never wanted our moments together to end.

He was that much fun to be around. In fact, they both were.

So, I guess you could say that my father and I collaborated with something we both did best.

He talked about his memories.

And I wrote about them.

In between, we drank a cold draft or two and laughed a lot.

These ensuing pages are the result of it all . . .

So, here's to you, Dad. Thank you for your service. Thank you for your heroism. And thank you for sharing your memories with us.

I often envision you up there, sitting on Heaven's bar stool with your U.S. Army buddies, reliving how you all did your part to win the big one.

Cheers!

■ JEFF SNOOK

Dad in 2017 at the age of 98, sipping a cold one in Florida, wearing his favorite hat.

CHAPTER ONE

"AM I DYING TODAY?"

There was that horrible question again, whispered from my father's lips. I heard him ask it over and over again during the month of November of 2018.

"Am I dying today?" he would ask.

And none of us could give him the answer.

Or even wanted to think about the answer.

This was a time I always had dreaded. As the years passed, and my father's age grew into his late 90s, I often wondered how the end would be for him.

How would he pass from this earth? Where and at what age? My father's side of the family lived lengthy lives—my grandfather Franklin Snook lived to be 98. Four of Dad's six siblings also lived into their 90s.

He was now 99 years and 10 months-plus old and approaching his 100th birthday on January 21, 2019, but now it became obvious to us that he would not reach that milestone of living a full century.

Leukemia finally was winning its long battle, taking over his frail body. He had been diagnosed several years earlier, but he didn't hear the doctor's diagnosis, so only me and Mom, along with my brother Bill and sister Becky, knew it. And we agreed not to inform him of the diagnosis.

He had what was called chronic lymphocytic leukemia, which grows slowly, and some patients endure it for several years before finally succumbing to it.

Thus, we all agreed: There is no effective treatment for someone of his advanced age, so why discourage him with such bad news?

Over that year, however, he started to lose more and more hair with each shower, a sure symptom of its devastation. Dad had always had a full head of dark hair, and he was noticing his hair loss, too.

"Look at this!" he told me one day that summer, running his hand through his thinning hair. "What the hell? I think I am going bald!"

He also often asked me, "Why am I so damn tired? I am sleeping 12 hours a day now . . ."

At times I wanted to, but I never could tell him the truth.

It was in the middle of the night on October 21 when he sat up in bed and was very confused. He didn't know where he was or even remembered Mom's name. He was talking gibberish, she said. He also was sweating profusely.

That is when she decided to call 911. The responding paramedics rushed him to the hospital in Ashland before doctors told her he must have suffered a slight stroke. Two days later, she admitted him to the nursing home down the street.

Mom was simply worn out at that point, having cared for Dad daily for several years. He hadn't been able to walk as well and needed to be pushed in his wheelchair everywhere outside of the house. His hearing impairment grew worse by the year. His blood pressure was high. He had diabetes. She had prepared his every meal, looked after all of his medication and waited on him, as the phrase goes, hand-and-foot.

She was very tired.

I flew from my home in Florida to Cleveland two days later and drove directly for Brethren Care Nursing Home. I met my brother Bill, who had just left his room, in the parking lot, and we walked back into his room to see him lying there in his hospital gown, frail and weak.

It was a sad sight.

"Look who's here," Mom announced as I walked in the room. "You've been waiting for him . . ."

Dad weakly held out his hand, which I shook gently before I hugged him. The way he looked at me . . . I could tell immediately that he realized the end was near.

"Am I dying today?" he would ask.

"I don't know Dad," I would say over and over again. "Only God knows . . ."

As I wrote in the Introduction, he had lived through the horrors of battle in World War II, spending almost four years of pure hell on earth too often in the Pacific Theater.

He had been drafted in the fall of 1941, before Pearl Harbor was attacked, and emerged from that grand event of world history more than four years later, with a Bronze Star and several other war medals.

But what he brought home—most importantly—was the rest of his life to live.

He didn't waste any time, asking that young secretary from work out just a few days after meeting her. Their first date was less than two months after he returned.

"He was the perfect gentleman," Mom said. "He always was a gentleman. I could tell right away that he was different from other boys I had dated. He had character and integrity and would always do the right thing, or at least he would try to. I always felt completely safe with him."

Following that first date, at least the way Mom told it, they both knew they were meant for each other, marrying on June 30, 1946, at First Christian Church in Ashland.

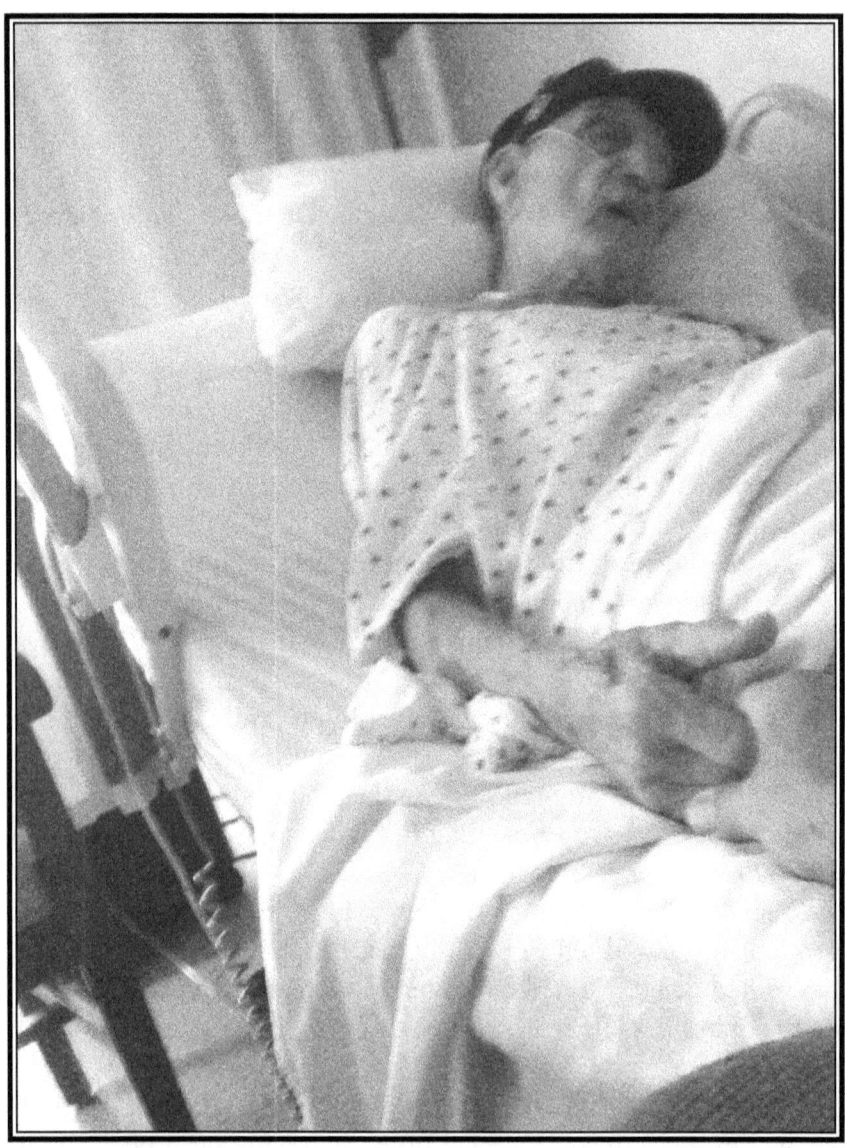

Near the end of his life, Dad wasn't talking much from his nursing home bed, unless he was thanking a nurse or an attendant who cared for him. But he could squeeze my hand. And of course, he wanted to wear his World War II Veteran's hat.

They had three children: Rebecca "Becky" was born on March 1, 1948; William E. "Bill" Snook Jr. on July 19, 1952, and eight years later, on March 21, 1960, I came along.

It wasn't until I was 14 when I began to fully realize what a great man my father was as well as the heroism he had exhibited in the past. But I had to hear it from someone other than him.

As a young boy, I didn't know anything about the war, his part in it, or the Greatest Generation in which he so perfectly symbolized. I didn't fully comprehend that he had fought for his country in faraway Pacific islands with names such as Saipan, Enewetak, Ie Shima (not to be confused with the more well-known Iwo Jima) and Okinawa.

Most of my knowledge of the war—and Dad's role in it—would come later, as I grew into adulthood.

It was June of 1974, when Mom and Dad decided to throw a small party in our backyard, in honor of a couple visiting us from New York for a week. They weren't just any guests, but one of Dad's buddies from the 27th Infantry Division. They had talked over the telephone, but they hadn't seen each other in the three decades since the war had ended.

"They were camping at Pleasant Hill Park, and he looked on map and saw Ashland was close by," Dad explained. "He called us and asked, 'We would like to stop and see you for a few days. Can we park our camper in your driveway? We'll stay in it if you don't have room for us.'"

So, that is what they did.

John and Cora Lewis camped out in our driveway for a week that summer. Before they arrived, Dad had told Mom that he didn't think either of them drank alcohol, so they would not be serving beer or wine at dinner.

"Then we drove to the grocery store because I had to get a few things and Cora asked me, 'Do you mind if I buy a bottle of wine for dinner tonight?'" Mom recalled.

From that moment on, the two couples who didn't know each other well got along perfectly. Mom and Dad decided to throw the party that following Saturday, inviting dozens of their friends from around town.

Anyway, on the afternoon of the party, I remember it was very warm. There I stood, minding my own business under one of our huge Weeping Willow trees in the backyard, munching on some shrimp cocktail watching my parents and 40 or so of their closest friends indulging with some adult beverages.

I surmised our guests must have been a special couple because we rarely had shrimp cocktail. I was taking in the scene, wiping cocktail sauce off my shirt when my dad's infantry buddy walked over to me.

John was carrying a camera when he struck up a conversation. I had noticed him throughout the week taking pictures of almost everything, from our trees to the birds to the horses at the farm across the street, all things I pretty much took for granted.

After some small talk about the weather and how Ohio was different from his native New York, and how much he loved our Midwest countryside, he got right to the point.

"Let me show you something, Jeff," he said.

He pulled out his wallet, which included one of those fold-down, plastic photo binders. It unraveled about two feet toward the fresh grass I had just mowed hours earlier.

"Look at these faces . . . my wife and all my favorite pictures of my kids. I have a great family. I love these pictures because of what my children mean to me," he told me.

He now had tears in his eyes.

Where is this guy going with this, other than thinking he must have been a really proud father, I wondered. The photos of his kids ranged from their youth to their early adulthood. Their names were Greg, Jerome and Nancy and they were 24, 22 and 20, respectively.

Then he pointed to my father, who had a beer in one hand and his other arm around Mom's shoulder.

"Look over there," he said. "What do you see?"

"Mom and Dad," I said.

"I see a hero," he said. "My personal hero."

What he said rattled me.

"That's a great man right there," John told me. "Do you know what he did? Did he ever tell you about me?"

No, he hadn't, I admitted. I truly had never heard of this guy before the week began.

"Well, let me tell you that every face in all these photos right here exists only because of your father," he said. "None of them would be possible without him. And I wouldn't be here talking to you today without him."

Those tears were now streaking down his cheeks, and he had my full attention.

"Well . . . did he ever talk about Saipan?" he asked.

Saipan?

What did I know about Saipan? I was just a naive country kid who had just mowed the yard, as was one of my weekly chores, got dressed and hurried to the appetizer table which held the shrimp cocktail. We had not taken any courses in school about American history just yet.

Anyway, John Lewis began to tell me his story. As I would learn later, it was in June of 1944, when the 27th was taking on mortar and machine-gun fire on the island of Saipan, where the Japanese army was entrenched. It was one of the fiercest battles in the Pacific—and winning it was paramount to winning the war.

The Allies desperately needed that island in which to build airstrips so America's bombers could take off within flying distance of Japan and other nearby islands in the Pacific.

But during an intense battle one night, John got hit with something in his side, felt an intense pain and jumped into a fox hole. He had an open wound and was in danger of bleeding out and dying right then and there, with no medic in sight on the front lines.

Within a minute or so, Dad jumped into the same foxhole to take cover, finding John already in there, gravely wounded.

He spent the next few minutes working frantically to save John's life, which I will describe in greater detail later, and it would result in a lifelong bond of two ex-soldiers. They got to know each other in the worst possible way, fighting for their lives in a foxhole with one of them seriously wounded.

Now here they were, some 30 years later almost to the day, sharing a drink and laughter in our backyard.

"I was a sergeant at the time and John put me in for the Silver Star, but they awarded me the Bronze Star instead," Dad explained to me. "I didn't really care about any medal at that point. I just wanted to live through the war. And so did John. So, I did my part as far as helping him achieve one of our goals.

"I always joked with him back then if he had been an officer, I would have gotten that Silver Star. And John would laugh every time I told it.

"Anyway, I guess we always had a special bond after that."

Dad had requisitioned some souvenirs from the Japanese army near the end of the war, things I saw in our basement over the years. One of them was a Japanese "knee mortar"—which essentially was a small grenade launcher with a base.

From April through September of 1945, Dad and the rest of the 27th were on Okinawa. Aside from combat, he also was managing H Company's motor pool at the time.

One day, he took a knee mortar from a heap of dead Japanese soldiers, wrapped it in a towel and stuck it under the seat of a Jeep. He then wrote down the Jeep number. When Dad arrived back in Tacoma, Washington, that October, he located the Jeep as it came off a troop ship, confiscated the weapon and stuffed it in a bag for his train ride back home to Ohio.

Now I am sure he broke some sort of rule by doing it, but at that point, what would they do to him?

Later that night, after John told me his story, Dad showed him to our basement. So, I followed.

I often had noticed this odd-shaped weapon, about 30 inches in length, sitting on the end of our bar along with Mom's bowling trophies, and I never gave it another thought. I never knew what it was, nor had I asked Dad about it.

I had no idea that it had been one of the most effective Japanese weapons of World War II, accounting for an estimated 40 percent of American casualties in the Pacific, according to the war historians.

Dad picked it up and handed it to John.

"John, this is the weapon that hit you," he explained.

John stood there in the bowels of our basement, staring at the piece of killing equipment and I wondered what must have been going through his head.

I didn't have to wonder too much longer, because the tears started running down his face again.

I really don't remember him saying another word. I think he was just too choked up to say anything. It was as if the trauma of that June day of 1944 came rushing back to him all at once 30 years later. He held it for a minute or so, then handed it back to Dad.

Within a day or two, John and Cora Lewis left our house and drove back to their home in Endicott, New York. I never saw him again.

But I will always owe him in ways I could never repay him.

What he told me that day started to change my perception of my father. In my eyes, he went from being a hard-working father, just another guy in town who went to his job every day during the week and tended the yard and our garden on weekends, to a brave World War II hero in only a matter of a few minutes.

That is the time it took John Lewis to tell me his story.

As I grew into adulthood and more years passed, what happened on that hot summer day of 1974 made me more than curious. It made me want to learn all about my father and his time in the war. He had told us many war stories over the years, including a lot of funny ones, but they had always been offbeat little tidbits or anecdotes. They never revealed his heroism.

We had been growing up in the shadow of a decorated war veteran and I just didn't realize it.

As he reached his 90s, that is when I wanted to know everything. He had saved at least one life, which had resulted in many other lives being lived. His bravery in battle also surely saved other lives along the way over those four years of 1942, '43, '44 and '45.

Now here we were, 73 years after the war ended, in a nursing home on the edge of town, his family gathered at his bedside, and unfortunately, his life was nearing its conclusion.

Dad's long journey had been well-lived, rich with great friends and family and memories, plenty of love and laughter. It was obvious that he had but a few days left.

It was if he wanted to know when his day was coming. Thus, he continued to ask the same question over and over again each day . . . one we hated to hear.

"Am I dying today?"

CHAPTER TWO

THE SNOOK HERITAGE

It had been a long, winding, amazing journey for our father from the time he was born in 1919 on the north side of Ashland, Ohio, to the nursing home on the south side of town.

The distance from his boyhood home at 1415 Cottage Street to that bed where he now rested for his final days was only three miles.

The timespan, however, covered 99 years, nine months and one week to the day he was admitted.

Throughout his long life, Dad only knew of his family history—his heritage, roots and ancestors—from what he had been told by family members over the years.

Having been born when he was, just two months after the end of World War I, he never learned how to use much technology, other than he became pretty good at handling that remote-control soon after my parents bought their first color TV sometime in the early 1970s.

He just began to learn the basics of computers near the end of his career when he managed the shipping and warehouse of a large frozen-food business in the early 1980s.

Also, because of his severe hearing impairment which started during the war and grew progressively worse over time, he rarely talked on the telephone over the last two decades of his life or so.

I still can clearly recall the final phone conversation I had with him. It was in the summer of 2006 after Mom and my sister Becky had flown from Cleveland to California. I was heading to the San Francisco airport to pick them up before the three of us would spend a week in nearby Carmel-by-the-Sea.

I called to ask if he had delivered them to the airport on time.

"THEY SHOULD BE ON TIME!" he yelled into the phone. "TAKE CARE OF YOUR MOTHER FOR ME! BYE JEFF!"

And that was it.

He couldn't make out any of the questions I asked in vain during that call which lasted just a minute or so. He gave me the information I needed, got to the point and then hung up.

Therefore, it always had been up to Mom to handle any telephone communication to and from him. She would relay any message he had for friends or relatives out of town. When I talked to her, I could always hear him in the background, saying, "Tell Jeff this . . . tell Jeff that. . . ."

And that's how we communicated from four states and 1,200 miles away.

So, naturally, like most people of his advanced age, he never learned how to access the Internet when it came along.

I, however, could and should have conducted my research of our family background much earlier. It wasn't until 2020, when the covid pandemic consumed the country and the world, and I had some time on my hands, I finally decided to dig into our family roots.

When I was finished, I know Dad would have been proud and intrigued by it all. And I would have absolutely loved to see the look on his face as I had read to him what I discovered about our family tree, and the details, dates and names of his ancestors which he never knew:

As far back as I could discover, a man named Jacob Schnug Schnuck, born on May 17, 1655, in Vielbach, Germany, would be my great, great, great, great, great, great grandfather.

There are SIX greats in there.

Jacob eventually married a woman named Anna Margreth Hauser, and they had a son in 1700, naming him Johannes William.

Johannes would be the adventurous ancestor we owe so much to, because from what I discovered, Johannes immigrated to North America from Germany sometime between 1718-38. Just as importantly, he made one other significant change.

Upon his arrival in New York, long before Ellis Island even existed, he changed the family name from Schnuck to Snook.

Johannes eventually settled in Amwell in the then-colony of New Jersey. He had married a woman named Cateron Ketcham, and they had a son in 1738, naming him William.

William Snook eventually moved to Hartley Township, Union, Pennsylvania, and married twice. He had one son with his second wife. Matthias Snook was born August 16, 1775—a year before the birth of the United States.

Matthias married a woman named Maria Christina Kleckner and they produced John Snook, born December 2, 1817. John married a woman named Mary Homan and they named their son, born in 1841, after his father.

John Snook Jr. grew up and married Sarah Ann Eighinger. They eventually moved even farther west to settle in the tiny town of Ashland, Ohio.

Ashland is the heart of Ashland County, in north central part of the state, almost smack dab between the state's two largest cities, Cleveland and Columbus. It is the town where our family tree planted its roots. Today, its population is slightly more than 19,000.

But back then, it was much less.

It once was a town anchored by its various factories, including one of the larger rubber and balloon factories, The Faultless Rubber

Company, in the world. Faultless moved to Ashland from Akron in 1907 and was the town's largest employer for almost 100 years. In fact, Ashland still is known as the "balloon capital of the world," and celebrates that title with an annual hot-air balloon fest each summer.

Other factories in town were the A.L. Garber Company, Meyer's Pumps and Hess & Clark. It also was home to a large Archway Cookies plant, which was later purchased by the Lance Company in 2008.

Also, Ashland was and still is a town surrounded by farming communities, as well as a significant Amish population.

And it is the town in which we were all born and raised.

John Snook Jr., the ancestor who led the family to settle there, was tragically killed in 1880, at the age of 39, in a timber-cutting accident somewhere north of town.

He would be my great-grandfather.

"John Snook Jr. created a school north of Ashland, called the Snook School," Dad once told me. "He really was known as an educator. But he died early . . . I never really knew the details of how he was killed, but I knew it involved cutting timber."

At the time he died, he left behind a nine-year-old son, who had been born May 8, 1871.

His name was Franklin E. Snook, my grandfather.

When I have told people over the years that my grandfather was born only six years following the end of the Civil War, during the Reconstruction period of the United States, many often have looked at me like I am crazy. Then I can always tell that they are doing the math in their head, trying to figure out how that could possibly be.

But it is true.

"Yep, we are stretched apart, that's for sure," Dad once said. "My dad was a very smart man and a hard worker, always working two jobs. He even once drove cattle from Texas all the way to Ohio in the late 1800s. He rode a horse and wore a pistol just like the cowboys in the movies.

"He married Mom late in his life. He was working as a foreman at Faultless during the week back then and also moonlighted on weekends as a butcher at the Sloan Meat Market downtown . . . he rarely took a day off.

"That's one reason we always ate well when I was growing up, even during the Depression. We had plenty of meat he would bring home after cutting it and we also planted vegetable gardens out back of our house."

And that also is how my grandpa one day met a girl 20 years his junior, Treva Mae Sprinkle.

"Mom was working at the telephone company back then and it was located above the meat market in the same building," Dad told me. "She walked into the meat market one day and that is how they met . . ."

They were married on July 7, 1912. He was 41 and she was only 21, which I am sure would have been almost scandalous at the time, especially in a small town like Ashland.

But from what I knew, from Dad's stories, they were happily married for the next 57 years.

From my limited memories of him, Grandpa Snook was very dignified and very, very quiet, at least by the time I knew him when he was in his 90s. I can still picture him sitting in his rocking chair in their living room smiling, not saying a word, wearing a dress shirt and tie. He always wore a dress shirt and tie, no matter what day of the week it was. Even in all of the pictures I have ever seen of him, he was wearing a white dress shirt and a tie.

As kids, we just didn't visit Dad's parents that much even though they lived in the same town, in the same five-bedroom, two-story white house on Cottage Street where Dad and his six siblings were raised. The house, built in 1914, still stands.

My grandparents, Franklin E. Snook and Treva Mae Snook, circa the 1950s.

FROM OHIO TO OKINAWA...

When we walked in the back door of it, on the first counter we came to, Grandma had placed a huge turkey roaster, where she always stored her freshly made cookies.

She would always tell us, "Go grab a few cookies!"

We went to Sunday dinner there perhaps only two or three times each year and spent several Christmas afternoons there over the years, after we had already opened our presents at home.

But for some reason, I just never felt comfortable there since things seemed so formal. I don't even remember the TV in the living room ever being turned on. And Sundays, at our house after church, was always reserved for watching football. I couldn't wait to get home just so I could watch the Cleveland Browns on TV.

But there was no doubt that Dad and his siblings had great parents, at least from all the stories he told me about them.

"Mom was a wonderful mother to us all. She was a giver, not a taker... She was such a great cook and made sure nobody was ever hungry. The homeless people had a way of marking the curb in front of our house with a stone, because they knew that's where they always could get a free meal. It was their way of signaling to the other homeless in town or who were passing through that they could get something to eat at that particular house.

"It would be normal for us to be sitting at the supper table with a stranger eating there with us. Mom wouldn't turn anyone who needed fed away if they knocked on the door asking for food. And she wouldn't have them eat outside, either. She had a big heart and cared about everyone, even the strangers who happened by our house during..."

My father's childhood was likely typical for Midwestern boys during the 1920s and '30s: He learned great values from his parents, went to school daily, church on Sundays, and was taught to always help others who were less fortunate.

And for that time period, there were many.

"I had what I thought a normal childhood was supposed to be," Dad told me. "We worked hard. We played hard. We loved sports. And we loved our parents and each other. There was no TV back then, so we listened to the radio just to see what was happening in the world. But unlike a lot of families at the time, we had plenty of food on the table. I never considered us to be poor like so many other families were."

Dad had a lot of siblings to love, or to sometimes argue and fight with. He was the fourth of seven children.

Each of them became very accomplished people in their own right.

Of his four sisters, Frances was the oldest, born September 7, 1913, six years before Dad came along. She became a registered nurse and served in that capacity for the U.S. Army during World War II. She later married and moved to Penn Hills, Pennsylvania and raised one child.

Alice, born April 10, 1915, never married. (Mom once told me that a young man broke her heart when she was in her 20s and she just never tried to find love again). She remained in Ashland and worked her entire career at Faultless.

Carrie, born December 18, 1917, married and moved to Fort Myers, Florida, where she raised seven children.

Betty, born January 27, 1924, also remained in town, and worked as a registered nurse at Doctor M.A. Schilling's office, where we all received our shots and whatever we needed when we were children. She married a man named Myron Ekey, who spent much of his adult life in a wheelchair due to multiple sclerosis. They raised two children.

As far as Dad's two brothers, Dad was especially close to his brother George, who was born December 26, 1920, and was only 23 months younger. While we were growing up, he and his family (Aunt Barb and their four children) lived on Sandusky Street across town, and they were very close to us. We saw them often until he was transferred through his job at Ohio Edison, and they moved to Springfield, Ohio, in August of 1973.

Richard was the baby of the family, born June 3, 1928. He married and moved to Euclid, Ohio, where he raised a family of three children.

To their older sisters, Dad and George were the lovable little brats who were very bothersome while growing up together.

"Piss and vinegar . . . ," Aunt Alice described to me once about Dad's boyhood antics. "He was just full of piss and vinegar!"

That was her way of saying Dad was mischievous. Alice was one who always got directly to the point.

"I often wanted to smack him on his head!" she said.

Dad admitted, "George was not as ornery as I was. But he did what I told him to do. I usually got into everything when I was a boy, and I did what I could just to annoy my sisters. We had only two toilets in that big house, so with nine of us living there, the girls often would have to use the outhouse out back.

"Well, in the winter that wasn't a very pleasant thing to do. They would bundle up in heavy coats and George and I would notice them. I would give him that look, and we would grab our baseball bats, wait until the perfect time, sneak around back and time it perfectly so we would deliver a nice loud thud to the back of the outhouse. You would hear whichever one of them was in there screaming bloody murder at us. Then we would run like hell . . .

"But I picked on George, too. I didn't want anybody at school or in the neighborhood beating him up. That was my job, but I really took it easy on him. I knew how to fight, and George didn't. When he got picked on by some older neighborhood kids, or got beat up, I took care of him . . . one day, I came home from school, and he was sitting on the curb crying his eyes out . . ."

"What's the matter?" I asked him.

"Some kid beat me up," he answered.

"He identified the kid, and I told him, 'You come with me!' The kid he named was a well-known troublemaker. So, we went over and knocked on the kid's door. When he answered, I grabbed him by the shirt and dragged him out into the middle of Cottage Street and whipped his ass.

"Then I told him, 'Nobody beats up my little brother—but me!'

"The truth is, George always was a gentle soul. He didn't like to fight with anyone. I am sure he got his gentle side from Mom. She was that way, too."

One of their neighbors on the other side of Cottage Street happened to be an elderly Civil War veteran who had been partially blinded on the battlefield. Thus, Dad did whatever he could to take care of the man, bringing his groceries home, running errands for him and taking care of his property.

"I would walk to his house and sit on the front-porch swing with him and then ask him to tell me all of his Civil War stories," he said. "I loved listening to him, hearing all of his battle stories.

"But he couldn't see well enough to mow his yard, and he couldn't afford to pay for it, either. Problem was, I wasn't yet strong enough to push those old manual lawnmowers . . .

"So, I would walk behind that mower in front of him and I became his eyes . . . I steered it as he walked behind me pushing it, providing the strength to get it through the grass. And that is how we worked together to mow his yard. He didn't pay me anything and I didn't want any money for it . . . I just wanted to help him mow his yard.

"I like to think he paid me with his war stories. I was fascinated by the Civil War, and I would sit and listen to him talk for hours. Even back then, when I was a kid, I guess I loved hearing war stories."

One of Dad's part-time jobs while growing up was working at the old Ashland airport, located just north of town on Route 250. A man named Walter Shuey, a trained pilot, operated the airport.

"Walt had been a mechanic in World War I, and he liked me hanging around the airport. I would ask him all about the war and he would tell me his stories . . . then eventually he gave me some odd jobs for a little money," Dad recalled.

"Anyway, he had bought a single-engine Stinson airplane, and he had added an extra seat to it. He would fly people around the area in that extra seat and he often flew it up to the Cleveland Air Races.

"Whenever he had that seat open, and I was allowed to go, he would always take me with him. Then when we flew back home, he would let me fly it into town visually until we got to about 1,000 feet. I had a lot of flight time in that thing, but I never got to land it. He wouldn't let me land it. I would bring it into the airport and then he would take over the controls."

At the Cleveland Air Races, sometime in the 1930s, Dad happened to meet a pilot who would become one of the most famous and influential aviators in American war history.

His name was Jimmy Doolittle.

"Walt knew him well," Dad explained. "One day, he introduced me to him. I actually shook hands with Jimmy. I remember the three of us stood there talking a long time. He asked me a lot of questions about what I wanted to be when I grew up, that sort of thing. He was a fascinating man. And to think he later became a national hero . . ."

Doolittle, a former World War I pilot, was later called out of retirement at the age of 45 after the Japanese bombed Pearl Harbor. He was appointed to plan a long-range bombing mission of Tokyo, which became the famous Doolittle Raid on April 18, 1942. (He was portrayed by Spencer Tracy in the movie *Thirty Seconds over Tokyo* and by Alec Baldwin in *Pearl Harbor*.)

Anyway, the Doolittle Raid was a huge success and helped turn the momentum of the war toward the Allies, before the atom bombs were developed and ready for use. He later served as a commander

William "Ed" Snook, Ashland (Ohio) High School, 1938 senior class photo.

FROM OHIO TO OKINAWA...

of the U.S. Eighth Air Force in Europe in 1944-45 and did not finally retire until 1959. He was presented the Medal of Honor by President Ronald Reagan in 1986. Doolittle died in 1993 of a stroke at the age of 96 and is buried in Arlington National Cemetery.

And to think, Dad once shook his hand and talked to him . . . years before the Doolittle Raid took place.

That gives me chills.

Still, Jimmy Doolittle was likely the second-most famous World War II pilot, following a man by the name of James Maitland Stewart, who will enter into the Snook family story a little later.

"I read a lot about the wars in school, from the Civil War to World War I," Dad explained. "That material was never boring to me. I wanted to learn why they started and how they were fought and how politicians conducted them . . . and I had two friends telling me first-hand stories of each of them, so I was ahead of the other kids when it came to that subject."

Besides war history, Dad was a natural-born sports fan. He played most of them, listened to them on the radio as a kid and watched them on TV much later as an adult.

"I loved every sport, although we didn't have TV of course to watch them when I was a kid," he said. "My dad had always been a big Yankees fan, and I rooted for the Indians as a kid. He just loved Babe Ruth. He took me to League Park in Cleveland a couple of times when the Indians played the Yankees."

Although he also played baseball and boxed a little, Dad's top sport was basketball. He was named honorable mention All-Ohio in 1937 and '38. What makes that interesting is that his junior year was the final year of the "center jump rule," in which the ball was tipped off at midcourt following each made basket. As a senior, the new inbounds rule took effect.

"It was a big adjustment," he said. "I was the captain of the basketball team, and we had some pretty good teams. But I knew I wasn't going to college. When I graduated from Ashland High

School in 1938, I didn't know immediately what I was going to do . . ."

Meanwhile, living only two streets away and several blocks to the south from their house, at 1113 Troy Street, was a 12-year-old girl. She was from a very poor family but was an A-student, would become a high school cheerleader and later blossom into a beautiful young woman.

Her name was Ferne Darlene Biddinger.

FROM OHIO TO OKINAWA . . .

CHAPTER THREE

~

WHEN THE WORLD CHANGED ONE SUNDAY

It seemed the country was changing rapidly in the late 1930s. The Great Depression, which saw massive unemployment and homelessness throughout the United States, was finally nearing its end and the economy was improving.

By 1938, President Franklin D. Roosevelt's "New Deal," a public works spending project to help get Americans back to work, was showing some results. The first minimum wage was established at 25 cents per hour, which led to Dad getting a 10-cent per hour raise.

A new house cost an average of $3,600 while a new car sold for around $860. Gasoline cost 10 cents per gallon, a postage stamp was three cents, and a loaf of bread sold for around seven cents. The superstars of American music were guys named Benny Goodman, Tommy Dorsey and Artie Shaw, who headed big-band orchestras pumping out swing and jazz. Rock and Roll had yet to be invented, as Elvis Presley was just a three-year-old toddler living in a shotgun house in Tupelo, Mississippi.

Overseas, a dictator named Adolf Hitler had plans to conquer the world, and while Roosevelt warned that Nazi Germany's rise was an increasing threat, he still wanted America to remain neutral.

Most U.S. citizens at the time agreed with their president, because memories of the first World War, in which the U.S. lost 117,000 soldiers, were still fresh in their minds even though it had concluded two decades earlier.

And it also was the year Dad graduated from high school.

A year later, on September 1, 1939, Hitler's troops invaded Poland, thus officially kicking off what eventually would evolve into World War II.

The following May, Germany invaded France, and the great war was expanding by the month because of the Nazis' aggression.

The United States enacted the Selective Training and Service Act four months later, creating the first peacetime draft in U.S. history. The government then imposed a total embargo on all scrap metal shipments to Japan, which had sided with Nazi Germany in its desire to take over the world. The country was rapidly losing its neutrality, and it appeared it was only a matter of time before it would become a large participant in the war.

Most men ages 17 to 35 were paying close attention to world events, either from listening to the radio or reading newspapers, fearing their futures would soon be dictated by America's ultimate decision whether to remain neutral or to join the expanding war.

Anyway, I'll let Dad tell it the way it was at the time . . . his recollections from a series of taped interviews over the years:

"After I graduated from high school in 1938, The Great Depression was still on for the most part, and there were not many jobs available, but I had one and I was happy with it . . .

"I had taken a printing course and had been working as a printer at A.L. Garber's for only 15 cents an hour. Then I soon got a raise to a quarter. Garber's was a manufacturer and one of the biggest employers in town, having something like 600 employees . . .

"I thought then I was making good money, and I also had a lot of friends working there, but I knew it looked bad as far as what was going on in the world. Everyone figured we would be in World

War II sooner or later, so I decided I would do my part: I decided I would join the navy.

"I rode my motorcycle up to Cleveland one day in the summer of 1939, to take the physical, but I was completely shocked when I didn't pass it . . . I had broken my nose playing basketball, and the navy doctors said I couldn't breathe properly. They also said I was flat-footed, so they rejected me."

After the disappointment of not getting into the navy, Dad knew he could either continue working, enlist in the army and see if he would pass that physical, or maybe wait to be drafted in the coming months.

It was May of 1941 when he decided to quit his job, with the agreement it would be there if he wanted it when he returned from completing his service to the country. He then organized a bucket-list trip with three of his buddies, who also were about to enter the military, taking a six-week journey across the country on their motorcycles.

Their names were Ted Deever, Ed "Buck" Bentle and Howard "Cockey" Morekel.

"I was 22 years old. We all knew we were going into the service at some point, and we thought, 'Who knows what will happen to us over the next few years? So, let's go see the country first and have some fun,'" he said. "At that time, we were young and naive, and I don't think any of us had ever been more than 100 miles from home . . ."

When Dad told his parents of the plan, they simply told him one thing: "Ride safely and don't speed!"

"At first, we were just headed to New Orleans and back because we had heard of how much fun it was. Then we all decided, 'Oh, well, let's go all the way to the West Coast' . . . so that is what we did.

"We left Ashland and averaged about 250 miles each day, first heading south to Kentucky, through Tennessee and Mississippi on the Natchez Trail and then along the Mississippi River. The

Dad, in 1941, on the back of his 1939 Harley-Davidson.

roads back then weren't that good. They were either brick, asphalt, macadam or oiled gravel, nothing like the wide-open, two-lane, smooth freeways we have today . . .

"Ted rode his Indian Chief and the other three of us rode Harleys. We wore matching uniforms, so a lot of people thought we were policemen on motorcycles. I had saved $220 for the trip, but we could buy gas anywhere from eight to 18 cents a gallon. When we saw a filling station, we would fill up because they were few and far between. For breakfast, we could eat at restaurants and get an egg with toast for a nickel. For lunch, we would eat a lot of hamburgers, which cost 10 cents most places . . . we also carried canned salmon and beans and often we just pulled over and ate lunch under the shade of a big tree. We would stop when we saw orchards and we ate a lot of peaches and apples . . .

"We went through Mobile on the Gulf and headed west until we reached New Orleans. We spent two nights at a hotel on Bourbon Street for two dollars a night. They were dormitory-style rooms. I never saw anything like New Orleans and a big city like that with hundreds of people were just walking around the streets everywhere . . . .

"Some of the people in the South still had a Civil War-type of mindset and may have still hated Yankees like us, so you had to watch what you said to them. Still, most people everywhere we met were friendly to us. They accepted us and we never had to worry about crime or all the things that happen today . . .

"It was the first time I ever tasted oysters—and I loved them immediately. From that point, I always loved them. We had a few beers on Bourbon Street, but we weren't drinking a lot of beer on that trip. Most of us drank pop . . .

"We took most of our baths in creeks along the road somewhere. I carried a bar of soap and powdered toothpaste. I would shave about twice each week, just so I wouldn't grow a beard . . .

"Somewhere out in the country in Louisiana, we stopped at a dairy farm to get some milk, and the farmer asked us, 'Anybody know how to milk cows?' I told him I did, so he let us all sleep in his barn for free, and when we woke up that next morning, I milked his cows for a few hours to pay him back. Then he had us up to his house for a nice breakfast. Most people usually welcomed you with open arms in those days. They weren't scared of four young unshaven guys on motorcycles like they would be today."

From New Orleans, the four rode their way west through Dallas.

"I remember riding by a school in Arlington and this large group of girls came running out to stand along the road and wave at us as we went by. They were all wearing high heels and dresses and they didn't look like any girls we went to school with . . .

"We then worked our way through New Mexico, Arizona and the desert. We finally made it all the way to Santa Barbara. I remember we found a citrus grove there and then we walked down to the beach, sat there and ate oranges while looking at the Pacific Ocean. I was just flabbergasted. The sand was so soft. We were used to Lake Erie sand. But that Pacific beach sand was just so soft on my feet. I will never forget it. I could have sat there staring at the Pacific all day. It was the first time any of us saw an ocean. We had only seen Lake Erie before that. We all tasted the salt water. We knew enough not to drink it, but we brushed our teeth in it . . .

"Ted had a great voice, and he started singing, 'My Bonnie lies over the ocean, my bonnie lies over the sea, oh bring back my Bonnie to me . . .' at the top of his lungs. You could say we felt like we were on the top of the world . . .

"Then we rode north along the coast to San Francisco, and we saw the Golden Gate Bridge. What a sight. When it was time to head back east, we started along Route 50. When we reached Colorado, I remember all of us racing to get to the top of Pike's Peak. The Rockies were just as beautiful as the Pacific Ocean . . .

"I remember Buck was riding tail then. We would always rotate what order we were in and when we got down to the bottom of the mountain, Ted and Cockey and I stopped to stretch our legs a little bit and Buck didn't show up. I threw my hand up to signal the first car that came by, and the guy stopped and said, 'I'll bet you are hunting your buddy . . .'

"Yep. Where is he?" I asked him.

"He told us an oncoming car had gone left of center and brushed Buck, knocking him off of his bike. So, we all headed back up that mountain and found him on the side of the road. He wasn't feeling too good. He had hurt his shoulder and arm, and he thought for sure he had a broken wrist. The other driver had stopped and told us he was a traveling salesman who was running late for an appointment, and he had drifted into the other lane. He didn't want Buck to call for the patrol because he could lose his job, but we were not anywhere near a phone anyway. His bike was smashed up and he wouldn't be able to ride it all the way back home. The guy handed Buck $50 and went about his way. We found a farmer who had a trailer and put his bike on the back of it. We took him and his bike to the nearest train station, where he bought a $16 ticket to get him through Chicago and then on to Cleveland . . .

"It took him 10 days to get back home and we took only seven. We beat him back home by three days. But he healed up pretty good in a few weeks. By the time we returned to Ashland, we had traveled more than 6,000 miles in six weeks, and we spent no more than $30 on gas and $60 on hotels per person . . .

"It was the best time of our lives, at least until that point, but we knew everything was about to change for us. We talked a lot about it, too. We knew we were all going into the service, but didn't have any idea a war would be coming right away. We were figuring each one of us would be in from 21 to 24 months or so . . .

"Then I got my draft notice when I got back. I can still remember reading the words, 'Your friends and neighbors have selected you

William E. Snook, U.S. Army, 1941.

to serve . . .' What friends? What neighbors? I thought that line was kind of funny. We were not in a war then, but I knew the military was always short of infantrymen and most draftees became infantrymen . . .

"So, as it turned out, I went into the draft, instead of getting into the navy. The draft was for 18 months of service at that point, and that sounded better than the navy commitment to me anyway, which would have been for four years. In the meantime, I had wrecked my Harley-Davidson motorcycle going up the Cleveland Avenue hill in Ashland. There was a small piece of road missing . . . I didn't see it and I hit that hole, going right over the handlebars and landing on my face. I must have rolled about 100 feet. I broke my nose again pretty bad, so now I was worried about that affecting my military status again."

My father's serial number was 35028489. He officially became a member of the U.S. Army on October 8, 1941.

Those four motorcycle explorers then went their separate ways to serve their country . . . and all four would serve in the Pacific Theater.

Buck joined the army and became part of General MacArthur's 6th Division. Ted joined the navy and spent the next four years at sea. Cockey would join the U.S. Army Air Force and would fly bombing missions.

Dad was part of the 27th Infantry Division, 106th Regiment, H Company.

"I said goodbye to all my friends, hugged and kissed my mother and sisters, shook hands with George," Dad recalled. "And I told them, 'I'll be back . . .'

"On my first day in, they sent me to Cleveland. I passed the physical with no problems. My broken nose and deviated septum never came up for some reason and I never asked . . . it was not an issue. Then they put us on a troop train to Fort Hayes in Columbus, where we underwent our first training for about one week: How to march, how to salute, who to salute, the what's and why's of the U.S. Army . . .

"Looking back on it now, I really think I adapted pretty well. I had played sports and always considered myself to be a team player, and it was not that big of an adjustment for me, but some guys struggled with authority. They didn't want anyone telling them what to do . . .

"At that time, however, it seemed like nobody wanted to be in the infantry because that was a hard life for most guys. I wasn't worried about the physical part of it. They assigned us to Camp Wolters in Texas, and we were sent down there from Fort Hayes. It was a new camp, and one of the nicest of its time, located in Mineral Wells, about 80 miles from Dallas. There were about eight battalions and more than 25,000 men there at the time. It was the country's largest Infantry Replacement Training Center . . .

"I learned how to handle a machine gun and shoot an M-1 rifle and we got in an awful lot of good practice on the shooting range. We also trained in maneuvers, hiking 20 to 26 miles on any given day with a half-pack, which weighed about 40 pounds, on our backs. I was in wonderful physical condition then and I would finish it and be home at our base camp an hour or two ahead of some of the other guys . . .

"I also was on the camp basketball team. Most guys on the team told the coach they attended college somewhere, so when he asked me if I had, I just said, 'Yeah, I played at Finn College,' thinking I would have a better chance to make the team. I don't know how I picked Finn College, and I didn't know if there was a Finn College, but I made the team anyway once they saw me play. We had a really good team, too. I think we won 33 games against the other battalions and lost only once. We also played some exhibitions against some small college teams in the area and never lost to any of them. We had a nice, big gym where we played. They had just changed the rules from the 'center-jump' after each basket to inbounding the ball like in today's rules . . .

"We got off every weekend because it was still considered 'peace time' at that point. So, I found plenty of things to do on Saturdays and Sundays. We did a lot of hunting. There was a horse farm right down the road and I could rent a horse for one dollar a day. I would ride them all over the place. We would go out on horseback, carry a canteen and go into the foothills and hunt for deer. By now, I was already considered an expert rifleman by the army's standards, and I later had a badge to prove it, so I didn't miss many deer. I could shoot accurately to a long distance with the naked eye . . .

"On the first day I went hunting, I shot a deer, and then I learned from the guy who rented the horses that it was out of season. I didn't know they had a deer season in Texas, so I covered it up with some brush and told the guy, 'Let's go back and get it later and you can have it,' so we did. We loaded it up in his flatbed truck and took it to his place . . .

"He told me, 'Come up one night this week and we will have venison for dinner.' He had a couple of little boys and a daughter, and we had a great dinner. But I didn't shoot any more deer after that. I just enjoyed riding his horses."

"They also put me in charge of the motor pool, and I quickly realized that the guy before me didn't know anything about it. It was all screwed up, so it was my job to fix it. And I also served as a guard in the stockade, mostly on the weekends . . .

"I can still remember some of the guys' names from H Company . . . Don Sloan also was from Ashland. Paul Schultz was from Marion, Ohio . . . Most of the guys were from New York or New Jersey . . . like Mickey D'Onofrio, Joe Majernik, Shorty Friedman, Stan Gardner, Jack Noble, Claude Stillwagon, Carl Rundberg, Herb Kinsch, Alan Merritt, Marty Emmer and Frank Kowatch, who lived in Pennsylvania "on the mountain side" bordering West Virginia,

Dad riding high at Mineral Wells, Texas, November of 1941, one month before Pearl Harbor was attacked.

as he always said. He was always making fun of West Virgina 'hillbillies' . . .

"One of my friends there who also was from Ohio said he always wanted to learn how to ride a motorcycle. There was one there, so I taught him, and he was pretty good within a week or two. After we all were shipped out later, that guy stayed on as a trainer and spent the next four years at Camp Wolters."

One day, Dad was buying some supplies in downtown Mineral Wells when he encountered something he had never witnessed before.

"I was walking down the street when a Black man saw me coming," he recalled. "He was headed in my direction, but as I approached, he just stopped walking. Then he stepped off the walkway onto the grass. As I passed him, he had his head down, looking as if he was ashamed. I had no idea how to react. It was the first time I ever saw that. You know, I have thought about that moment all my life, and all these years later, I would like to go back and shake his hand, to stop and talk to him to let him know that's not the way I thought it should have been. But I guess that's the way it was in the deep South. And I'll be honest, it really shocked me that day."

In just a few weeks, everything changed. Dad's future, and that of the United States and the entire world for that matter, was about to enter a new era.

"I was working at the stockade, where they put the guys who screwed up, or the guys who went AWOL, or who didn't play by the rules. It was a Sunday, when suddenly somebody came running in and yelled, 'The Japs just bombed Pearl Harbor!' . . .

"We all looked at each other and asked the same question: 'Where the hell's Pearl Harbor?' It was a U.S. territory back then and not yet a state, and not that well-known to most people, including us. I admit that I had never heard of it. None of us had.

"Now we knew at that moment everything would change very quickly. President Roosevelt then gave his 'A Day Which Will Live in Infamy' speech which we listened to on the radio that we had mounted on the back of a transport Jeep. You could hear in his voice that he was really upset. We wouldn't know all the details until later, but when we did find out, all the guys were emotionally ready to go fight right then and there. We may not have been ready as fighting units, but knowing it happened on a Sunday morning in peace time made us angry as hell . . .

"Congress then declared war, while the ships in Pearl Harbor were still burning. The war was on, as far as us being in it. And we all knew that meant we would be in the middle of it very soon."

Dad in his U.S. Army dress uniform, 1941, Camp Wolters, Texas.

CHAPTER FOUR

FROM CAMP WOLTERS TO FORT ORD TO PARADISE

After Pearl Harbor was attacked, and Americans were suddenly united to fight another world war, Dad's 106th Regiment of the U.S. Army's 27th Infantry departed Camp Wolters and headed west on a troop train.

The country may have still been in shock for weeks to come, but its soldiers, airmen and seamen now were preparing for battle.

"My company was full of guys from New York and New Jersey, and they were just different guys than me, a Midwestern guy. They were brash and boastful, and cocky as hell. I eventually grew to like them, most of them anyway, but traveling by train with all of them wasn't always so easy . . ." Dad said.

"They wanted to go kick the hell out of the Japanese army right away, but I could tell that many of them, if not most of us, were still not ready to fight a war. We just hadn't had that much training or seasoning yet. We were very green."

For the second time in six months, after never leaving the state of Ohio for his previous 21 years, he would find himself in California: The first time on the motorcycle trip with three close buddies who were having the time of their young lives, and now via a troop train along with hundreds of guys who were fighting mad . . .

"They sent us to Monterey Bay, California, to a place called Fort Ord. We lived in tents at first, and then they moved us into the barracks when they were cleaned and ready. We were told that the Japanese would soon be invading the West Coast, so we had to be ready to fight and it was our job to stop them . . .

"I really was very worried then, because I think we would have gotten slaughtered. As I look back, I think it took our guys about two years to get caught up to the Japanese army. I know they could have invaded us (in California) and hurt us severely if it had happened. We wouldn't have survived it, and we were expecting it every day . . .

"We had built outposts up and down the Pacific Coast, from Santa Barbara to Monterey all the way up to San Francisco, and I was running the motor pool at all those points and in between. Our job was to supply the outposts and give them what they needed. Our guys in those outposts were dug in and always on edge, fearing the invasion . . .

"But it never came. Knowing what I know now, I really think that the only thing that saved our butts was the width of the Pacific Ocean. All these years later, I read that (the Japanese) didn't have the supply ships to pull it off, but if they had tried, I really believe they would have overrun us pretty quickly by the end of 1941 or early in '42 . . .

"By the end of February, when we were told we were about to ship out again, they were using civilian ships as troop ships, so I ran a lot of convoys from Fort Ord to San Francisco to load the USS *Lurline*. It had been a cruise ship, but they had pulled off all the mirrors and chandeliers and made it into a troop ship. It already had made a few runs to Hawaii and back by the time we helped load it for the final time . . .

"Then we all got on it. What they didn't tell us was they snuck about 100 nurses on that ship at the last minute once we were all aboard. They didn't want us knowing they were aboard . . .

"On March 10, 1942, we left around midnight, and I walked out on the deck of the *Lurline* to watch us sail under the Golden Gate Bridge. What a sight for a kid from Ashland, Ohio. Ted, Buck, Cockey and I had just seen the bridge from our bikes that previous year, but it was more impressive to go underneath it. I could see it very well under a little moonlight and city lights that night and it was an awesome sight . . .

"We were headed for Hawaii, sailing next to the USS *Aquitania*, another troop ship. We went directly south for about 100 miles along the California coast, figuring the Japs wouldn't have any subs in that area so close to the coast. Then we zig-zagged the whole way at full speed, always knowing a Japanese torpedo could take us out at any moment. That fear was always in most guys' minds. It was in mine, too. There were 50-caliber machine guns around the decks . . . armor piercing . . . which made us feel a little better I guess, but we all knew that wouldn't protect us from a sub . . .

The U.S. troop ship USS Lurline, *pulling into Sand Island in downtown Honolulu, Hawaii. The famous Aloha Tower is in the background.*

"Most of those guys in my unit had never been on a boat on a lake, let alone a ship on the ocean, and they were throwing up all over the place. Most of them were seasick. I got tired of smelling it after a few days. I had fished on Lake Erie so often that a rough sea didn't bother me, but the smell did . . .

"Eventually, five days later, we made it. We pulled into Sand Island in downtown Honolulu, and the first thing I saw were the Japanese internment camps. Most of the Japanese on the Hawaiian Islands had been loyal to America, but the government stuck them in camps fearing they were spies or traitors after Pearl Harbor was attacked. We acted as guards at the internment camp for the next few days . . .

"I was just relieved we made it, because I was tired of seeing guys throw up, and happy that no torpedo took us out. Then we all went to see the damage at Pearl Harbor. I looked around the harbor and the sight of it just broke my heart. It was even worse than I had imagined. There were still almost 20 ships down at the time. The fires were out, but it still was a stinking mess. I could smell that burning oil for weeks. It was an awful sight. I saw the *Arizona*, the *Nevada* and the *Utah* . . . all down. The *Oklahoma* was turned over and they still were trying to cut holes in the hull to retrieve the bodies . . .

"It was just a slaughter in that first wave, and I stood there picturing what it must have been like. At that moment, I developed a tremendous hatred for the Japanese. I admit it—I did. These guys died in their bunks, in their sleep. It was a Sunday morning. It was peace time. They were somewhat more prepared for the second wave more than an hour and 50 minutes later . . . but it was still a cowardly attack, and I will always feel that way . . .

"I met George Welch, a pilot who shot down four Japanese planes. He told us what happened that day and how awful it was, and what struck me was that he was so young-looking. I don't think he had ever shaved. He was regarded by all the guys as a hero . . . he later received the Medal of Honor . . .

"We stayed on Sand Island for about the first 10 days and then we transferred to Schofield Barracks, which was located in the hills above Pearl. They had a PX there where we could buy anything we wanted. We could buy a pack of cigarettes or a can of beer for a nickel. I started smoking a little back then and continued throughout the war . . .

"One day, Eleanor Roosevelt visited Schofield. We were all lined up and she walked by as if she was inspecting the troops. I remember one of the officers close to me said, 'My God, what a homely woman!' . . .

"The big 10-wheelers would transport us from Schofield into town and the first stop was Hotel Street, where all the prostitutes worked for $10. I would see so many young sailors get off the ships and then walk directly toward Hotel Street and then line up by the hundreds on the stairs. They even set up stations where they treated them for crabs or whatever VD they would catch . . .

"That wasn't for me, or for any of my close buddies that I knew of. We would stay on the truck until it got to Waikiki Beach and then hop off and go get a cold beer at Fort DeRussy, or find some little bar we could afford. Even in Honolulu, we carried loaded .45s on our sides. And we were usually limited to two beers anyway, so the guys wouldn't get into trouble . . .

"One time, we walked into the Royal Hawaiian, the nicest hotel there was. They called it the 'Pink Palace' and we sat there on the veranda sipping cold beer, watching the sun set over the Pacific. That was paradise to me. Waikiki Beach was the most beautiful place I ever saw. The sand felt so soft, and you could see Diamond Head right there. I fell in love with it right away . . .

"A week or so later they shipped us to the Big Island on a smaller interisland ship. We were based at Parker Ranch in Waimea on the northern part of the island. I was shocked at the scenery there, too.

It looked like I had pictured Montana would look. I could see snow on the top of Mauna Kea, an extinct volcano . . .

"Parker Ranch was a large cattle ranch, and it had 90,000 head of beef at the time and 130,000 acres of beautiful landscape. There also were plenty of horses and sheep. They had kicked the horses out of the barns, cleaned them up and put bunks in there for us. We lived in the barns for about a month until our camp was built . . . then the horses got their barns back. I would take a horse and go out and hunt pig and let me tell you, that Kalua pork was very tasty . . .

"Our main job was to protect the Big Island from an invasion. We had expected it in California and didn't get it, but we were still somewhat on edge. We knew Hawaii was closer to Japan than California and it would be easier for them to reach. We set up tents and started to build pill boxes along the coast facing the west. Many of those pill boxes are still there . . .

"I was a staff sergeant of transport, running the motor pool again like I had in California, so I had the responsibility for the

A view of the snow atop Mauna Kea from Parker Ranch in Waimea, Hawaii, where Dad was based for most of 1942.

100 miles or so from Hilo to South Point and then north to a small town of Hawi, replacing fuel, trucks, spare parts, whatever was needed. I traveled the island extensively then . . . there was still an ordered blackout and martial law in Hawaii, and we traveled a lot at night. I really got around that entire island, and most people who have never been there just don't realize how big it really is. And that is how I got to meet a lot of Japanese-Americans on the Big Island, but at the time you really didn't know who to trust. Over time, I discovered that they all were very trustworthy, and they didn't like the attack on Pearl Harbor any more than we did . . .

"Our guys had stationed machine guns all along the coast. We also had heavy weapons, such as water-cooled 30-caliber machine guns. We had mortars that were so accurate we could drop a shell 1,000 yards away into a bushel basket. We were scrambling to do our best to be ready in a hurry . . .

"One day I was on road patrol when I came upon a vehicle which was broken down. I stopped to help. The guy standing next to it told me he was an engineer for the county and his job was to take care of five miles of growth along the roadway and he had a small crew with him . . .

"I looked at his truck and I could tell he had some water in his fuel, so I blew it out and put a little fresh fuel in there and it started right up. Then I added five gallons of gas for him. He told me that after Pearl Harbor happened, they had to use the reserve gas on the Big Island, and it most likely had water in all of it because it had been in holding tanks for a long period . . .

"The guy was so happy and thankful. He gave me his address and pointed out the direction where he lived and said, 'Come for dinner . . . any night you want!' . . .

"So, a week or so later, I took him up on it. I went to visit him in the small town of Captain Cook. When I turned my Jeep onto his property, I saw it was a ranch-style house sitting high on a hill and overlooking the Pacific. It was a beautiful place . . .

"His name was Henry Kailikole and he was 40 years old. He was half Chinese and half Hawaiian. His wife's name was Elizabeth. She was full-blooded Hawaiian. I got to know them very well, well enough that she told me their story: They had raised seven or eight children, but none of them were their own. They had taken in nieces, nephews and cousins. Elizabeth was 38 and she later told me that she could not bear children, but Henry had always wanted to have kids, so they took in kids all the time . . .

"Elizabeth was an entertainer and had a beautiful singing voice. She had a troupe of girls that worked for her, and they did the hula, as she sang at shows all across the Hawaiian Islands. On Sundays, the army had put on shows to try to keep us entertained, but they weren't as good as Elizabeth and her girls, so one day I asked the captain, 'I know this Hawaiian group who entertains everywhere—can I bring them in?' He was all for it, so I took a 10-wheeler and drove 50 miles and picked them up. That night, they put on a great show for us . . .

"You can imagine having all these beautiful Hawaiian girls dancing the hula and all the guys just went nuts when they saw them. They loved me for bringing them in . . .

"Over time, I grew close with Henry and Elizabeth. She treated me as her long-lost son, the one she never had. She even called me 'Sonny Boy,' and I called her 'My Hawaiian Mom.' They were just wonderful people. Henry told me to call him 'Pop.' So, that's what I did. They became my 'Mom' and 'Pop' away from home. I had no idea then that we would become lifelong friends . . . She really was just like a second mother to me and would do anything for me. I guess she knew I was far away from home and about to fight for the country she loved, too, even though Hawaii wasn't even a state then. Mom didn't like the Japanese for what they did at Pearl Harbor any more than I did, but she had several Japanese friends who had nothing to do with it, and she realized that. I met so many

Dad and his "Hawaiian Mom," January 9, 1973. This photo was taken at her home in Captain Cook, Hawaii, 31 years after they first met.

great people through her and they were a mix of all the nationalities on the islands: Hawaiian, Japanese, Chinese . . .

"I could write my own trip tickets then and sign them myself, so I could take weekends and stay at their house whenever I wanted just to get away from the guys and the barracks. They had a guest house in the back which I made my little home away from home. They would throw luaus down at the beach or at their house and I would be the only service guy there. I would wear Pop's clothes, which were too short on me, but I still thought I died and went to heaven . . . I got to know all of their friends and family members and they treated me as if I was a member of their family . . .

"On most Sundays, I would go with Mom to the Catholic church down the road and she would play the organ for the congregation. It is the famous 'Painted Church,' which is now somewhat of a tourist attraction. They call it that because its walls and ceilings are hand-painted murals. It sits high on a hill overlooking the Pacific . . .

Above: The famous 'Painted Church,' in Captain Cook, Hawaii, where Dad attended Sunday services in 1942.

Right: A photo I took in 2021 from within the entrance of the church, facing the Pacific.

"She would write letters to my real mom back in Ohio when I was in Hawaii, to let her know I was okay and that she was taking care of me. Mom often would send her a letter addressed for me. I got to talk to Mom a few times on the phone from her house that year, too . . ."

Most of Grandma's letters to Dad informed him of what was happening back home with the rest of the family, and always, how his brother George was doing in the U.S. Air Force in the European Theater.

One, however, contained heartbreaking news.

The bomber containing Howard "Cockey" Morekel, one of his buddies on the motorcycle trip just a year earlier, had been lost at sea in the Pacific on a flight from Hawaii to Australia.

"I never felt so bad in my entire life as the day I read that letter. Cockey was such a nice guy. He graduated out of Polk, and we met playing basketball and became friends right away. I taught him how to ride a motorcycle and that is why he bought one . . .

"He was a flight engineer, just like my brother George. They never found his plane or any of the remains from his crew. It was so sad. Anyway, it made me wonder if any of us would make it back home after the war."

While Dad and the 27th Infantry spent most of 1942 in the Hawaiian Islands, someone whom he already had met was making headlines. His actions as a pilot provided the first swing in the momentum of the war toward the Allies in the Pacific.

"Remember how I mentioned meeting Jimmy Doolittle in Cleveland when I was a kid?" he asked. "Well, I had no idea at the time while we were in Hawaii, but he was becoming an American hero for a second time . . .

"We would learn all this later, but in early April of '42, the USS *Hornet* sailed out of San Francisco under the Golden Gate just as we had earlier on the *Lurline*. It carried 16 B-25 bombers, which normally can't fly a long range. Their mission was to eventually get as close to Japan as possible without being detected and then just bomb the hell out of Tokyo as payback for Pearl Harbor. It was basically considered a suicide mission . . .

"Jimmy was the organizer and lead bomber, so they called it the 'Doolittle Raid.' It took place on April 18 and over time it became legendary, because it was a huge success, and that was probably the earliest victory of any sort for our side. I read where there were 80 pilots and crew on those 16 bombers and 71 of them made it back home. The other nine were executed in brutal fashion when they landed in China and I always felt so bad for those guys, knowing they had no chance to survive, but they had sacrificed their lives for the greater cause . . .

"What I would have given to run into Jimmy Doolittle again at the Cleveland Air Races after the war just to shake his hand, thank him for the morale boost and have him describe what that mission was like. Then the battle of Midway in May of 1942 seemed to be the another turning point, because we had been on the defense ever since Pearl Harbor . . .

"The fun was over for us, too. After about nine months protecting the Big Island and also living it up with Mom and Pop and their extended family on the weekends, I guess our intelligence had determined a Japanese invasion was not coming . . . just like it never came in California. They transferred us back to Oahu, mainly to get more training on the Higgins boats, the landing crafts, and how to charge the beaches. We knew we would be doing a lot of that across the Pacific. At the time, I hated to leave the Big Island and swore I would come back some day to see Mom and Pop . . .

"One day we were on the North Shore of Oahu, and we were charging the beach when a marine with us fell overboard. That was the worst place for that to happen because of the high surf. It is the same spot where they still hold all the world surfing events. I was on the deck and saw that marine go down and he must have hit his head, because I could see that he was unconscious as soon as he went underwater. I could see him underwater because the ocean was so clear. Somebody tried to dive to save him, but they couldn't reach him. They finally rigged an anchor and brought him up on it, but it was too late. He had either drowned or died from a head injury, and I always wondered what the government told his parents about his death when they were first notified . . .

"What was always so sad to me was losing guys when we were not even in battle, or by stupid ways. We lost guys when their appendix would rupture, for example, when no doctors were around to save them, or in careless training accidents: One time I saw a guy loading a mortar and he was in a hurry and put one shell down too early and it exploded, wounding the three guys standing right there with him. It was an awful sight. Then another time, this lieutenant was operating a flame-thrower which could shoot out a flame in an arc of about 50 to 75 yards, but he didn't twist the oxygen knob tight enough and the thing exploded on his back. He had no chance.

"Another time at Schofield, we were training to crawl under barbed wire. The sergeants were shooting machine guns above the wire as part of the drill, training us to stay down. One guy stuck his head above the wire and took a bullet to the head. So, when we are done with the drill, one guy is lying there dead . . .

"Stuff like that, just like this marine falling overboard to his death on the North Shore, always made me mad. Those were the first deaths I saw in the war, and those were stupid mistakes. And I knew many more were coming . . .

"Anyway, we got our training in on landing on the beaches. It was now early in 1943, and it was time for us to ship out of Pearl Harbor. We knew we were headed for battle someplace in the Pacific, but we just didn't know where."

CHAPTER FIVE

THE SIGHTS, SOUNDS AND HORROR OF SAIPAN

The successful Doolittle Raid and the battle at Midway were the first signs that American forces, still motivated by the sucker-punch at Pearl Harbor, had started to take the fight to the Japanese in the Pacific Theater.

After being reassured Hawaii was safe from a Japanese invasion, the 27th Infantry was ready for battle and would be on the move in 1943. What the men of the 106th Battalion did, however, was a lot of sailing the high seas of the Pacific, thousands of miles from their home base in Hawaii to first the Gilbert Islands and back and then to the Marshall Islands and back.

"At this point, we had plenty of training on just about everything we would need in battle," Dad explained. "It was time to go fight somewhere. We were about to do our part, and now I thought all of our guys were ready for it . . .

"Remember, we had to have floating reserves all over the Pacific because most of these islands were more than 2,000 miles from Honolulu, and it would take a week to 10 days to get back to wherever they needed us in a battle. We would sail out of Hawaii, and we never knew where we were going until usually the second day out. Then they would break out the map, and tell us, 'Now, here's what we will be responsible for . . .'

"The Japanese used a lot of those little islands as staging areas, and we had to take them out and capture the islands. We needed all of those islands to build air bases so we could control the Pacific with our bombers . . .

"We came in at Makin Island on the very north end of the Gilbert Islands, but we never even got off the ship during that battle. In three days, it was all over. The marines and a few other army units had wiped them out. They didn't even need us, so we headed back to Hawaii . . .

"One thing I noticed was that everybody was made up differently, as far as being brave, or letting fear overcome them when you are about to go into battle—or think you are going into battle. I never saw much fear in the guys who were around me, but we always heard stories of other guys who let it consume them. When we were back in Hawaii, a shot rang out in the middle of the night when a guy from E Company committed suicide. Someone said he was scared to death of going into battle. The army would cover that up and call it an accidental shooting, and I am sure that is what they told his family . . . .

"After four weeks in Hawaii, we left again. On the second day at sea, they broke out the map and told us, 'Guys, we are going to the Marshall Islands . . .'"

They landed unopposed on Majuro Island, on February 1, 1944, and completed its seizure of the entire island in only two days.

"It was called 'Operation Flintlock.' The Japs had a small naval base there, but we never knew how many of them we would face when we landed. There could be 50, 100 or 1,000 . . . we just never knew. We outsmarted them by landing in a narrow gap in the middle of the island at about four in the morning. One group of us went south and the other went north. I think I could have thrown a baseball three or four times across that island since it was so small . . .

"What we learned there was those Japanese soldiers were not that good of fighters, but there probably were only 100 or more of them there and it really wasn't much of a fight. We came in behind a group of them and pinned them against the ocean and they had nowhere to go. That is when we hit them with flame-throwers. I could hear them screaming. That is a vicious way to die. We took them out in only two days, and I never fired a shot. We didn't lose one guy . . .

"We always had to do a mop-up for stragglers or guys that were hiding from us. They didn't want to surrender, and we had been told that ahead of time. They were told NOT to surrender—and we accommodated them every time. That's what happened on Majuro. I think we captured three of them and the rest either committed suicide or we killed them . . .

"Then we went to Enewetak on the western side. It was probably 30 miles long. We took that island in three days. Again, there was little resistance. When we were done with Enewetak, we sailed back to Hawaii in late February to get rested and to prepare for our next battle."

On May 25, the 27th boarded troop ships and sailed out of Pearl Harbor again. Two weeks later, on June 6, American troops stormed the beaches at Normandy, France. It would go down in history as the most famous invasion of World War II and it turned the momentum toward the Allies in Europe.

When that was happening, more than 16,000 soldiers from the 27th were headed toward Saipan, which is more than 1,400 miles southeast of Tokyo, but almost 4,000 miles from Hawaii. Control of it was crucial to winning the battle of the Pacific.

Saipan spans 14.5 miles long and 6.5 miles wide, a total of about 44 square miles.

In the Pacific Theater, it would be the site of the biggest and most important invasion—and come only nine days after the Normandy invasion, although it never would garner the worldwide attention D-Day did.

But its outcome would go a long way toward determining the outcome of the war.

It often has been called "The D-Day of the Pacific."

And it was Dad's own D-Day.

He recalled it this way . . .

"Nothing we went through to that point had prepared me for what we would experience next. We knew that every one of those islands we took would get us a step closer to Japan, and a step closer to winning. We also knew that they had complete control of Saipan. We pulled offshore on June 14, and again, we were expected to be floating reserve there. We were told we were there to support the marines who would be invading soon."

In the heart of the island is Mount Tapochau, reaching a height of 1,550 feet. Unknown to the American commanders, there were thousands of Japanese soldiers embedded there with a clear view of the beaches, just sitting in wait for the American invasion.

American intelligence had estimated there would be about 15,000 Japanese soldiers waiting, but they wouldn't know exactly what type of resistance their troops would face until the invasion started.

It was planned for the early morning hours of June 15.

But first, for three days, U.S. Navy ships bombarded the island with constant shelling. The American commanders expected that would take its toll on the Japanese army. However, they took cover in well-fortified caves and had been so deeply entrenched, it had not been as successful as expected.

What the American commanders also discovered: There were more than double the number of Japanese soldiers embedded on Saipan than they had estimated.

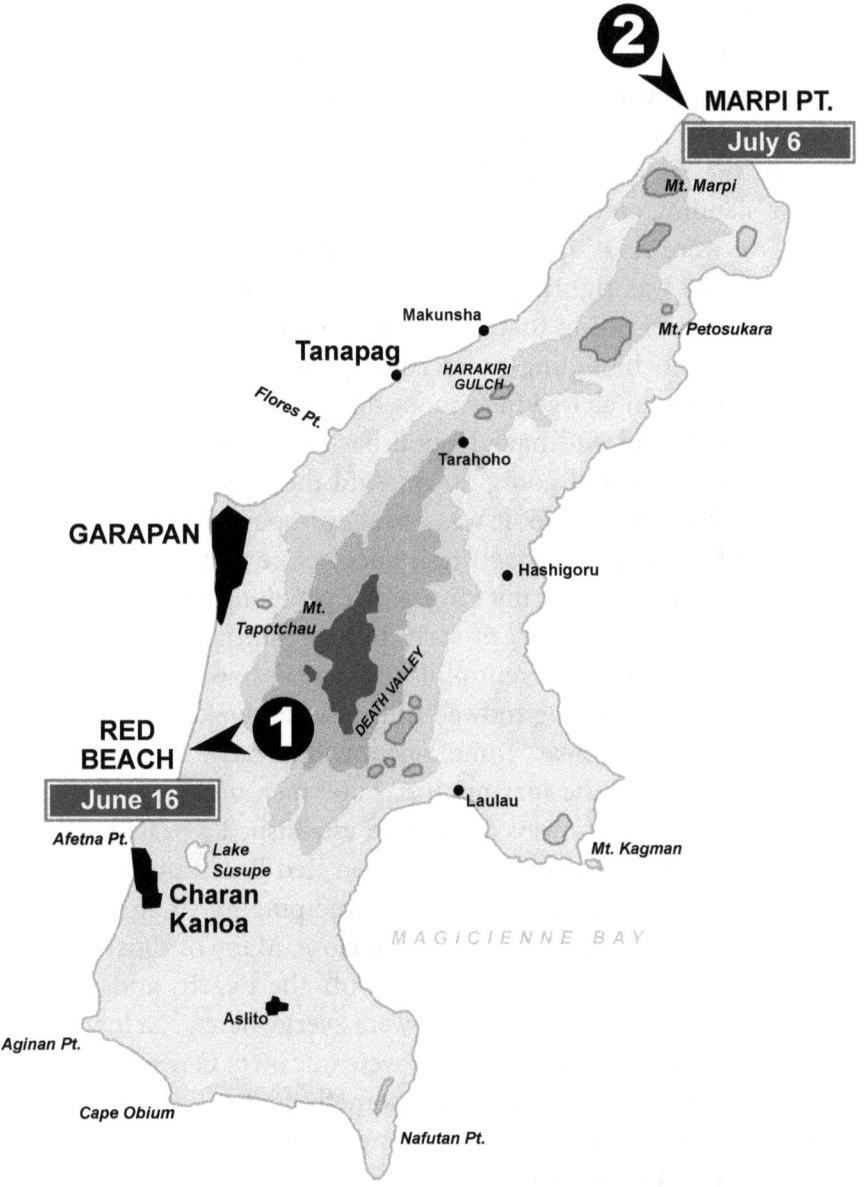

Dad and his unit came ashore on Saipan on June 16, at Red Beach (1), and spent the next three weeks fighting their way to Marpi Point (2) to the north.

That miscalculation would result in a costly and deadly battle.

When the marines stormed the beaches before sunrise on the 15th, expecting an easy path through the island, instead they were greeted with fierce resistance.

As the sun came up, Dad watched it all through binoculars while standing on deck of a ship.

"We were floating right offshore, and I could tell everybody on our side was fighting for their lives. I could see through my binoculars everything that was going on and it was awful. What I saw was a bunch of gung-ho marines getting slaughtered . . .

"They would charge in without taking cover, maybe get 100 or 200 yards inland and have to pull back immediately. I could see them taking fire and going down. And the Japs were shelling the beaches from above, too. It was a real eye-opener to see that, since we hadn't encountered much resistance before that . . .

"I'll be honest, us army guys didn't get along with the marines too well. We had a rivalry of sorts, but we didn't want them killed, either. We just had different philosophies on how to fight a battle. As we saw them getting mowed down, we all looked at each other and said, 'We're up next. Tomorrow it will be us.'"

It is estimated the marines lost 2,000 men on that first day. By the end of the day, however, they had established a beachhead.

"That next morning, we came in on Red Beach on our landing crafts, and immediately, I could hear the pinging sound of bullets whizzing by me. I knew they were all close. Many of those marines hadn't gotten more than 200 yards off the beach, and it was a horrible sight to see. Dead bodies were everywhere . . . a lot of them from both sides, but most of them were our own. Our guys wore GI combat boots, while the Japs wore something that looked more like a tennis-shoe type of boot. With some of the bodies, that really was the only way I could tell . . .

"We immediately took cover and took turns looking through our scopes to scout for the Japanese before we moved any farther. I was looking through one on that first day and remember seeing one Jap standing behind a tree, taking a pee. Suddenly, he just dropped over. I knew one of our snipers got him . . .

"Our main problem trying to work our way inland had to do with all the bodies. We almost had to climb over them or move around them to make any progress. The smell was horrible, too, and the blow flies were everywhere. It was a bad sight. But we slowly worked our way inland by taking cover and then running like hell . . .

"It was June, so it was hot, too, I had two canteens full of water, two medical kits, about 200 rounds of ammo for my M-1 and six to eight grenades, with five clips for my .45 which I had on my waist.

A squad of 27th Infantry soldiers walking from the beach toward the front lines on Saipan in late June of 1944.

I also carried three knives and a gas mask in case we needed it for some type of chemical attack . . .

"Those grenades always came in handy. Once you pulled the pin, you had about five seconds to get rid of it. I would throw it like a baseball, and sometimes it exploded in the air before it landed, but the shrapnel would do a lot of damage if you could time it to explode about four or five feet off the ground above a group of Japs . . .

"We started pushing toward Aslito Airfield, then digging foxholes to sleep in every night. I always attached my bayonet on my M-1 before I went to sleep, or tried to sleep, just in case somebody rushed me at night, and I had to act quickly . . .

"In combat, you never got to bathe, and we all smelled real bad within a few days. I didn't know it then, but I was about to go more than three weeks without a bath. That's one thing you never see in the war movies, but your personal hygiene goes all to hell. If I saw a puddle of fresh rain somewhere, I would take out a small towel and give myself a quick bath sometimes . . .

"At night we would dig our foxholes on a reverse slope so we could look out at the ocean. I could see our ships about three to five miles offshore. At times that was reassuring and at times they seemed a million miles away and there was no way they could help you . . . some of our foxholes were big enough for three to five guys. And some of them would be interconnected . . .

"Some of the guys carried cigarettes and would light one and pass it around, and I smoked a little then, but we had to cover them so they wouldn't glow in the dark. We would try to get some sleep and always have one guy alert and awake. The rest of us would cover our heads and try to get an hour of sleep, but it was always so loud with gunfire. Sometimes it was close and sometimes it was in the distance . . .

"What we noticed on Saipan is that the Japs would crawl underneath debris from the houses or buildings that would be flattened and then fire at you, so they were hard to reach. We started working our way into the highlands, but we had very little shade or cover . . .

"We had some small firefights here and there as they retreated into what was called 'Death Valley,' aptly named as it turned out. On the third day ashore, we came up to about the middle of the island and I saw a flash out of the corner of my eye to my right. It was coming from under a house from one of their snipers. I hit the ground and crawled about 20 yards to a point where I could see him. The house was set up on logs and I saw him lying under there. So, I threw three shots under there. His firing stopped. Some of our guys then rushed the house and pulled him out. They pulled a medal off his chest. It was from Manchuria, which one of our guys told me it meant he was older and must have been in their earlier war with China. They handed me that medal and some yen out of his wallet, which was covered in blood . . .

"I wanted to honor him in some way, so I kept them both. I just never had the courage later to ever ask any Japanese person what the medal stood for. It sounds awful to say, but I just didn't feel that bad because I knew he was killing our guys . . .

"Then on June 25, the battle got real intense. They pinned us down and we lost four or five men right away. It was just constant fighting, constant firing and running for cover. One thing I know happened on Saipan was that a lot of our guys got it from friendly fire. It happened all the time. There was chaos and confusion at times . . .

"I heard a 'pop pop pop pop' and I hit the ground. The Japs were firing knee mortars at us. The shells were about the size of a baseball. I could see them firing them from 500 to 700 yards away. It was one of their most effective weapons. They would put them in the ground, then drop a shell in them and aim them our way. They were just reigning mortars on us one after the other . . . they would land and there would be a huge bang concussion, and the mortar would split apart in two or three pieces and throw shrapnel in any direction . . .

"A friend of mine, who took care of our weapons, was Joe Majernik. He was just a little guy, but he could fix any weapon there was. Joe wore thick glasses. I went down behind the rear wheel of a Jeep and he was kneeling at the front of it. He was cleaning off his glasses when I just got the feeling that he wanted to stick his head up to see what was going on, so I told him, 'Joe, just stay down, don't stick your head up . . .'

"But either Joe didn't hear me or didn't listen, I don't know which. I barely got the words out when he stuck his head up and a small piece of a knee mortar shell hit him on the side of the head. I knew right away he had bought it. He was gone. I heard someone yell 'Medic! Medic!' but we didn't have a medic near us anyway and there was no saving him. I will never ever forget that moment . . .

"I didn't have time to process Joe's death, because right after that is when our radio man got hit by shrapnel from a knee mortar. He ran into a depression, or a small foxhole. Then I jumped in there after him."

That radio man was John Lewis.

"John was moaning and groaning really bad. I saw a small entrance wound in his lower side and told him, 'Hey John, you didn't get hit too bad.' But then I rolled him over to check his back, and I think I could have put my fist in that exit wound in his back. It was that big. He wasn't bleeding at the mouth, so I gave him some pain pills. I gave him my canteen and he slugged down some water, which I later learned from a medic was a big mistake. I shouldn't have done that. I took the biggest pack I had, sprinkled Sulfa on it and stuffed it in that hole in his back and then wrapped it as tight as I could . . . I told him to hold his hands over the wrap . . .

"Can you move?" I asked him.

"He just moaned a little and I knew he would be gone soon. I told him I was going to put him over my shoulder and start running.

"'AW!! NO WAY I CAN DO THIS!' he screamed.

"'We have no choice, John! We have got to get out of here!' I told him.

"John was bigger than me, but I got him over my shoulder, climbed out of there and started blowing my whistle and yelling 'MEDIC! MEDIC!' as I ran back toward where I thought the medics would be. We all carried whistles in battle just to call for the medics. I knew I had to get him back at least 200 or 300 yards, or to where I thought I could get a medic to come to him because he would die in that hole . . .

"I made it back and found a medic, who put hm on a stretcher. I told John that he was in good hands now, that he would be fine, and that I would catch up with him later . . . even though I didn't believe any of it. I really figured he was a goner, and I would never see him again. But I didn't want him to see that in my eyes, so I lied right to his face. What else could I do? I then ran back to where we were when he got hit . . .

"We had to pull back after that, since we were taking so many casualties. Then we were in an area where there were a lot of trees. I had my back against this big tree as cover and took out my knife and carved 'S-N-O-O-K' and the date into the tree. I thought, 'If I buy it here, at least someone will see this years later.' But we worked our way out of there and then started advancing again . . .

"It took us seven days to get through Death Valley to the hills on the other side of it . . . when we finally gained more control toward the north of the island. I would drive my Jeep near Marpi Point, where they had built an airstrip, once or twice each day, taking supplies to the front line. I never failed to come around this certain curve without a sniper taking a shot at me on every trip. But he always missed, fortunately. Obviously, he was either a bad shot, or he had 200 or 300 yards or more to shoot, I don't know which . . .

"I had grown tired of it and figured sooner or later, he would get lucky, so one day I told some guys, 'That's enough of that shit . . . let's go get this sucker.'

"I got eight guys together and we went back up there. We needed him to fire again, so we could spot him. He fired on us, and we saw him . . . it looked like he was dug in pretty good. We surrounded him and we all threw grenades into where he was. We pulled his body out and I could tell he was very young. He weighed about only 120 pounds, and it looked like he had been dug in there for several months, because he was so dirty . . .

"But at least I knew I could drive my Jeep around that curve now without him taking a shot at me each time. After that, one of my guys in the motor pool took a bad angle there and rolled his Jeep. Four or five guys went flying out and the Jeep rolled over him. His name was Lawrence Gardner. He had a real bad head injury, and I never saw him again . . .

"We were making progress every day, but everything came to a head on July 7. The Japanese must have realized they were losing Saipan, so they decided to banzai attack us. They came in the middle of the night by the thousands . . . we had to shoot flares up in the air so we could see them to shoot them. We would shoot flares and then we could see the sugar cane moving, so we knew they were in there. They were like ants crawling through the sugar cane . . .

"We constantly reminded each other, 'Don't shoot high, shoot low . . . they will be crawling on their bellies' . . . then they would come charging out, start shooting, then turn and run back. You had to time firing at them to be at the closest point, before they would turn around . . . We opened fire on them all night and we also had our big Sherman tanks shooting over my head. It is no wonder I spent the rest of my life hard-of-hearing from my right ear. They were losing their goal, which was to break through our line and then circle around us . . .

"Our sister regiment, the 105th, was right there with us that night. I just kept firing that night, almost all night long. You just didn't have any idea if you were hitting or killing someone, but you fired at what moved. You would think I would be scared to death, but you know I wasn't for some reason. It must have been adrenaline. I had about 35 men under me there and I felt responsible for them, including non-combat guys like cooks and messengers. I think that is what prevented me from being scared. But I wasn't brave, either. To say that would be pure bullshit. We all had a job to do, and we did it . . .

"By the time the sun came up, it was a horrible sight. I never saw so many dead bodies in my life. That banzai battle took about 30 hours, but we outlasted them. We lost a lot of guys, but they lost even more. It was just a simple slaughter. I think more than 4,800 Japanese died that night, from what I read later . . .

"Near the end, the island had a lot of disease. There were dead bodies everywhere. They were bloated from the heat and the sun, and you could smell it in the air. Blow flies were everywhere. Birds were circling us from above because of the smell . . .

"I walked around when the fighting stopped and at one spot, I saw where one of our boys from the 105th had put up one hell of a fight. He was a lieutenant named O'Brien. He got caught behind the lines and they had tried to rescue him. He was slumped over dead by the time we got to him, but there were about a dozen Japanese bodies lying around him. I could tell from that he had fought to the very end . . . probably ran out of ammo. Then they bayonetted him and cut him all to hell after he was dead. That really pissed me off. They later gave his family his Medal of Honor."

William J. O'Brien, of Troy, New York, was 44 when he was killed. He received the Medal of Honor posthumously on May 9, 1945, for his bravery in Saipan.

"I will never forget him because he didn't fall back with the rest of us when he had the chance to. Then he got trapped and couldn't get out . . . some of the guys who were trapped behind O'Brien ran out of ammo and had to swim out into the ocean to survive. Most of them who made it far enough got picked up by our PT boats . . .

"After battles like that one, we picked up our dead on the battlefield as quickly as possible and loaded them onto army trucks. We took special care to lay them with their feet facing up. But we had so many they would be stacked like cordwood. There would be several people deep on a truck and I hated to see it . . .

"As far as the Japs, we didn't take such special care. Hell, they didn't even take the time to recover, let alone bury their own dead when they could, so we didn't hurry with it either. Guys would be assigned to lasso them by their legs and drag them into these massive ditches we dug. Then we would bulldoze dirt over them as they laid shoulder-to-shoulder. It still is one of the most heartbreaking things a man could see. And I never will forget it as long as I live . . .

"We would plant a stick in the ground above the dirt mounds, with the number of bodies, such as '80' or '300' written on it and that was it. We buried all the Japanese that way . . .

"You know, they had been told that we were inferior fighters to them, which was probably true at the beginning of the war. But as time went on, like by the time Saipan happened, they really found out different. We put a lot of pressure on them and gave them no time to rest when we were chasing them. I was in good shape then and could run five miles at a time with my pack on my back without stopping . . .

"Toward the end, we pushed them toward the ocean and then we surrounded them. They had no place to go. Our planes dropped fliers written in Japanese 'to surrender and you will be given food and water and treated well.' But we knew they wouldn't surrender. That is not what they were trained to do. They either feared they would be tortured by us, or that they would rather die with honor than surrender, or maybe it was a little bit of both, I don't know . . .

"That final week on Saipan we were doing a lot of mop-up duty, searching for stragglers who did not surrender. One day, we were escorting a few engineers who were using satchel charges and flame throwers to get them out of the caves. We were walking on a footpath around the mountain, when suddenly, a Japanese captain and two of his soldiers surprised us. They walked right into us. I was at the front, and I noticed them before they noticed us, so I had no choice but to open up on them. I shot them all before they ever raised their rifles to their shoulders. I just reacted."

It was a kill or be killed situation, something often seen in war movies. Dad always credited the M-1 Garand for keeping him alive in situations like that. It was the most common semiautomatic rifle American soldiers carried, versus the slower bolt-action rifles the Japanese soldiers were issued.

"I loved that gun. We had a big advantage with that M-1. I fired it so much on Saipan that I had to replace the barrel after each big firefight. I wore a couple of ammo bandelier belts around my neck, because I never wanted to run out, but I came close at times."

During the final two weeks of the battle on Saipan, Dad started losing a massive amount of weight and was running an increasingly high fever. He was growing weaker by the day. His wisdom teeth were fully impacted. He also had severe dysentery.

"By the end of it, all I could do was run out quickly, shoot and then run back for cover. I was very weak. A medic took my temperature, and it was 104. I was eating nothing but bullion and pea soup through a straw. The medic gave me some white, chalky substance for my dysentery . . .

"You can imagine what I looked like, being that sick, and living and sleeping in a muddy hole in the ground for almost a month. I would run and jump into a fox hole and have diarrhea all over the place, and if there was another guy already in there, all I could do was apologize to him. Our foxholes were unsanitary to begin with and I was making them much worse. It's really a wonder I didn't get shot by one of my own men because of it . . .

"Toward the end, our planes started dropping DDT on the island. It was like a misty rain falling down on us. Then for the next week or two, you wouldn't see one fly or mosquito. I always wondered what that stuff did to your body."

The army raised the U.S. flag on July 9, two days after the banzai attack failed, and immediately started to build airstrips. The remaining Japanese soldiers refused to surrender, and the fighting ended when there no more left to kill.

Afterward, Dad said his company received intelligence that the famous female pilot, Amelia Earhart, who had been missing since 1937, may have been captured and held somewhere on the island.

(One coincidental fact about Earhart: She had been on the USS *Lurline* from Los Angeles to Honolulu with her Lockheed Vega airplane secured on deck December 22–27, 1934. The voyage came a month before her record-breaking Honolulu-to-Oakland solo flight. It would be the same ship Dad and the 27th sailed on just less than eight years later, from San Francisco to Hawaii).

Once Saipan was secured, one of the tasks was to ask civilians if they had seen her. They were each given pictures of her to show them.

"We had been told there was a chance she was there somewhere, but since her airplane disappeared seven years earlier, none of us thought there was any chance we would bump into her. I am sure it was bad intelligence. I don't know how they expected us to do it anyway, since we didn't speak Japanese and they didn't speak English, but hell, we never had the chance to ask anyone . . . ," Dad said.

When it was over, thousands of Japanese civilians and the few Japanese soldiers who had survived or hidden successfully from the final mop-up jumped to their deaths at two locations, called "Banzai Cliff" and "Suicide Point."

The Japanese commanders had emphasized supposed American brutality, claiming the U.S. soldiers were bloodthirsty and would torture them if captured. They also had convinced the civilian women that they would be raped if captured. Of course, that was not true, either. It is estimated that there were more than 5,000 who committed suicide after the fighting was over.

"I watched through my binoculars as Japanese women would hold their children and jump off the cliffs into the ocean . . . I saw some of them landing on the rocks below. They just believed their government which told them we were evil, and that we would torture them . . ."

Dad always claimed it was one of the worst sights of the entire war.

The medics of his unit then convinced him he had to be admitted to a medical tent they had constructed by the beach. He now weighed 140 pounds, his mouth was full of blood, and he was sweating profusely from the high fever.

"I was just skin and bones when it was over. They laid the wounded in two rows on cots. There must have been about 50 of us in there," he said. "That first night, I was scared to death in there. I kept dreaming the Japs would bust in there and shoot us all. I was delirious. The medical personnel wanted to take my M-1, and I struggled with them, screaming, 'YOU ARE NOT TAKING MY RIFLE!' So, they laid it right beside my cot, but I am sure now that they had unloaded it first."

After three days in the medical tent, when a room opened on a hospital ship floating offshore, he was moved there.

"The first day I was on there, this big doctor who weighed about 300 pounds put his knee on my chest and pulled out my infected wisdom teeth without giving me any anesthetic. He held my teeth in his hands, and they looked huge, and they were covered in blood."

"That's why you were in so much pain!" the doctor told me.

"He then diagnosed me with Dengue fever. I asked him, 'What the hell is that?'

"It's not good," he said. "It can kill you if it is not treated."

"He told me I had been bit by an infected mosquito."

One day as Dad recovered in his room, one of his buddies stopped for a visit. In the course of the conversation, the guy mentioned John Lewis.

"I asked him, 'Yeah, what about him?'"

"Well, he was telling me what you did to save him," the buddy explained.

"I said, 'WHAT? YOU MEAN HE'S ALIVE? HE MADE IT? WHERE IS HE?'"

He was shocked to learn that Lewis not only was alive, but he was starting to recover following surgery, and his room was down the same hallway of the ship. A doctor then helped Dad into a wheelchair and pushed him down the hallway to see for himself.

"He wheeled me in there, and there was John, smiling. I couldn't believe it. I told him, 'I can't believe you survived that wound, but I never was going to tell you that at the time.'

"That was the last I saw him. He was shipped back to Pearl Harbor, and they admitted him to Tripler Hospital. When he was well enough, they sent him to San Francisco and then discharged him and he returned home to New York . . .

"Years later, John found my address and wrote me a long letter of how the doctors told him I saved his life. But I never saw him again until he and his wife Cora visited us in Ohio that one summer. John could never thank me enough, but at one point I told him, 'John, I know you would have done the same thing for me if I had been hit instead of you.'

"He put me in for the Silver Star, but they ended up giving me a Bronze Star, which was fine with me. I didn't care. I always told John if he had been an officer, I would have got the Silver Star . . . he knew I was joking."

John Lewis was awarded a Purple Heart for his wounds.

Dad spent five days on the medical ship.

"They released me, and I caught a boat ride to the beach. I then hitched a ride with some guys from another unit in a Jeep back to the northern part of the island where I was told my unit was. They got me as close as they could, and then I walked the final mile," he said.

"I wanted to be a part of them starting the construction of the new airfield. That was the whole purpose of winning the island in the first place..."

Saipan marked the first defeat of the Japanese army in Japanese territory, and it shocked the military leaders back in Tokyo. General Hideki Tojo had promised the Japanese citizens that the Americans would never take Saipan. Tojo resigned a week following the end of the battle, which was very costly—to both sides.

"He had helped design the Pearl Harbor attack," Dad said. "To me, he was a coward."

The Japanese army lost more than 32,000 soldiers and more than 10,000 civilians, by most estimates. The Americans lost more than 3,000 soldiers, including Joe Majernik and William O'Brien, and another 13,000 were wounded, including John Lewis.

They were three statistics of war, but three that were very personal for Dad, because he talked about them often over the years.

"It really was hell. The things I saw during those three or four weeks of battle on Saipan I will never forget as long as I live."

CHAPTER SIX

BOATING AND FISHING "UNFAIRLY" ON R&R

After Saipan had been fought and ultimately won, there was no understating its importance toward total victory for the Allies in the Pacific Theater. The new airfield runways would be ready by October of 1944, as the Americans began launching B-29s headed to the Philippines, to other islands close by in the Marianas chain and to the Japanese mainland.

As for Dad and most of the 27th Infantry, they had been pulled from Saipan on September 4 and were headed for some well-deserved rest and rehabilitation.

And no soldier needed it more than he did.

"We got out to sea, and we got our papers that we were going on some R&R, which I needed, but we didn't know where," he said. "I was hoping it would be in New Zealand or Australia because I always wanted to see those countries, but it turned out to be a place called New Hebrides . . .

"It was a chain of islands occupied by the French and British, located east of Australia. We arrived on September 13 to a tiny island called Espiritu Santo, where they had already built a large U.S. Naval base, supply depot and airstrip . . .

"But I had to spend the first eight or 10 days there at the navy hospital. I was still recovering from the Dengue fever. It turned out I also had a bad concussion, the doctors told me, and I wasn't able to hear much at all. I still was low on the list of patients, because doctors and medics cared more about bullet wounds and blood loss than what I had . . .

"Anyway, I slowly started to recover, and I knew I had to put some weight back on, but it took some time. I had no muscle mass on my body, and I basically was nothing but skin and bones. I got to eat a lot of black olives and peanuts in addition to normal food they served us like mutton and spam, which I always hated. But to this day, I love black olives and peanuts . . .

"When I got out of that hospital, I discovered the place was beautiful. There were huge rows of coconut palms, nice bays and beaches, places to swim. During the mornings, from about 6 a.m. to noon, we still were doing some light training and basically regrouping. In the afternoon, we could do what we wanted, and at night, they had outdoor movies for us to watch. But I wasn't much of a movie guy back then, so I don't remember watching one movie . . .

"At times, it actually seemed like we were on vacation somewhere in the South Pacific, which I guess we were in a way. Me and some of the guys who I was close to usually went fishing each afternoon. But I admit we didn't fish 'fairly,' since we didn't have any tackle or fishing poles. We would wait for the tide to come into this little bay, and then I would toss a grenade into the water and all kinds of fish, like snapper and grouper, just floated to the surface. They were stunned. So, I told the other guys how it worked and that became our method of fishing . . .

"We would scoop them up and have plenty of fish to eat. The cooks gave us one of those large, deep-frying pans, and we fried them every night. One day, Captain Willie, who was not well-liked by the men, came to me and asked, 'Who has been killing all of these Red Snapper the guys are eating?'

"'I have. Been using grenades.'

"I thought I was about to get a real ass-chewing for wasting grenades, but he then he told me, 'Well, keep it up! The morale has never been higher since the guys started eating all this fish instead of mutton and spam!'"

One day, Dad and some buddies were by the beach fishing when he spotted a familiar face.

"There was a guy from my hometown, Dwight Richey, who I knew had been on Saipan, but I had no idea if he survived it. This little outboard boat comes puttering up to us and there was Dwight on the boat. That is when he told me his incredible story: He had been pinned down on the beach at Saipan and ran out of ammo, so he had no choice but to swim out into the ocean, where one of our destroyers picked him up. It was an amazing story of survival . . .

"He and his buddies told us they were shipping out soon—they were sending them all the way back to Saipan to help with the building of air strips. They asked us if we wanted to buy their boat. It was about a 22-footer with a six-cylinder motor on it. It was me and three other sergeants—Maynard Levitz, a guy named Runyon and Jack Noble.

"I said, 'Of course we want it . . . but how much?'

"They wanted $600, but we didn't have that much money on us, so we ended up chipping in $100 each and we bought it for $400. Almost every day after that, we went fishing on that little boat. We took it to other little outer islands all the time . . . One day we came up on one tiny island, which was about five miles away, and as we pulled into a dock, a Frenchman came running out, yelling, 'Hey, hey, come on in . . . glad to have you!' . . .

"I don't think he was used to seeing many people. We gave him some of our fish and he gave us some of the wine he had saved. We drank some wine and had a nice conversation with him . . .

FROM OHIO TO OKINAWA...

"We also had met this French cattle farmer, who told us he couldn't ship his beef because the war was going on. So, we worked out a deal: We would give him fresh fish, and he gave us a lot of fresh beef. Now we had all the steak we could eat, too. There were dairy cows there, so we had fresh milk. There also were vegetable patches. We always had plenty of beer there, but we didn't have ice, so it was warm, and I never could drink warm beer . . .

"We got permission from the army to set up an area with thatched roofs on this guy's plantation where we could feed 40 people at one time, twice a day. We even had French fried sweet potatoes. I always loved them. Everything was served family style,

A recent photo of the bay at Port Orly, Espiritu Santo, which now is called Vanuatu, where Dad and his buddies from the 27th enjoyed "fishing" for snapper and grouper while on R&R.

and the guy charged $1.25 per man. We just had to sign up ahead of time on his calendar we made."

But Dad's boating fun ended abruptly one day.

"Noble was out on the boat with another guy, and they hit an outcropping about 300 yards offshore. The boat sank and they had to swim to shore . . .

"I told Jack, 'Hey, you owe me $100!'

"He said, 'Will you take $50?'

"I did—and that was the end of my boat investment. But I got my $50 worth on that boat. We had so much fun running around those little islands."

Their R&R time there, however, wasn't without a little stress. Dad said some of the guys were already experiencing PTSD symptoms after the horror of Saipan and he never knew when it would surface.

One day during lunch, a guy in his unit grew tired of a bug flying around his plate of food.

"So, he just pulled out his .45 and started firing at it!" Dad said. "It's lucky we didn't get shot eating lunch because of him."

Then one night, another guy they had nicknamed "Chief," because of his Native-American heritage, completely snapped.

"God, Chief was a big strong guy," Dad said. "We had those big Browning 1919 machine guns, which set on a tripod, and it usually took two or three guys to carry them when we had to move them. But Chief could pick it up, along with the tripod and the ammo belt, and run full speed with it. That's how strong he was . . .

"I also think he was the bravest man I ever saw. We were taking fire on Saipan once and he ran right through it to get to a strategic spot where we needed that machine gun. I always wanted Chief on that big gun, because he was the only one who could carry it by himself, and nothing seemed to scare him. But he was still a private because he was getting busted for getting drunk all the time . . .

"Anyway, even on Espiritu Santo, I slept with my M-1 and .45 next to my bunk, and I set my boots right there to jump into. One night I was sound asleep when I heard a machine gun close by and I thought we were under attack. I jumped into my boots, grabbed my M-1 and looked out to see what was going on . . .

"It was Chief. He was drunk. Apparently, he had too much warm beer, and he was shooting at the tops of the officers' tents. I snuck up next to him, turned my rifle around and hit him square in the side of the head with the butt of it. I really was lucky he didn't shoot me right there . . .

"He went down and then he looked up at me and said, 'Gee, Sarge, you about killed me!' He then went on and on about how much he hated all the officers. I told him, 'You big dumb Indian! You can't kill our own officers! You know better than that!' . . .

"I really thought the shit would hit the fan, but not one officer came down to our tents to see who was shooting at them. Even on the next day, nobody said a word about it. Nothing ever came of it, and we kept our mouths shut."

Espiritu Santo became well known worldwide a few years later after James Michener wrote *Tales of the South Pacific*, on the island. That led to the play *South Pacific*.

Today, it has been renamed Vanuatu, a well-known tourist attraction with plush hotels, aqua water and white sandy beaches.

"It sure was beautiful," Dad recalled. "We spent that Thanksgiving and then Christmas there. I spent four Thanksgivings and four Christmases, '41, '42, '43, and '44 in the army, but the final one was the best Christmas because Saipan was over, and we were having so much fun on that island . . .

"You would never think we would be having fun during a war, would you? Some days and weeks we were fighting for our lives on some island like Saipan, covered in mud, and we had not bathed or shaved in a long, long time. We smelled bad and I didn't know if we would live to see the next day . . .

"Then here we were, resting between battles on some beautiful island in the middle of the Pacific, palm trees all around us, thousands of miles from home, laughing and joking with each other, as if we didn't have a care in the world. At the same time, we always knew there was another battle ahead for us and we all had that fear it may be our last . . . . that is what our lives were like for almost four years."

On March 25, 1945, the 27th's R&R had come to an end. And despite two guys flipping out and shooting either at bugs or officers' tents, nothing died but a bunch of fish.

They then boarded troop ships again and sailed from Espiritu Santo, headed out to sea to rejoin the fight somewhere closer to Japan.

CHAPTER SEVEN

OKINAWA

Now that Saipan was under U.S. control and the marines had raised the flag on Iwo Jima on February 23, 1945, an event that led to one of the more famous photographs ever taken, the next major objective for American forces in the Pacific was to take Okinawa Island.

Okinawa, 66 miles in length, seven miles wide, and a total of 466 square miles, just east of mainland Japan, was being held by an estimated minimum of 130,000 Japanese forces, and it was considered the final obstacle toward total victory in the Pacific Theater.

That is, unless Japan would not surrender even if the Allies took the island, and President Truman would decide it was necessary to eventually invade Japan's mainland.

As Dad and the 27th Infantry were leaving New Hebrides, General Simon Buckner's 10th Army, and thousands more troops from the 2nd Marine Division were about to storm the Okinawa beaches in "Operation Iceberg."

It was late March.

"From New Hebrides, when we got out to sea about 200 miles, all we could see were ships," Dad recalled. "There must have been thousands of them. And all of them were ours. On the second day out, we were told we were headed toward Ulithi in the Caroline Islands, west of the Philippines.

"But we ended up as a floating reserve there and never got off the ship. From there, we continued on to Okinawa."

Japan's defense of Okinawa was considered to be its strongest and deepest of any island of the entire war, since its military leaders sent most of its remaining forces there as a last stand of sorts. It was defended by General Mitsuru Ushijima's 32nd Army and the 44th Independent Mixed Brigade. Then they had added 9,000 Imperial Japanese Navy troops. Ushijima also ordered almost 40,000 civilians to serve as reserve militia and laborers as support personnel.

In other words, it was well-fortified, and the ensuing battle would be bloody and costly.

Ushijima stationed his primary defense in the southern part of the island while the northern territory was up to Colonel Takehido Udo's forces. Japan also planned large-scale kamikaze attacks on the U.S. fleets they believed to be arriving soon.

They anticipated correctly.

American ships poured into the area surrounding Okinawa in the final days of March and the naval bombardment of the island began April 1, before 50,000 soldiers of Buckner's division stormed the beaches. Surprisingly, they encountered no resistance and quickly established a beachhead and began pushing inland. It was the trap that Ushijima had planned. He had figured they could surround the American soldiers on three sides at a place called the Shuri Line, and it initially worked, as the Americans suffered heavy casualties.

A week later, Dad's unit arrived.

"We pulled into a place called Nakagusuku Bay on April 9. We were a floating reserve for a few days when the fighting had started, but then we got off and established our position along the coast. We joined up with part of four army divisions which were headed to the south part of the island . . .

"I had no idea, but it was about to be a bloodbath like it was on Saipan, only on a much larger scale. We formed a long line of troops and pushed toward the mountain, toward the Shuri Castle, which I read later was built in the 14th Century. We were told that was the Japanese headquarters and taking it was crucial, but we really struggled trying to get up that mountainside, trying to climb foot by foot every night . . .

"The Japs didn't bury their dead there, either, just like on Saipan. They were lying all over the place. It was a stinking mess. There were the Blow flies, and it was a highly diseased area. The bodies were bloating. It was the most depressing thing. We had to go slow, because it was muddy and raining some of the time . . .

"That was the most miserable time as far as I was concerned. You almost couldn't breathe, because it was the worst smell you can imagine. Bodies laid there for almost a week. We were facing fierce shelling from the Japs each day, because they were losing the war and getting desperate. They had those big 155-millimeter guns and some other big artillery, which could throw a shell 10 to 12 miles . . .

"I was right there at what they called the Shuri Line on the southern part of the island when the shelling from both sides got as intense as anything I ever experienced. There were a bunch of caves and caverns on Okinawa, and we were going through them one by one. But we were being bombed constantly. And we were still taking some fire from the caverns and caves. They would run out and shoot four or five rounds at us and then run back into the caves . . . we suffered tremendous losses daily, mainly because of the terrain and mountains. It was hard to fight there . . .

"I remember we had to build a bridge of pontoons to get across a river one night and we had a suspicion the Japs had pulled back off that area, so we would be in the clear. It was true, they were hiding, waiting for us to get to the other side. It was about 250 yards across the river . . .

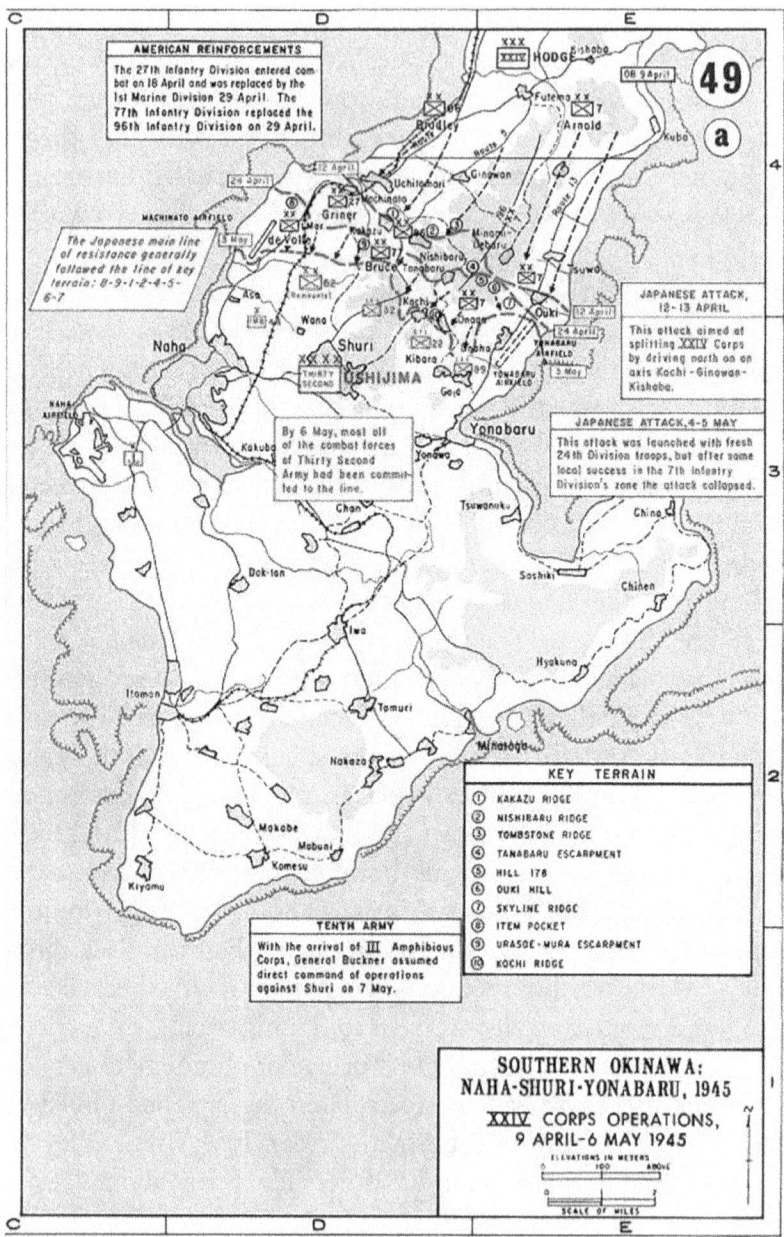

This Okinawa map details the U.S. forces' invasion and battles, which included Dad's 27th Infantry, of April to June of 1945.

"I hadn't crossed it yet when the captain came to me one night and told me to take some guys and get across this river fast. We needed to establish water, food, and ammo dumps on the other side for the guys already there. We already had somebody on the other side with a flashlight. When he would blink his flashlight, I knew I could go. So, I took some guys and went as fast as we could and we made it across without being noticed . . .

"Then the next morning, when day broke, all hell broke loose, because the Japanese saw the bridge and started bombing it with some big artillery rounds, but they were having trouble hitting it. They changed to aircraft bombing and put the bridge down real fast . . .

"I was about a half a mile away, watching it when I turned to a buddy and said, 'I think we are going to get it now.' As soon as the words were out of my mouth, a shell went right by my head. I never heard it, but I felt the heat of it go by me. It landed about 15 yards behind me and threw me straight up into the air. When I came down, I twisted my knee . . .

"I was really hurting. I thought I was bleeding, but there was no blood anywhere. The right side of my face was completely numb. I couldn't hear anything out of my right ear, either. It already had been damaged at Saipan. But our medics were so occupied with open wounds at the time that they didn't have time for me. I just laid there for a while . . . one eventually got to me and dragged me into a foxhole. Then a few minutes later, that same medic got killed . . .

"I could feel the shells going into the ground and then exploding underground. The earth was shaking, and that shook me right to my core. I thought I was about to buy the big ticket.

"I was scared to death, I'll admit it. I had been in war for more than three years, and I really feared getting it near the end. They say you can't see a bullet coming out of a rifle, but I know you can see the shells coming out of those big guns—and I saw that on Okinawa . . .

"We finally got dug in on a hill, digging some foxholes, but they had their artillery zoned in on us pretty good. When there was a break in the shelling, I climbed out to check on two of my guys who were in another foxhole when I saw that a shell had dropped directly into their foxhole, and they got incinerated. There were no boots, no helmets, no nothing left of them . . .

"I was never really afraid of combat until those moments on Okinawa, especially when I saw what an artillery shell could do to the human body. It could make it just disappear . . .

"After just seeing my guys get obliterated by that artillery shell, I was stuck in a foxhole, scared to death. It was the most scared I had been in the entire war. My hands were shaking. I had nowhere to run to, and I prayed for a sign from God to save me. I then looked up from the foxhole to see a rainbow. It was so clear—and it was nighttime. That was my sign, my miracle, I told myself. I know it sounds very hard to believe, but it happened—I saw that rainbow . . .

"And I got out of there the next day, but I had a headache you would not believe for several days. My face was so numb that I couldn't feel it or shave it . . .

"Our sister division, the 94th Infantry, had made a breakthrough of the enemy line about a mile from us. They came in with a dozen or so Sherman tanks with bulldozer blades on them to root out the Japanese's fake tanks. We had wasted too much ammo on their fake tanks . . .

"I saw a couple of our tanks with bulldozer blades moving along . . . and then I could hear it when they hit a yardstick mine the Japs had planted in the ground. Those big tanks would fly about 50 yards up into the air—just an incredible sight to see . . .

"But our big guns eventually beat theirs. It probably took us 14 or 15 days before we could neutralize what they had. The one advantage we always had over them in the war is that we could replace our losses with reinforcements, but they couldn't. But during the early battles of Okinawa, that was not the case for us. Our division had taken heavy losses in just a few days, and we got word we needed to pull back and re-tool. We had started losing people and not getting them replaced, and we were nowhere near full strength. I think our casualty rate on Okinawa was more than 40 percent. We were told a few marine platoons were coming in to relieve us . . .

"As we walked out, I shook hands with a few of them as they walked in, and I said, 'You are welcome to this mess.' Most of them were nice guys, but this one marine looked right at me and said, 'Watch the real men take care of these Jap bastards!'

"I told him, 'I will watch you real men die if you fight this battle like you normally fight!'

"I will never forget that. He just kept walking. I always wondered if that cocky marine made it or not. We army guys always thought they just did not fight smartly. They were young and brave, but they were so gung-ho that they would charge in and get slaughtered standing up facing the enemy, like I saw on the first day at Saipan. Okinawa was a place full of mountains and hills and you couldn't go charging at the Japanese anywhere or you would get mowed down. And sure enough, many of those marines died on Okinawa . . .

"After we got relieved, they told us we were headed right next door, to invade the tiny island of Ie Shima. Our regiment got on three LSTs and took off at dark, so their suicide pilots wouldn't see us. We ran those boats fast for about 40 miles from the south part of the island and headed northwest to Ie Shima and landed with no problem. We got off and established a beachhead quickly . . .

"But as soon as we got off, our boats immediately came under kamikaze attacks. Their planes were buzzing everywhere. I saw them hit an LST right in front of me. The stern floated free and the bow stayed on the beach, but I don't think anybody was in it . . .

"About 75 to 100 of them came in on a one-way trip. They were that desperate. They were young pilots. We knew that they were running out of men, so they had started drafting down to the age of 13- or 14-year-olds two years earlier and had trained them to fly. They knew they were going to die for the emperor. You find it hard to understand they wanted to die for a cause, which was to take as many of the enemy as they could take . . . .

"But once you got off an LST, you knew they couldn't hit you. We started up through the foothills of Ie Shima, and made contact with some Japanese soldiers and started pushing them back immediately, but there wasn't much resistance there . . .

"One of our jobs was to protect the small airfield with some marines and guys from the 77th Infantry who were attached to us. We would lay back and watch a Jap airplane land on the tiny runway there. Then all these guys would get out of it, almost huddle like a football team, and take off running in different directions. They would run to our planes sitting there and drop grenades in them. But now we had stationed Jeeps with 30-caliber and 50-caliber guns patrolling those runways and we just wiped them out the next few times they tried to do it . . .

"We mopped up that island rather quickly, although there were a few casualties, one of which really saddened me, which I will talk about later."

Once Ie Shima was secured, on April 22, the 27th was sent back to Okinawa where they were needed again, since the fighting was still fierce. American fighter planes and bombers started flying out of the new Ie Shima airfield runways on May 13.

"After we got back, we were above a little peninsula one night when I dug a foxhole and then put a tent over it. I was almost asleep, when I heard some guys making noise outside. One of our spotters in an outpost had noticed two smaller boats with little outboards coming ashore right below us . . .

"We knew they weren't ours, but we could clearly see people on them, so a few of the guys with machine guns opened up on them until they stopped moving. We waited for daybreak and then went down there to inspect the boats. There were 15 bodies lying there, but among them were six women . . . I don't know if they had been married couples or what. They were very young. We figured they must have been on another little island and were sneaking back to where they lived, but why they did that in the middle of a war, especially at night, I have no idea . . .

"I always felt so bad about that, but we didn't know. It was dark and we thought they were Japanese fighters sneaking up on us, but you remember those things later. That was terrible."

The battleship *Mississippi* had shelled the headquarters at Shuri Castle on Okinawa for three days from May 25-27, and it eventually burned. Dad said once that happened, he knew the Americans would take the island.

"We didn't know if their commanders would come out and surrender. Most of them committed suicide before we could kill them. I think we ended up taking 200 who surrendered, and that was a huge thing. We hadn't seen that before—they just hated to surrender . . .

"But that didn't mean they were all surrendering. They still had some firepower left and most of them who remained were going to go down using it. One day we were down by the bay, where we had landed in April, when one of our chaplains walked by me and asked, 'You got any toilet paper?' I handed him a roll and he walked into the woods . . .

"He was just about done when they started shelling us again. He came running by me with his pants down around his ankles. He pulled them up and kept running. I said, 'Hey, where's the rest of my toilet paper?' A roll of toilet paper in the war was like gold. But he just kept running . . . it seemed like everybody on Okinawa had diarrhea at the time. My buddy Marty Emmer was in the woods doing the same thing, and then he came running out before he could finish, too . . .

"The next day, not too far from that spot, is when Buckner got it."

The highest-ranking U.S. officer to die in World War II, General Simon Buckner was surveying a battlefield when an artillery shell exploded nearby. Its shrapnel pierced his chest. After the war, the U.S. renamed Nakagusuku Bay to Buckner Bay.

"I have always called it Buckner Bay," Dad explained.

By the time it concluded, the battle for Okinawa was the deadliest of World War II.

General Simon Buckner, left, on Okinawa days before he was killed on the island on June 18, 1945, the highest-ranking U.S. officer to die in World War II.

The Americans suffered some 48,000 casualties, with more than 12,000 killed or missing. Killed in action were 4,907 from the navy, 4,675 army soldiers, and 2,938 marines, counting the naval losses at sea and on the surrounding islands.

The battle resulted in more than twice the number of American casualties than the Guadalcanal Campaign and Battle of Iwo Jima combined, with Japanese kamikaze pilots causing the U.S. Navy to suffer more casualties than any previous battle in the Atlantic or in the Pacific.

One casualty on the island turned out to be Dad's close friend.

When the fighting finally concluded, he couldn't find fellow sergeant Jack Noble, who had run their boat aground on Espiritu Santo a few months earlier. He started asking around about Jack's whereabouts, and that is when someone told him he had been killed in combat just a few days earlier.

"That was all of our worst fears," Dad said. "To buy it near the end of the war."

Okinawa was the largest land-sea-air battle in history. The value of it was significant, as it provided a safe harbor for American ships, troop staging areas, and airfields in close proximity to Japan.

It also was the final major battle before the start of the atomic age of warfare, which was about to change everything.

CHAPTER EIGHT

MEETING ERNIE PYLE

As you could imagine, there were limited communications and media reports during the war for Dad and his buddies in the 27th from the time they were first stationed in Hawaii for the last nine months of 1942 and then while fighting somewhere in the Pacific from 1943-45.

They were constantly curious, however, how the war was progressing in the European Theater, as well as what was happening all around them in the Pacific.

They devoured pages of the *Stars and Stripes* newspaper whenever they could find it. And the war correspondent's work they read the most was that of Ernest Taylor Pyle.

To the soldiers on the front lines, Ernie Pyle was one of them, because he had been embedded with the troops in Europe for the first three years of World War II. He ate with them, slept in fox holes next to them, dodged the same bullets and bombs they did and told their stories to the American public along the way.

He was revered by U.S. servicemen everywhere.

Pyle had been a roving correspondent for the Scripps Howard newspaper chain 1935-41. His specialty had been writing in-depth stories of the lives of ordinary people in rural America.

FROM OHIO TO OKINAWA...

But after Pearl Harbor was attacked, he began his career as a war correspondent and was embedded with troops in Europe. Pyle covered the Battle of Britain, as well as military campaigns in North Africa, Italy and France, before traveling to the Pacific in January of 1945 to accompany the army and the marines.

"We all knew who Ernie Pyle was . . . he was very famous," Dad explained. "Everybody at one time or another had read his stories of the war. He was respected by all of us, because he would get down in the dirt with the guys. He didn't cover it from the safety of being behind the front lines. We all knew he loved to interview the dogface guys like us.

"We would get *Stars and Stripes* occasionally, but it was always weeks old. That's how we found out about Normandy, but it was always well after the fact."

Pyle, an Indiana native, had won a Pulitzer Prize in 1944 for his coverage of the war during the year prior. By April of 1945, he was embedded with the Army's 77th Infantry in the Pacific. He had just filed stories of Japanese kamikaze pilots attacking U.S. troops in Okinawa when the 77th landed on the tiny island nearby, Ie Shima.

The 27th, and Dad, was already there, having just arrived from Okinawa. Their assignment was to guard the small airstrip.

On April 16, Dad saw a Jeep approaching him and his H company buddies, who were walking on the road near the beach. It appeared to hold four soldiers, but once it got closer, somebody recognized that there were only three soldiers—and the famous war correspondent was riding in the back.

"Somebody next to me said, 'You know who that is? That's Ernie Pyle!'" he recalled.

"It was a big deal when I saw him. He was in the back of a Jeep, and it slowed down so Ernie could interview some guys. He was just a little fella, very thin and that big helmet on his head made him look even smaller. When he finished talking to a few guys, he was shaking everyone's hands as the Jeep slowly went by us.

"So, I stuck my hand out, too, and shook his hand as he moved by us. I found out later that the guy in the front seat of the Jeep was a lieutenant colonel by the name of (Joseph) Coolidge, who was the commander of the 305th Regiment."

The area was thought to be cleared of any Japanese soldiers, but two days later, that Jeep—carrying Coolidge, two other officers and Pyle—came under intense machine gun fire at the exact same spot. They jumped off and scrambled for cover in a roadside ditch along the road by the beach.

According to Coolidge, as they laid in the ditch, Pyle asked him, "Are you alright?" Then he made a fatal mistake, the same one Joe Majernik had made on Saipan, when he raised his head. Those were his final words.

He was hit immediately with a sniper's bullet to the left temple, killing him instantly. He was 45 years old.

The news spread quickly among the troops and made headlines coast-to-coast back in the United States. After spending more than three years writing about soldiers, bullets, bombs and death, America's most beloved war correspondent had become a casualty of the war.

Once the 77th wiped out the remaining Japanese soldiers, including the one they figured had killed him, Pyle was quickly buried next to other casualties on Ie Shima. He was laid between an infantry private and a combat engineer. He was one of only a few American civilians killed during World War II, in addition to those 68 at or near Pearl Harbor when it all began.

"We came back around there the very next day, and I rode right by that spot where he got hit. We stopped where they buried him to take a moment to honor him," Dad remembered. "They just buried him under a pile of dirt right there along the road. Then they took two large artillery shells to make a cross. They stuck his helmet on top of it."

"We secured that island right after Ernie died, and then some army engineers came in working like a bunch of beavers, working 24 hours a day to build an airbase. There was a lot of lava and coral there, like in Hawaii, so it made for a tremendous airbase. I think they had one airstrip built in 10 days and they eventually built three," Dad explained.

Former First Lady Eleanor Roosevelt, who had just lost her husband, Franklin Roosevelt, six days earlier, had often quoted excerpts from Pyle's war stories in her newspaper column, "My Day." She paid tribute to him in her column the day after his death: "I shall never forget how much I enjoyed meeting him here in the White House last year, and how much I admired this frail and modest man who could endure hardships because he loved his job and our men."

President Harry Truman said: "No man in this war has so well told the story of the American fighting man as American fighting men wanted it to be told. He deserves the gratitude of all his countrymen."

Pyle became the only civilian to receive a Purple Heart, posthumously of course. Today, the Journalism School at Indiana University is named in his honor.

Four years following the end of war, before the U.S. returned Ie Shima and Okinawa to Japan, Pyle's body was removed and buried at the National Memorial Cemetery of the Pacific—aka "The Punchbowl"—in Honolulu.

When Dad and I last visited it together in 2010, I pushed him in his wheelchair over to the shade under a line of huge trees on the left side of the entrance road, where we found Ernie's grave.

I will never forget watching him, almost as if he wanted to go back in time and speak to him if only to tell Ernie to keep his head down, just like he did for Joe Majernik, who is buried on the opposite side of the entry road.

The 77th's makeshift sign honoring war correspondent Ernie Pyle after he was killed on Ie Shima.

My photo of Ernie Pyle's grave, taken in 2021, at the National Memorial Cemetery of the Pacific in Honolulu.

I never realized this until that day, but Dad had to be one of the few men who ever saw both of Pyle's gravesites: The initial makeshift grave on Ie Shima and his final resting place on Oahu.

He was very solemn that day, seeing it for the first time.

"It really was a damn shame," he said, looking down at his gravestone. "If he had just kept his head down that day, he probably would have survived the entire war and then lived a long life and written so much more about it. I will never forget seeing that pile of dirt on Ie Shima, knowing the great Ernie Pyle was under it . . . and I shook his hand just two days before.

"You know, when you are in the middle of a war, you don't think about it as much because you are thinking about how to survive it all yourself, so you don't take too much time crying over someone else's body, or over their grave.

"But being here now is very different . . ."

His voice trailed off. He didn't have to finish the sentence. I knew what he meant.

CHAPTER NINE

UNCLE GEORGE AND HIS FAMOUS COMMANDER

While Dad was doing his part on the battlefield in the Pacific Theater, his younger brother George was doing the same in the air over Europe.

George W. Snook was a flight engineer and top gunner for the 445th Bombardment Group of the U.S. Eighth Air Force, which was dropping bombs on Hitler's Nazi forces.

With the oldest of their siblings, Frances, a nurse in the U.S. Army, I am proud to say that the Snook household in which seven kids grew up at 1415 Cottage Street had contributed its fair share to America's successful war effort.

But that was commonplace with families across America.

Patriotism flowed freely, perhaps more than at any time in our country's history. Many war historians agree that Nazi Germany's march across Europe and Hitler's plans to take over the world galvanized the United States like no other period in its history.

Then the Sunday morning attack of Pearl Harbor by the Japanese, bringing the first American bloodshed to the expanding war, instantly spurred men and women coast-to-coast to contribute something to the cause.

FROM OHIO TO OKINAWA...

It was just as Japanese Admiral Isoroku Yamamoto had predicted after the attack, when he stated, "I fear all we have done is to awaken a sleeping giant and fill him with a terrible resolve."

That line made it into several Hollywood movies, and it was debated whether he actually said it. Nevertheless, Americans were angry. They were fighting mad. They indeed were filled with a terrible resolve, and therefore, they took action.

They were, from every walk of life or profession, ready to go to battle. Rich, poor, black, white—it just didn't matter. They wanted a part in fighting, and eventually winning, the war that would save the world. No matter their occupation, fame or financial status, it seemed everyone wanted to join the fight.

That included the famous, from nationally known entertainers to Major League Baseball players, such as stars Yogi Berra and Ted Williams, to college and pro football players; to movie stars such as Clark Gable, Henry Fonda and Jimmy Stewart, who left their extremely profitable careers behind to enlist.

In fact, after his wife died, leaving Gable depressed, he wrote a personal telegram to President Roosevelt, asking permission to enlist in the army. It was granted. Once that news became public, Hitler, one of Gable's greatest fans, offered a $5,000 reward to any of his troops who could capture him and bring him to Germany.

Hitler's plan failed, however, and the actor returned to the United States safe and sound once the war ended. For his service in battle, he was awarded the Distinguished Flying Cross, American Campaign Medal, European-African-Middle Eastern Campaign Medal, and the World War II Victory Medal.

Fonda had claimed he no longer desired playing "fake war" roles in films, that he wanted to do the real thing, so he also enlisted in the U.S. Army in 1942. Working in operations and air-combat intelligence in the Central Pacific, he was later awarded a Bronze Star and Navy Presidential Unit Citation for extraordinary heroism.

Paul Newman, a Cleveland native, had enlisted in the navy. He was a torpedo bomber and also flew as a radioman-gunner. His squadron was attached to the USS *Bunker Hill* at Saipan in June of 1944, the same time Dad was there. Eleven months later, the pilot of his flight crew suffered from a severe ear infection and was forced to ground their airplane so he could be treated.

Thus, Newman stayed behind while the rest of the squadron was transferred to the Bunker Hill which was supporting the fight of Okinawa, also at the same time Dad was there. Only two days later, they were among the 396 men on the ship who were killed by a kamikaze attack.

After the war, Newman returned to Ohio, attended Kenyon College on the G.I. Bill, which was established in 1944, took drama and acting courses, before becoming a movie star.

Which brings me back to my Uncle George.

George's service during the war was anything but ordinary, largely because his commanding officer was none other than James Maitland Stewart—America knew him simply as Jimmy, the Academy Award-winning actor.

He had already starred in *Mr. Smith Goes to Washington* and *The Philadelphia Story* for which he won an Oscar—before joining the battle. That tells you all you need to know about the character of the man.

In today's world, it would be similar to a young Tom Hanks leaving Hollywood behind to join the army to actually save a Private Ryan somewhere in Afghanistan.

Imagine that for a moment.

By all accounts, and there have been many books written about him and his service to the country, Stewart always felt the call of duty while growing up in Indiana, Pennsylvania.

His paternal grandfather fought for the Union Army during the Civil War, serving under Gen. Philip Sheridan and a young officer named George Armstrong Custer. His maternal grandfather fought at Gettysburg and Fredericksburg. As a boy in the 1910s, Stewart would sit on his grandpa's knee, hearing his stories about the war that preserved the United States. They surely were similar to the Civil War stories Dad had heard from his blind neighbor while growing up.

In the following years, Stewart's father Alexander had sent him German helmets and other mementos he had collected while fighting in Europe during World War I. As a teenager, Jimmy would utilize those real war artifacts as props for his high school plays and musicals.

Given his heritage and what was at stake at the time, Stewart believed it was his calling and his duty to serve. He believed he had no choice, no matter what his agents and Hollywood producers told him.

However, there was a hitch when his draft number (Draft Board No. 245 in West Los Angeles) was called in February of 1941. Stewart, 32 at the time, stood 6'3" and weighed only 138 pounds—five pounds less than the mandated minimum weight.

Thus, he was rejected. That didn't stop him, however. He decided to go on eating binges to gain the necessary weight in order to become eligible. Weighing exactly 143 only one month later, he enlisted in the Army Air Corps as a buck private, assigned to Fort MacArthur near Los Angeles, thus becoming the first Hollywood actor to enlist before December 7, 1941.

Stewart always had a great interest in flying and had earned a civilian pilot's license in 1935, after taking flying lessons for several years. Three years later, he had his commercial pilot's license. By all accounts, he was an excellent pilot and was sent to Mather Air Base in Sacramento a month after the Pearl Harbor attack to serve as a flight instructor for the B-17 and B-24 bombers.

By then, he had been promoted to a second lieutenant. For his entire time at Mather, he constantly requested to be sent overseas to join the fight. Of course, given his status, he could have stayed in the U.S. and trained pilots for the duration of the war.

Finally, commanders relented and gave in to his persistent requests. He was sent to Tibenham, England, in November of 1943. There, he became a lead pilot of B-24 Liberators in the 445th. He soon became the commanding officer of a squadron and flew 20 bombing missions himself, many deep over Nazi-held territory.

My Uncle George, Dad's younger brother, participated in most of them—and they both had their share of close calls.

On February 25, 1944, Stewart led several bombers on a mission to Nuremburg, Germany. One particular B-24 Liberator with a distinctive name was the Stewart group's lead plane that day and had just dropped its load when it was hit by an 88-millimeter shell from German anti-aircraft fire.

However, the shell did not explode upon impact but traveled by the radio operator through the airplane's bomb-bay door, amazingly knocking the 50-caliber machine gun out of the gunner's hands while he was firing at trailing German fighter planes. The huge shell also ripped off the armor plating behind the pilot's seat, before blowing a huge hole in the left side of the plane, directly over the name of the plane, *Nine Yanks and a Jerk*.

It was simply unbelievable it had entered and exited the B-24 without nicking one of its 10 crew members or exploding upon impact.

The packed parachute and boots belonging to the B-24's flight engineer/top gunner immediately blew out of the large hole and another parachute followed. The crew realized their lives were riding on the crew's ability to work together to somehow land the damaged bomber somewhere safely.

After dropping his bombs, Stewart saw that the Liberator was in trouble, as did several other pilots on the mission. He slowed his airplane to survey the damage while flying alongside the wounded bomber. When he saw the size of the hole, he didn't think there was any way he would ever speak again to those 10 men who were under his command.

They were flying dead men, he thought.

The pilot, Mack Williams, immediately dropped the plane to a lower altitude so the crew could remove their oxygen masks and communicate easier as the flight engineer/top gunner checked the damage.

"We got a lot of problems!" the engineer/top gunner immediately yelled to the crew.

The hydraulic lines and the landing gear had been damaged, so he was forced to crawl into a tight space to pinch off the lines with a pair of pliers. Without working hydraulics, he then had to crawl into the nose of the bomber to manually push the nose wheel down into the landing position.

The crew realized the landing would be nearly impossible for all to survive, but they had no choice but to attempt it.

As it approached the runway in Tibenham, Williams and the engineer decided to have the other seven members of the crew sit in the tail to balance the weight. They all gathered there, crouching in a crash position. They believed this would keep the weight off the nose wheel, which likely would collapse upon impact. The flight engineer then positioned himself between Williams and co-pilot Douglas Pillow to count down their altitude and announce their air speed so they could focus on the landing.

Upon impact, the nose wheel collapsed, just as they had expected, and the plane suddenly veered to the left. The airplane's belly scraped along the runway and sparks flew from both sides. When it finally ran off the runway, the plane collapsed into a field. With the sudden stop, Williams hit his head hard on the instrument panel, opening a big gash, producing a scar he would show off for the remainder of his life.

Remarkably, everyone aboard lived to tell about the mission, the unexploded shell and the heroic landing which made it successful against all odds.

Stewart came running over to the plane, as the crew members jumped out thrilled to be alive.

"Mack, when I saw that hole in the side of the ship, I thought you were a goner," he told the pilot.

The crew members took turns sticking their heads through that huge hole as the gunner/flight engineer, who often carried a camera, took their pictures.

That B-24 became quite an attraction that day, as other bombing crews heard the tale and immediately scurried over to stare at the gaping hole.

That engineer/top gunner, the man who had lost his parachute and boots, then pinched the hydraulic lines, pushed down the nose wheel and afterward became the crew's chief photographer in the celebration and back-slapping once the ordeal was over, was hailed as a hero that day.

That man was Uncle George, who was only 23 at the time.

The miracle of that mission became so well known that one of the crew member's sons, Scott E. Culver, wrote a book about it, *Nine Yanks and a Jerk,* titled after that B-24 and its 10-man crew. Another book, *The Last Voices,* by Elizabeth Cassan, also detailed that flight.

"I had to give my pilot Mack a hell of a lot of credit," George is quoted in the latter book. "He had done everything right. He brought that damn airplane in tail-heavy, dragged her right down the runway. We turned off the main runway and the damn thing collapsed, which I knew would happen. Everyone had done their share. There wasn't any discussion or argument with anybody. I was in charge of that damn airplane, and no one ever argued one bit, even Mack. He never argued with me.

Uncle George snapped this picture of the aftermath of a miracle landing after the famed Nine Yanks and a Jerk was hit with an unexploded shell in mid-flight.

"We accomplished what we had to do, and we landed and walked away . . . and that's a good landing! Jimmy immediately came up to see how we were. He was the first one to meet us as we crawled out."

The mission also became known among its members as the "Lucky Number 13."

Most of the crew had left the U.S. for Europe on November 13, 1943, flew its first bombing mission together on December 13 over Kiel, Germany, and for most of them, this was their 13th mission together.

"I believe firmly in the saying, 'God was my copilot,'" George once was quoted in a Springfield, Ohio, newspaper, recalling the flight. "Hell yes, I do!"

Of the German anti-aircraft shell that didn't explode, he said, "Fortunately, it was built by slave labor, so it was a dud. It didn't explode. If it would've been a live one, I wouldn't be here telling you this story."

Shortly after that mission, Stewart climbed down from the control tower one day and Uncle George stopped him. He had his camera in hand and had a request. He told Stewart to look casual, since he wanted a candid photo of his commanding officer.

The huge hole in the bomber was soon repaired and the Liberator was returned to service but with a different crew.

On April 12, 1944, Williams and his crew including Uncle George were flying in another bomber to its right when *The Nine Yanks and a Jerk* took enemy fire once again. This time, the famous plane went down in a ball of smoke, crashing in a field in Belgium. Eight crew members had parachuted to safety, but two others went down with the plane.

Today, there is a memorial marker where it crashed.

Uncle George's final bombing mission occurred June 27, 1944, taking out a tactical target somewhere in France, the same time Dad and the 27th were experiencing the heaviest of combat during their invasion of Saipan, half a world away.

Commander Jimmy Stewart in this photo taken by Dad's brother, George Snook, 1944, Tibenham, England. This photo has never been seen by the public or published anywhere before. (Photo courtesy of Tom Snook.)

He had flown the maximum 30 successful bombing missions. Thus, for much of 1944, he worked with Stewart to repair whatever mechanical problems pilots reported once they returned from their bombing missions.

They would greet the pilots upon return and conduct an instant debriefing. Then they would make an adjustment or two or whatever as needed. Once finished, Stewart would hop into the pilot's seat and Uncle George would take the co-pilot's seat, as they conducted test flights to ensure their adjustments had worked before sending another pilot up in that particular bomber.

"I flew with him several times," George said. "He was a prince of a guy. He wasn't a movie star to us. He was an excellent bomber pilot and a first-rate officer. He was a pleasure to serve with."

Afterward, George became a flight-engineer instructor and managed an NCO Club in England for the remainder of the war.

One of Uncle George's passes to leave the base, signed and approved by Captain James (Jimmy) M. Stewart, his commanding officer.

FROM OHIO TO OKINAWA...

Stewart had earned the rank of colonel by the end of the war, and he was beloved by virtually all of the men who served under him. Their consensus was that he was a natural-born leader, admired for his bravery and leadership, especially given that his Hollywood status made none of it a requirement.

By the time he returned home, he had so many medals pinned to his chest—The Distinguished Flying Cross with two Oak Leaf Clusters, The Distinguished Service Medal and the French Croix de Guerre—that there was no doubt he was a true war hero.

Several reports claimed Louis Mayer wanted him to film a movie about his heroic days as a pilot and he refused, thus leading to the termination of his contract from MGM Studios. The first movie he starred in upon his return was *It's a Wonderful Life,* made by Liberty Films, filmed from April to July of 1946.

To think that the real George Bailey was in Europe commanding an entire bombing squadron, which included Uncle George, just one year earlier, is nothing short of incredible.

In the movie, however, it was George Bailey's younger brother Harry who came home a war hero.

In reality, it was Jimmy himself who fit that role.

By all accounts, he never talked much about his World War II service once it concluded. He had been close with all those who served under him, but those relationships faded after the war. He never showed up at any of their reunions or would accept any of their invitations to weddings or other social events once he stepped foot back on U.S. soil.

Also, to his credit, he wrote into every one of his movie contracts that the studios could never use his war record to promote its films. He never wanted to profit, or have anyone else profit, off his service to his country.

Just like with Dad's, Uncle George's experience in the war was something I never realized until my teen years when the actor's name was mentioned while my parents were playing a game of euchre one day with my aunt and uncle at their house.

"The actor Jimmy Stewart?" I remember asking Uncle George. "You knew him?"

"Yes, you could say I once knew him," he said laughing.

When the war was over, Uncle George, like Dad, was well decorated. He had been awarded several medals, including the EAME Theater Ribbon, a Bronze Star, Good Conduct Medal, Air Medal w/3 Oak Leaf Clusters, and the Distinguished Flying Cross.

He later became the commander of the American Legion in Ashland and often gave speeches about his bombing missions and the famous actor who had once commanded his squadron.

But I never heard either of the Snook brothers brag about all those medals they had earned, rather appreciating what they represented, their contributions and survival of the war and the fact they served on the winning team, if you will.

In the last few years of his life, Uncle George was appropriately recognized for his heroics, serving as the Grand Marshal of a Veterans' Day parade in Springfield, where he and his family had moved in 1973. He often gave interviews for books and newspaper articles, and just like Dad, he was one of the more patriotic men I ever knew.

George Snook died September 28, 2019, in Sylvania Ohio, at the age of 98.

Today, his Kodak camera, with which he snapped those historic photos of Stewart as well as the giant hole in the B-24 Liberator, sits on display at the Champaign Aviation Museum in Urbana, Ohio.

All these years later, I smile when I remember my father and his brother enjoying their adult years together: Playing cards, vacationing in Florida, grilling steaks, drinking beer, attending Ohio State football games, doing all the things that close brothers did as they grew older and raised families.

It was remarkable to think what they had experienced on opposite sides of the globe while fighting for their country at the same time and barely surviving at times—while the only communication they shared was through the letters they received from their mother back home, letting the other know that his brother was alive and well, still doing his part.

Today, Jimmy Stewart is regarded as one of Hollywood's legends, having starred in such major motion pictures directed by Alfred Hitchcock as *Vertigo* and *Rear Window* and also in my all-time favorite Christmas movie.

And whenever I watch any of his classic movies these days, I still can't help but think of one of my favorite uncles and his remarkable and heroic role in World War II.

Sergeant George Snook, flight engineer/top gunner, U.S. Eighth Air Force.

CHAPTER TEN

THE END OF WORLD WAR II

By mid-July, 1945, U.S. President Harry Truman was notified that America's top-secret development of an atomic bomb, which began three years earlier, was ready for use after a test in the New Mexico desert had been successful.

Thus, as the Allies pushed closer to Japan, conquering all the islands in the Pacific at a huge cost in American lives, he faced one of the biggest decisions in human history: Continue to wage a deadly ground and air war, which ultimately would lead to an invasion of Japan's mainland; or use this new weapon, which would obliterate a Japanese city and kill thousands of its citizens.

The loss of American life on Iwo Jima in June was more than 6,200 soldiers. On Okinawa it was more than 13,000. Truman believed that an invasion of Japan would resemble "Okinawa from one end of Japan to the other."

The price would be hundreds of thousands, if not a million or more of American dead and wounded.

"We didn't know it at the time, but our military leaders were planning an invasion of Japan for later in 1945," Dad said. "As I read about it later, they were expecting about half a million casualties, and that was a conservative estimate, in my opinion."

Historians agree that Truman believed one atom bomb deployed onto a major city in Japan would prompt an abrupt surrender by the enemy, which had started the fight almost four years earlier by bombing Pearl Harbor in Hawaii.

Therefore, his decision, as courageous as it was, became clear.

On August 6, 1945, an American B-29 bomber, the *Enola Gay* piloted by Paul Tibbets, dropped the world's first deployed atomic bomb over Hiroshima, Japan. The explosion immediately killed an estimated 80,000 people, and thousands more would later die of radiation exposure.

Truman announced: "Sixteen hours ago an American airplane dropped one bomb on Hiroshima and destroyed its usefulness to the enemy. If they do not now accept our terms, they may expect a rain of ruin from the air, the like of which has never been seen on this earth."

U.S. Senator Richard Russell, of Georgia, among several others, immediately urged Truman to drop more atom bombs on Japan, but the president responded in a telegram, "I know that Japan is a terribly cruel and uncivilized nation in warfare, but I can't bring myself to believe because they are beasts, we should ourselves act in that same manner. For myself, I certainly regret the necessity of wiping out whole populations because of the 'pigheadedness' of the leaders of a nation, and I am not going to do it unless absolutely necessary."

However, Japan did not surrender as he expected. Its military leaders vowed to fight to the bloody end.

Thus, it became necessary.

Truman approved another atom bomb to be deployed, and three days later, a B-29 dropped it on the city of Nagasaki, killing at least 40,000 people.

Finally, Japan had had enough.

Emperor Hirohito then announced his country's unconditional surrender in a radio address on August 15, citing the devastating effect of "a new and most cruel bomb."

With that, the deadliest war in human history, with between 60 million to 85 million fatalities, including more than 407,000 Americans, by all estimates, was finally over. That is, at least on paper.

"We had no idea about the atomic bomb or anything about it. We were fighting a battle every day," Dad said. "Guys still were getting shot and killed in the days after that . . . We heard something on the radio. Then word had filtered through our officers to us. We were close enough to Japan to listen to Tokyo Rose on the radio just because she played American music. At that time, it was just like with Pearl Harbor, because all of us asked the same question, 'Where the hell is Hiroshima anyway?'

"Tokyo Rose was always trying to lower our American G.I.s' morale by reading made-up 'Dear John' letters to us over the air. And her message got to my buddy Claude Stillwagon, who was one of my drivers. He had a girlfriend when he left before the war, and they were gonna get married, because I think she knew she would get benefits if he died in battle, according to what he told me. Then they agreed to get married when he returned, or if he returned . . .

"She sent him two 'Dear John' letters in 1945, and he was a mess. I told him, 'Now listen, you have to ignore all of that and focus on yourself. Then when you get home, sit down with her and work it out. It will be fine.' I had no idea if it would, but I was just trying to get him to focus on what he needed to do to stay alive at the time . . .

"Anyway, after the first bomb dropped, I don't know what took them so long to surrender. I guess the Japanese were trying to get the best deal they could, but three days later, we dropped another one. It was the right thing to do by President Truman, and I will always feel that way. A small bomb on a house or factory kills a few people. An atom bomb kills thousands. And war is all about trying to break the other side's will to fight it . . .

"But at the time, we really didn't know anything about the ramifications of those bombs. Word slowly filtered to us that the aftermath was more awful than you could imagine. We were still focused on fighting, so we never knew how many people were killed . . .

"That so-called surrender didn't stop the Japanese army from fighting or taking shots at us."

On the very day Hirohito announced Japan's surrender, American soldiers on Okinawa were dealing with their own problem—and for once it had nothing to do with combat.

A U.S Army Jeep stuck in the mud after the monsoon that hit Okinawa, August of 1945.

"On August 15, we got the surprise of our lives: We got hit by a monsoon. I had never even heard of a monsoon. It just rained cats and dogs for one day after another. We were camped on the low side of a hill and the water ran down that hill right through our tents. Mud flowed with it. It was awful. Then our tents fell over into the mud . . .

"We had to somehow put them back up in the pouring rain. We dug deep to post the center pole and then we double-tied everything. Those were just terrible conditions. We slept in a foxhole every night, covered in mud. There were mudslides and it seemed like it would never stop raining. There were also dead Japanese soldiers lying everywhere and the stench was something you wouldn't believe. They would be lying there, covered in mud, or they would come sliding down a hill in the rain and mud. It was something I would never forget . . .

"Trying to exist in that mud was terrible . . . I had to prop my cot above the water line and then drain the rainwater off my food to try to eat it. It was like that for days . . .

"After the monsoon finally moved through and it started to dry up a bit, we had gone through a valley when we spotted about a dozen cattle. Some of the guys came to me and asked, 'Can we have a vehicle with a big winch?'

"What are you going to do with it?" I asked.

"We are butchering those cattle and hanging them out to dry," one of them said.

"So that's what they did. They butchered them, rinsed them out with seawater, put mosquito nets over them, and let them hang overnight. Once they cooled down, they cut them up, cooked them and for about the next four days, and we all ate high on the hog. Everybody was running around with a big steak hanging out of their mouths."

Soldiers of the 27th then were told they were being sent to the mainland of Japan, but on a peace mission, something called "garrison duty." They were not being sent there to fight.

Dad said, "And that's when they also told us that anybody with 100 points can be relieved now and go home if they wanted."

The U.S. Army had devised a system to determine who could return home when the war had ended: "The Adjusted Service Rating Score." The soldiers simply called it "the point system."

Each soldier received points according to their months of service, months of service overseas, number of battle campaigns, medals earned, and number of dependent children back in the United States. Of course, Dad was not married and had no children, but he had enough points to return home.

"I had 114 points, and I was able to go home if I wanted, but my captain wanted me to go to Japan with the rest of the unit," he said. "When he came to me for my final decision, I told him I was ready. I was just tired. I was weak, and I felt I was lucky I had survived to that point. I didn't know how we would be received in Japan, so why take the chance? I figured, 'Why would I want to go to Japan and maybe have someone take a shot me over there after I survived the entire war?' . . .

"When I told the captain my decision, he almost begged me with tears in his eyes to go with them. He said, 'Ed, you fought this whole war, why not see it through? Please see it through with us!'

"I said, 'No, I am headed home!' I just had had enough. I had spent more than three and a half years overseas, and more than four years away from home. We had won the war . . .

"And to this day, I regret that decision. I should have gone to Japan with other guys in my unit. I always wished I could go back in time and change my mind on that, but I can't. That was my biggest mistake of the entire war . . .

"As I was being relieved, one of my drivers brought a guy to me and said, 'This guy says he is from your hometown.' It was Earl

Iceman, who was from Jeromesville, Ohio, a tiny town outside of Ashland. Earl walked up to me and said, 'Ed, I hear you are going home—and I am your relief!'

"I told him, 'Well, where the hell have you been the last four years?'

"Then my outfit left Okinawa and went to Kagawa, Japan. Earl told me later that they were received very well. But I got on a troop ship, which had come from somewhere in Europe, and was headed to Fort Lewis, Washington. I was going home."

CHAPTER ELEVEN

VICTORY ACCOMPLISHED, RETURNING HOME

For that lengthy journey on a ship from Okinawa to the state of Washington, totaling almost 5,800 miles across the Pacific, Dad had plenty of time to process the previous four years.

The fresh memories of bullets flying by his head, the bombs and mortar shells dropping all around him, and the friends he saw die next to him were horrible. What's more, the sudden quietness, headaches from his severe concussion, his sudden hearing impairment, the nightmares and the "what-ifs" from the battlefield didn't make it any easier.

"I was having trouble hearing and having trouble sleeping. But I figured I was lucky to get through that many battles with only the injuries I had," he said. "What if I was one or two feet this way or that way at times? I would have bought it, especially on Saipan and Okinawa . . . I did a lot of 'what if?' thinking.

"You always hear people talking about timing and being in the right place at the right time. Well, I always thought about that after our battles during the war. After four years, it takes its toll on you. It all took its toll on me. Watching guys who I knew die around me also took its toll on me."

Since its arrival in the Pacific, the 27th Infantry Division had 1,512 men killed in action, 4,980 wounded and 332 more who later died from combat wounds.

"I think we lost more than 20 guys from my H Company, and I got to know them all by the time they died. I have thought a lot about this over the years, but we lost more than 405,000 men in the war. You know, if the (atom) bomb had been developed a year or two earlier, the total number may have been half of that, because we lost so many men near the end of it, like on Okinawa . . .

"I look back on it and war itself is terrible. You lose friends who fought next to you. You watch them die. You always wondered if you would be next. But you can make it bearable with the right mindset, and I think I did that. I tried not to get too close to any one guy because I knew if he died, it would be even worse, and I would have a much tougher time to get over it. It was bad enough as it was. I lost a lot of friends, and you took that personally. It hurts. It hurt then and it always will, knowing they didn't come home to start a life like I did. I was carrying two sets of dog tags home, and I knew lot of my friends' dog tags had been sent home to their wife or parents . . .

"I had been away from home for more than four years. It had been a long war. It had been very stressful, and I was very tired, but I also was very thankful I had gotten out of it alive. I was only 26 and hoped I had a good life ahead of me . . .

"When I had time to process all of it and think back, another thing I always wondered about were the friendly-fire deaths. When the families were notified of a guy's death, if it was by telegram, it would just be labeled "killed in action." The families would never know exactly how their son or husband died. He could have been shot by an overanxious comrade standing 30 yards behind him, a guy who either panicked, or was a bad shot, or was scared, or all of the above . . .

"I saw it happen. It happened all the time. We lost 405,000 men in the war and I always wondered, how many of them died from our own guns? There was never an investigation after a battle, like into Pat Tillman's death (2004, in Afghanistan) in today's time—and the family would never know . . .

"With all that artillery fire, bombs dropping everywhere, bullets flying, aircraft flying above you and tanks moving around you, confusion reigns. Combat is not drawn up on paper and then carried out easily. When the army, navy or marines screwed up somehow, resulting in their own people dying needlessly, the government and the higher-ups didn't want anybody to know about it."

Those were some of the thoughts that consumed Dad as he sailed back to the United States. Life wasn't pleasant on his final journey aboard that troop ship, either, other than the reminder he had survived and would get to see all of his loved ones again.

"It was overcrowded. The people who were already on the ship had been on there for four weeks, so there was not much food left," he said. "We had some beans and cornbread and not much else. They had only powdered eggs, which was never one of my favorites, but I forced them down because I was so hungry."

It was late September when the ship pulled into dock near Tacoma, Washington.

"It was at daybreak and there was so much fog I couldn't see anything," he said. "After we landed, I saw Red Cross people greeting everyone getting off the ship, giving out oranges, grapefruit and milk. There were girls dancing and music playing . . .

"They took us by truck to Fort Lewis, where they gave me a very light medical exam. Afterward, I walked outside, and I saw a lot of apple orchards there. I told the MP guarding the gate that I wanted to walk down the street to get some apples.

"You are not allowed to go down there!" he told me.

"Are you going to stop me?" I asked him.

"He said he wouldn't. What were they going to do, court-martial me after fighting the war because I wanted an apple? There were Red Delicious apples as far as I could see. I hadn't had an apple in over four years. I noticed a guy along the road there and I asked him, 'How about a couple of apples?'

"He saw my uniform and told me, 'I will give you all the apples you want!' Then he handed me a bushel basket of them. I walked back to get on the troop train and started giving a few to the guys. When my basket got low, I told them, 'Go out there and get some more!' So, a few guys left and came back with several baskets of apples . . .

"Our train was headed east, and since I was a sergeant, they made me a troop commander. I was responsible for 46 guys, making sure they got off where they were supposed to get off and things like that. I had their discharge papers, and I knew where each one was supposed to get off . . .

"We stopped at a lot of small towns for coal, and I would always get off to stretch my legs. There were some hardened troops on that train. They had been away for so long like I had, and they didn't care much about anything at that point . . .

"When we pulled into Lincoln, Nebraska, the conductor told everyone, 'When we blow the whistle three times, you had better be coming back to get on board.' I walked downtown and looked around, and the bars and restaurants were overflowing with G.I.s coming home from the war. Guys were going crazy, running around with three beers in their hands, and girls were walking in and out of all the bars. It was one big celebration . . .

"The conductor blew the whistle three times, and I got back on. Then he blew it another three times and eight of my guys were not on board. I told the conductor that they were probably drunk somewhere and would just have to catch the next train coming through. Nobody seemed to care. What could they do to them? It's not like they would be court-martialed for it. The war was over, and they were getting discharged anyway."

From Lincoln, the troop train continued east to Camp Atterbury, Indiana, where Dad would be discharged. Ironically, his oldest sister Frances was a U.S. Army nurse stationed there. When he arrived, he had 12 papers without the men who needed them, so he gave the papers to the commander in charge.

"I lost 12 guys, but I am sure nothing happened to them," he said. "Although I always wondered about it. I underwent my final physical at Camp Atterbury, and they gave me all the shots I needed. My skin was blotched from the sun in the Pacific since I had my shirt off so much. I looked almost two-toned, tanned in some places and completely white in others. The doctor told me given time, my skin pigmentation would return to normal . . .

"When I went into the service in 1941, I weighed 168 pounds, and I like to think I was solid muscle. I had been in excellent health. When I was discharged, I weighed 134 pounds and was pretty much skin and bones . . .

"The doctor told me, 'You got a lot of weight to gain back!'

"I said, 'Doc, nobody gets fat on army food. I've had Dengue fever. I went days in battle with nothing but water out of a canteen, some spam out of a can, which I hated, or some beans or powdered eggs. Did you think I was going to gain weight?'

"But I was officially discharged. I was now a civilian."

It was October 8, 1945—four years to the day that he had first put on an army uniform in Cleveland.

Dad reconnected with Frances, who gave him good news.

"I didn't have a car right away, so she told me, 'My car is in our garage. It needs a valve job, a brake job and some other work. If you take care of all that, you can drive it all you want until I get out and come home.'

"Then I called home, and told Mom, 'Your long, lost son is coming home! I'll be in Crestline (Ohio) tomorrow, can somebody come pick me up?'"

He also made one more telephone call, to the Big Island of Hawaii to his "Hawaiian Mom," Elizabeth Kailikole, to let her know he had survived the war.

"When I got to Crestline the next day, George was there to pick me up. He had gone into the air force after I left home and he got out before I did, so I never once saw him in uniform."

When Dad walked into his childhood home at 1415 Cottage Street, he hugged everyone in sight and then he saw an 18-year-old standing in the room. It was his youngest brother, Richard.

"Richard was just a little kid when I left," he said. "I didn't recognize him at first."

Dad then walked into the garage and saw his Harley-Davidson still there, covered under a tarp just as he had left it four years earlier. After he had repaired Frances' car, he now had two forms of transportation.

On one of those first few days home, Dad and George engaged in a wrestling match on the living room floor, as brothers often do. They knocked over an end table and broke a lamp. They each looked up to see their mother sitting there, thinking they were in big trouble. But she had a huge grin on her face.

She just told them, "Don't worry about it . . . my boys are back home!"

Everything was not perfect, however.

"I had had that severe concussion, or two, which still gave me headaches. Both of my ears were badly damaged from all the shelling and big guns, so I had bad earaches. I still couldn't sleep well at all. And my language was quite salty. We didn't have a lot of time to de-program and adjust to civilian life. I had to stop and think before I would converse with people. I think it might have been common, but I don't know."

When he checked at A.L. Garber's Manufacturing, his old job was waiting for him, just as the bosses had promised.

"So, I went back to work there. I had been in the small press room when I left in 1941, and when I came back, I asked if I could move to the composing and casting room. They let me do that, so I had a new position."

Three weeks later, on October 30, Dad noticed a blonde secretary sitting at a desk. He was told it was Neil Biddinger's little sister. Her name was Ferne, and he introduced himself.

"I had known Neil before the war, but I never knew he had a little sister," Dad said.

Ironically, on the day he had been discharged, October 8, it had been her 19th birthday.

An archived photo of the casting room at A.L. Garber's Manufacturing in the late 1940s. Dad is on the left. Two good friends, Walter "Ducky" Arndt and Herb Carr are on his right.

FROM OHIO TO OKINAWA . . .

He was almost eight years older, but she went out with him anyway. They went on their first date on November 30, 1945.

From that day on, they rarely spent a day apart over the following seven decades.

Ferne D. Biddinger, in one of her modeling shots as a teenager.

CHAPTER TWELVE

THEY WERE MADE FOR EACH OTHER

From that very first date, Ferne Biddinger and William E. Snook—my eventual parents—seemed like they were meant for each other, despite their large age difference.

Even though they had grown up just blocks from each other on the north side of Ashland, they were still seven grades apart in school, so they had never met until Dad returned from the war and went back to his old job.

"I think we fell in love within a few dates," Mom said.

She was born October 8, 1926, into a very poor family. Her parents Mina and Clair Biddinger just didn't have much—in possessions or money.

But they did have plenty of love to go around with their four children: Paul, who was 14 years older than Mom; Neil, another World War II veteran and the only member of the family Dad knew, was 10 years older; and Florence, who was seven years older.

Mom was an A student, obviously very studious, and always beautiful, especially when she was a teenager and then into her early 30s. She actually did some local modeling jobs for small pay. She had that glamorous Hollywood look with long curly blonde hair and stood 5'8" when she was younger.

Mom and Dad on their honeymoon on the south shore of Lake Erie, July 1, 1946.

FROM OHIO TO OKINAWA . . .

She had spent plenty of time from 1942 to '45 writing letters to G.I.s overseas for a school project aimed at encouraging U.S. forces fighting in both theaters of the war.

After that first date within months of returning to his hometown, Dad knew very soon, too, that he would someday ask that secretary to marry him.

"When I came back from the war, it wasn't that I was looking to get married right away . . . I was still adjusting to being a civilian again, to working again, to putting weight back on," Dad told me. "But then I met your mother . . . and I knew from the first date. I would never meet another girl like her."

Dad was not a well-educated man, at least not formally, but he was right more often than he was wrong. He developed great instincts—as a youngster, before the war, during the war which led to his survival of it as well as once he was a veteran back home—and could judge character as well as anyone I ever knew.

Eight months following that first date, they were married on June 30, 1946, at Ashland's First Christian Church on Cottage Street, just blocks from Dad's childhood home, and one block from the high school they each had attended.

Dad still didn't own a car then, so he borrowed his sister Frances' car which he had repaired in late 1945 so she didn't have to spend their honeymoon on the back of his Harley-Davidson.

New cars were hard to come by then, because of a production shortage in the aftermath of the war. The auto assembly lines had been backed up during the war and were now trying to catch up to the demand from the millions of veterans returning home.

"We went down to the Chevy dealership on Cleveland Avenue and we put our name on a chalkboard, which listed the order of who was next in line for a car," Mom explained. "When a car came in and your name was at the top, you could buy it or pass on it. Then they crossed your name off of the chalkboard.

"About once each week, I would walk to that dealership to see where our name was on the list. When it reached the top, we got a blue, two-door coupe with a white top. That was our first car."

They borrowed money from her older sister, Florence, to buy a tiny two-bedroom house for $6,500 at 509 Snader Avenue, where they lived until 1958 when they moved to a new three-bedroom home on King Road just south of Ashland.

His new bride couldn't help but notice how what he had gone through on the battlefield had affected Dad both mentally and physically, even though she had never known him before the war.

"I knew his ears were badly damaged when I met him," she said. "He was not deaf, but he had severe nerve damage from the war. His right ear was much worse than the left. He was told by the doctors that hearing aids wouldn't do much for him.

"And he had frequent nightmares, too. When we first were married, if he ever heard an airplane at night, he would sit straight up in bed like he was still in battle."

Dad underwent surgery on his right ear in Dayton, Ohio, sometime in the early 1950s, but the results were not productive in repairing much of the damage.

"That surgery didn't help me," he said. "I was just never the same hearing-wise after the war. And I went into the service with perfect hearing, perfect eyesight and perfect skin. I came out of it somewhat damaged, especially my hearing, and it was always frustrating."

The 27th Infantry hosted annual reunions, usually in Syracuse, New York, but Dad didn't attend his first one until years after the war.

"We stopped to stay with a buddy from our unit, Frank Kowatch. He lived in Uniontown, Pennsylvania," Dad recalled. "Now Frank lived on a mountain, and he had been a coal miner before the war, but he had always made fun of West Virginia 'hillbillies' during the war. It was his constant joke.

"But once I saw his place, I asked him, 'Frank, how could you ever make fun of West Virginia guys all those years? This place is really in the hills!'"

But Mom and Dad remembered the visit for another reason.

"One night his wife asked us, 'I am going to fix pizza for supper, is that okay?' Dad recalled.

"I looked at her and asked, 'Pizza, what is that?' We didn't have pizza places in Ashland yet. Neither of us had ever tasted it. And we loved it . . . that is hard to believe now that was the first time that we ever ate pizza.

"Frank had been one of my drivers in the motor pool during the war, and he got hit with something on Okinawa and had a real bad concussion, so I tried to take care of him. Everything I told him to do, he did but he was like a docile dog from that point. He just couldn't remember or hear anything for weeks, so I just let him rest and recover. His hearing never really came back, either, but his mind got better over time."

One major change Dad made 13 years after returning home was a bad habit he had picked up during his time in the service.

One day in 1958, two years before I was born when my sister was 10 and my brother was six, they were riding in the backseat of the family car. Dad took a cigarette from the pack, stuck it in his mouth and asked Mom for a light, so she pushed the lighter on the socket on the car's dash.

When it popped and was red hot, she blindly handed it to him without looking at him, just as he bent his head down to move his cigarette toward it. The hot end of the lighter seared him directly above his nose, right between his eyebrows, and left a circular burn mark that lasted for weeks.

"I remember that so well," my brother Bill told me. "I thought Dad was going to blow up at Mom, but he didn't."

He just calmly put the lighter back into its socket on the car's dash, removed the cigarette from his mouth and tossed it out the window. He never lit another one for the rest of his life.

"I picked it up when I went into the army," he said. "Most all of the G.I.s smoked back then. And that is why so many of them died in their 60s and 70s. It was a nasty habit, but I kicked it that day when the car lighter burned me."

Following the war, mostly through letters and cards, Mom and Dad stayed in touch with several men and their wives from the 27th: Frank, Marty Emmer, Claude Stillwagon, Carl Rundberg, Herb Kirsch, Stan Gardner, Alan Merritt and a few others she had met at his army reunions.

During those get-togethers, Dad and his army buddies always toasted the guys who didn't come home, men like Joe Majernik and Jack Noble.

And as far as Stillwagon, after receiving those "Dear John" letters from his girlfriend on Okinawa near the end of the war, he eventually convinced that girl, Sarah Shreve, to marry him. The couple had two daughters, four grandchildren and two great-grandchildren, and were married for 60 years until September 19, 2006, the day he died at the age of 87.

"It all worked out for Claude, just as I told him it would," Dad said. "Although I really didn't believe it back then . . . I just wanted him to focus on what he had to do to stay alive."

And of course, there was John Lewis and his wife Cora, who visited our home for a week in the summer of 1974, the week he told me the incredible story of the day in June of 1944 when the shrapnel from a knee-mortar shell ripped into his side on Saipan.

One day in the 1950s, Dad was walking down Main Street in Ashland when he bumped into an old childhood friend by the name of Cloice Proctor. They hadn't seen each other since high school in the late 1930s.

Mom and Dad on June 30, 1965, the day of their 19th wedding anniversary, in the backyard of the house in which Dad grew up.

After some small talk, which led to their stories of the war, Proctor said, "I was on Saipan in 1945. You didn't happen to be in that big battle there the year before, did you?"

After Dad confirmed he had, Cloice told him, "I SAW THE TREE WHERE YOU CARVED YOUR NAME AND THE DATE!"

"I couldn't believe it," Dad said. "I was just flabbergasted! I never, ever figured anyone but a Japanese citizen or soldier would see it someday and then have no idea what it meant. I was pinned down and just took a minute or two to leave my mark showing I had been there, just in case I bought it that day.

"And then a guy I knew from my hometown saw it . . . what are the odds?"

Dad just seemed to have a habit of beating the odds over the years. Surviving motorcycle crashes and so many close calls on the battlefield was proof enough. But he also had a knack for being in the right place at the right time, such as meeting Jimmy Doolittle before the war and Ernie Pyle just two days before he was killed on Ie Shima, before then meeting the love of his life while at work one day immediately after returning from the war.

As the years passed in the 1950s, Dad assimilated back to civilian life very well, not suffering from any PST symptoms other than the times he set up in bed when he heard an airplane immediately after the war, as Mom recounted.

Dad, second row, far right, pictured with his city championship—"The Printers"— fastpitch softball team in 1949.

For the most part, he did all the normal things married fathers did while raising a family in the Midwestern United States during the time.

He immediately started playing fastpitch softball on the team that represented his printers' division at the factory in which he worked, A.L. Garber's.

He and Mom were very social: They had plenty of friends around town, and usually did things as couples, such as playing in card clubs such as bridge or euchre. They attended Saturday night dances at either the local Elks Club or the American Legion, where he once served as the post commander.

He loved to fish for perch or walleye in nearby Lake Erie, and he and his fishing buddies took me and my brother Bill often. He hunted for rabbits and took us with him from the time I was only eight—but he never shot a deer following the war. And given that deer-hunting where we grew up in North Central Ohio during hunting season each December was very popular, he was in the minority.

"I can't shoot anything that big or beautiful," he once told me.

His stance duplicated a scene right out of the movie *The Deer Hunter* the award-winning Vietnam movie Dad never watched. I had the feeling he already believed he had done enough killing in his lifetime.

He never was a golfer, either, having played just a few rounds in his entire life. And I don't ever remember him playing tennis in his entire life. But I know he loved the smaller version—he was an excellent table-tennis player and kicked my butt often when I was a kid. He also loved to play basketball at the local YMCA and did so through his mid-80s.

The other things he loved were gardening and yardwork. We always had a small garden on the south side of our house each summer, as Dad nurtured such vegetables as the tomatoes, lettuce, onions, rhubarb and radishes he had planted.

As far as travel, Mom and Dad did what they could afford—they would take us on an annual car trip to Florida each spring and they often saved to visit Hawaii, as I will get to later.

He and Mom traveled to France once in the 1980s, only because he wanted to see Normandy.

"That cemetery above the cliff there took my breath away," he told me when they returned. "I could relate to what those guys went through. They came into the beaches so low beneath enemy fire from the Germans . . . a lot of those guys just had no chance to survive. And seeing that broke my heart."

Unfortunately, he never made it back to the island of his own D-Day.

And he mentioned missing that goal often.

"I always wanted to go back to Saipan as I grew older," he told me more than once. "I would have wanted to see the beach where we landed, see Death Valley again, see Marpi Point, maybe somehow find that tree, if it was still standing, and see my name in it . . . but I never made it back. I always regret that."

As the years passed, it seemed he grew even prouder of his service to his country. He never wanted to forget the people he served with, either and he always said he was proud of them, too.

It seemed that they all went to war as wide-eyed young men angered by the attack on Pearl Harbor and not having any idea what to expect. They came out of it almost four years later as hardened vets in some ways and yet even more appreciative of life in ways they never realized before. They had made it home, unlike thousands of others who died in battle. They survived and they were on the winning team that saved freedom. That was a large source of their pride, too.

"We talked about that a lot at our reunions," Dad told me. ". . . Just how lucky we were to be able to live the rest of our lives, something other people took for granted."

Herbert Kirsch, Marty Emmer, Mom and Dad at a 27th Infantry Reunion, at Fort McClellan, Alabama, 1990.

For most people, shooting the bull or "telling war stories" is just a cliche' or a meaningless phrase. But for Dad and his army buddies, it was literal. It was real.

And of the ones I met, I could tell that they all realized that their war stories were worth retelling.

I attended one of his army reunions with him in Orlando, and as I sat at a large round table having a drink with his infantry buddies, I was impressed with how vivid their memories were after all those years. They remembered dates, details of their battles and even specific conversations.

"Jeff, you have no idea how tough a guy your dad was back then," Marty Emmer whispered to me during a cocktail party. "He was one of our bravest. He was one of our toughest, even though he wasn't one of our biggest. He would never tell you this, but he was mentally and physically one tough son of a bitch!"

I told Marty, "Believe me, I saw that side of him while growing up, but I think he's mellowed a little bit now . . . the war and what happened in those years will never leave him. It is a large part of who he is."

"It is a large part of all of us," Marty said. "We can't just easily forget something like that."

CHAPTER THIRTEEN

WE WERE BABY BOOMERS

My parents didn't wait long after they were married to start a family.

My sister Becky, born March 1, 1948, came along just 20 months after they were married; and my brother Bill was born four years later, on July 19, 1952.

However, Mom and Dad were 41 and 33 years old, respectively, by the time I came along on March 21, 1960. Thus, obviously, I was the baby of the family by a wide margin.

That age gap became a huge thing to me over the years, too. Both of my siblings were out of the house by the time I was 10 years old, and thus I spent the last half of my childhood basically raised as an only child.

We were three kids fathered by a World War II vet, part of the 76 million who made up the so-called Baby Boomer Generation—those children born from 1946 to '64.

It's really amazing to consider that there were about 132 million people in the United States in 1940, the last full year before the country entered the war. The birth rate stalled like a car running on bad fuel from 1942 to 1945 when more than 16 million men were overseas for anywhere from one year to four years doing their part in the war effort.

Naturally, when they returned, married and started families, the nation's population exploded.

I often had sensed throughout my childhood that Dad had wanted *only* two children, therefore explaining the big age difference among the three of us.

I once believed it affected his attitude toward me somewhat, at least for the first 16 or so years of my life. There were many times

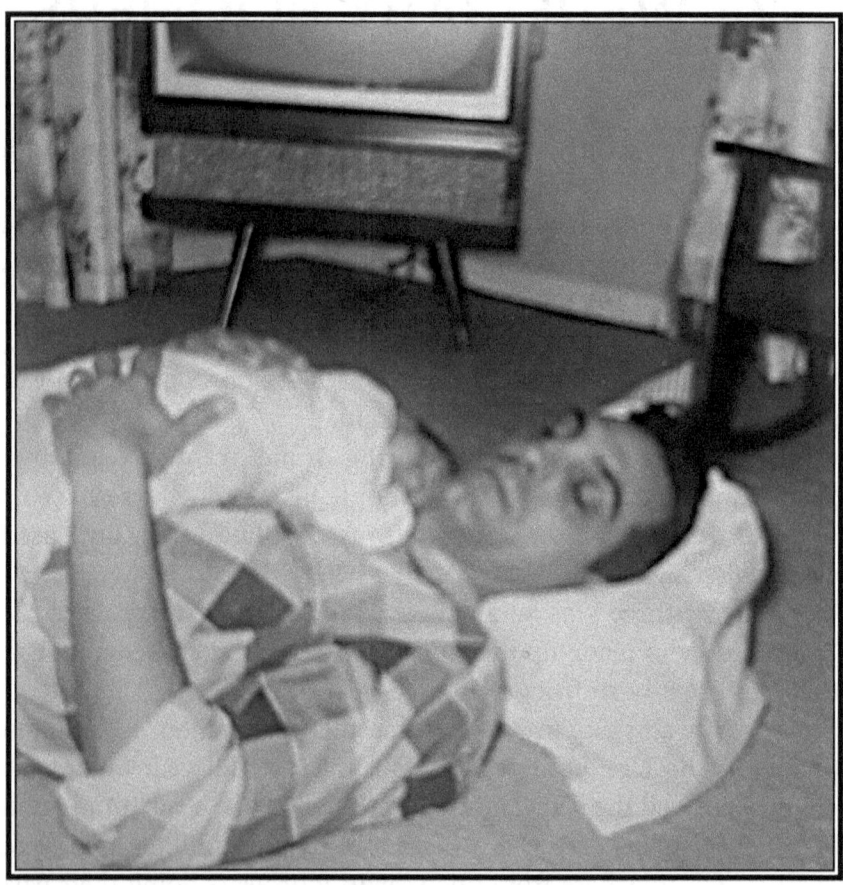

Taking a nap on Dad's chest, one week old on March 28, 1960. Notice the television, then considered state-of-the art.

when I was younger when it seemed that he snapped at me for small things or maybe disciplined me too harshly for the simplest of missteps.

At least that's the way I felt.

I regarded him as a strict disciplinarian, although I was "spanked" only twice in my life. The first came when Bill and I were wrestling in the living room when day and we broke something.

"Just wait 'till your father gets home!" Mom warned us.

She was right. Dad took us downstairs and took a yardstick over my butt. Problem was, it broke in half. Thus, he had nothing left but to take off his belt and whip Bill's behind. I got the better of that deal.

Then when I was about 11, he was lecturing me about what he deemed my lethargic attitude toward my assigned yardwork chores. When I thought he had finished, I grabbed my bike and took off out onto the country road to the south. However, I guess he wasn't done with the lecture, because when I got about two miles away, he pulled his truck up next to me, got out and took that big right hand of his across my butt. It was the hardest spanking I could imagine.

"Now get back to the house and finish your work!" he demanded.

It was the final time he ever laid a hand on me, other than to put his arm around me—or to give me a hard foul on the basketball court.

After the two seasons in which he coached my T-ball team and then my little league team, he may have attended three or four of my baseball or fastpitch softball games over the years by the time I graduated college in 1982 when Dad was already 63 years old. Mom and Becky were usually there, but I never expected Dad to show up.

He was always working during the week or doing yardwork around the house on the weekends.

Those feelings I had subsided gradually once I went to college. He seemed more caring and loving. I don't know, maybe he was just waiting for me to grow up. Once I graduated from Ohio State, and

Becky, 13, Bill, 9, and me as a one-year-old in 1961.

started working full time, things turned around for us for good. He retired three years later when I was only 25, and through the next four decades until he died, we spent much more time together than we did when I was a kid, and we became very close.

But it was a closeness I never sensed while growing up.

There is no doubt we understood each other much better, too.

In fact, he admitted my suspicions one day in the late 1980s.

We were headed to grab a beer and some oysters when I was driving and he was sitting in the passenger seat. I don't remember how the subject came up, but while we were stopped at a red light, he began to reveal the story I always suspected: He had indeed wanted only two children largely because of the cost it took to raise kids.

I realized Dad never made a lot of money, first as a printer from 1945 to '72 and then as a warehouse manager at a wholesale frozen-food business for more than 10 years before he retired. If I remember correctly, I think he was making only $700 per week by the time he retired in 1985.

As I said, he didn't have a college education, but he was still one of the smartest people I ever knew. When it came to common sense, I like to think he had a Ph.D.

However, Mom always wanted three children, he told me that day, and she had to undergo some sort of special surgery in 1958 or '59 to become pregnant for a third time. He relented, as he usually did when she wanted something.

And that is how I came along.

After finishing telling me the story that day, he looked at me with glassy eyes and said, "I am sure glad she talked me into it. You are a wonderful son . . . and I am very proud of you."

I will never ever forget that, because I had never heard those words before.

From that point on, I understood him better and we became very, very close in his later years. I had always loved and worshipped him anyway, just as my siblings had, and as most kids then regarded their fathers.

Once he retired, he also seemed to mellow tremendously and I believe that had something to do with having no more children to support financially.

I always knew he was a great man, one who stood for all the right things. And now, as I grew older, he became more like a best friend to me.

Anyway, back to my childhood . . .

We three kids grew up in a three-bedroom ranch style house in the country on King Road, two miles from downtown Ashland. I loved that old house, which my parents bought shortly after it was built in 1958—two years before I was born. My siblings knew that tiny house on Snader Avenue for a few years of their youth, but the house on King Road was the only home I ever knew.

There was a large horse farm located across the road from our house, and I often would sit on the fence, petting or feeding the horses. Our tiny rural neighborhood contained seven other houses, and it was surrounded by woods and several large cornfields. There was a nearby lake containing frogs and fish and several "creeks" which kept me, and the neighbor kids, busy all summer long.

That house had one problem, however, although we didn't even realize it wasn't common: It had only one bathroom and no shower.

I will never forget the number of times I had to do a dance outside that bathroom door waiting for a family member to finish whatever they were doing. There were times, mostly in the summer, when one of us was forced to walk out behind the house and take a pee in the grass under the stars. But it never bothered me.

I just thought it was common until I went to college. When I told my college roommates I had grown up in a house with one bathtub, one toilet and no shower, they could not believe it.

"How the hell did you get the shampoo out of your hair?" one freshman roommate asked me.

"Shampoo?" I answered. "I usually washed my hair with a bar of soap."

And I know we never had a conditioner, either.

When we grew up, Becky always joked that our parents were so cheap that they would never run separate baths for each of us because of the water bill.

She told me they worked their way up according to age. Thus, I would get the first bath, then Bill would jump into my water after I finished and then she was left with the dirty water for her bath. At least that's the way she told it.

Looking back on it, I really believe Becky was right about that bathwater thing, because our mother never wasted a nickel. Perhaps that is because she once remembered her father walking two miles in the snow to return one which he had borrowed from a friend.

Our parents paid cash for everything and never owned a credit card until they were in their 50s. If I remember correctly, they paid $12,500 for that house on King Road and eventually sold it 36 years later in 1994 for $92,000. (For some reason, once we were grown and out of the house, Dad added a small bathroom with a walk-in shower in their master bedroom).

If I walked into my childhood bedroom today, I am sure I would be shocked—because it was so small. I believe my bedroom was 10 feet by eight feet. I had a double bed in there, a nightstand and not much else.

We didn't have air-conditioning, either, which was very common in Ohio for the time our house was built in the 1950s. On hot summer nights, I often slept with the windows open a foot or two to allow a breeze through the screens, if there was a breeze on that particular night.

More often, there was none at all and I would lie there sweating until I fell asleep.

It seemed I was often visiting the local emergency room for one reason or another—a frog-gigging incident lodged in my lower left leg by a neighbor kid, a fall from the couch onto the coffee table and I even once bit a hole in my tongue while playing basketball in elementary school.

But the fourth time I headed to the ER was the worst yet, and it illustrates just how honest and honorable my parents were.

My best friend from elementary school, a blond kid by the name of Mark Anderson, invited me to his house one day after school. His family pet was a very large German Shepherd. I was in the yard minding my own business when that giant dog approached me. I petted it for a moment before it suddenly jumped on top of me fangs first. It began biting me just about everywhere. I was only 12 and I was flat on my back, thinking I was going to die right then and there.

That big dog even ripped into my nose. Then as I raised my arms in defense, it ripped into both of them, too. It also bit my forehead right at my hairline.

Fortunately, Mark's dad happened to be home and pulled the dog off of me or I surely would have been mauled to death since I was so small, and that big dog had complete control over me. I wasn't strong enough to fight him off.

When it was over, I was a bloody mess. By the time the ER doctors were done with me that day, I had almost 80 stitches in my body: Twenty-six in my nose alone, 36 more in my arms and 12 in my forehead. (Getting stitches at the ER seemed as common for me as a kid as getting a haircut).

My parents later learned that the dog had bitten the mailman a week or two earlier and yet nothing was done about it—and they were absolutely furious. I remember sitting at our kitchen table, those large black stitches protruding from my nose blocking my vision, my left arm wrapped in a sling and my hair shaved back around one of the bites, as Mom and Dad discussed whether to sue the Andersons.

Anyway, they had no choice but to put the dog down after it had injured me so severely. My parents ultimately decided not to sue because Mark was a good friend, and they realized it likely would have ended our friendship. Back then, people just didn't sue other people as they do today even if there was pure and obvious negligence, but I am sure it would have resulted in some money being paid out by the insurance company.

My parents, however, didn't care about making a buck off someone else even if they had just cause to do so.

From the time of my childhood through today—I am 65 as I write this—I also have had several near-death experiences in which I somehow miraculously escaped.

The first one happened when I was 14. One Saturday in the winter, Dad wanted me to help him unload some trash from his company van at a place called Polar Foods on the north side of town, where he supervised the warehouse and managed the trucking routes. The company sold frozen foods to just about every restaurant and franchise you could think of.

Anyway, it had snowed earlier that morning and he left the van's engine running. The transmission was in park while I stood about 20 feet behind it, my back to the van, emptying the trash bags from the back of it.

Dad got in the van and was slowly backing it up, but with his boots wet from the snow, his foot slipped off the brake pedal onto the gas pedal. I can only reason that I must have heard the engine rev because something made me turn around. I saw the van speeding in reverse and heading directly at me.

I just reacted and dived headfirst into a large snowdrift as the van crashed behind me into the pile of trash. When it came to rest, it was propped up on a trash pile and the rear wheels still were spinning. Dad came running around the driver's side screaming my name, searching for me.

He had figured the van had run over me, as he dropped down to his knees to look underneath it. I was covered in snow on the other side where he couldn't see me, my heart pounding. I was young, but I realized immediately how close I had come to dying right then and there.

"Dad! I am over here . . . I am okay!" I yelled.

He came running over to me.

"Oh, thank God! . . . My foot slipped!"

I was covered in snow, but this time, I didn't have a scrape on me and no trip to the ER would be needed.

Eerily, it would not be the final time I had to dive out of the way of a moving car, amazingly, having two more near-misses in my later years in Florida when an elderly driver had mistaken the gas pedal for the brake pedal.

Maybe I had Dad's luck, I don't know.

"Please don't tell Mom about this! She will never forgive me!" he pleaded with me that day.

I kept my word until I was well into my 40s, when the story slipped out one day while we were having a few drinks.

"Dad . . . remember that time when you almost ran over me with the van?" I asked him in front of Mom.

"WHAT?" she asked.

I then told her the story of that snowy day, as Dad shook his head and smiled.

"You got lucky that day!" he joked.

"So did you!" I told him.

When Mom left the room, he whispered to me, "You know, I hadn't thought about that day in years. Someone was watching out for us that day . . ."

CHAPTER FOURTEEN

~

THE WONDERFUL WOMAN DAD FELL IN LOVE WITH

Our mother's heritage isn't much different than our father's—the Biddinger family tree, just like the Snook side, also extends back to Germany.

Mom's father was a descendant of a man named Adam Budinger, who was born in the tiny village of Dorschel, Germany, in 1698. Adam would have been my great, great, great, great grandfather. He and his wife Anna and their four children voyaged to North America aboard the ship *Samuel,* arriving August 30, 1737.

Through the next three generations, their surname Budinger changed to Bedinger to Bettinger and finally to Biddinger by the time their descendants migrated west to settle in Ohio.

Myron Filmore Biddinger (1856-1918) and Minerva Annette Phillips (1861-1925) had a boy, Clair Odell Biddinger, on July 30, 1887, in Ashland. That boy would be my grandpa, Clair Biddinger, who later married Mina Irene McBride, who was born June 11, 1893, on March 6, 1912. Mom's mother was of Irish descent.

They had sons Paul Myron Biddinger, born December 18, 1912 (exactly nine and half months after they were married) and Neil Floyd July 12, 1916, and then daughters Florence Bernice April 4, 1919, and our mother, Ferne Darlene, who was born October 8, 1926.

They lived in a less-than-modest, two-story house at 1113 Troy Street, about eight or nine blocks and two streets away from Dad's childhood home.

Grandpa Biddinger is the only one of my four grandparents of whom I have no memory

Everyone called him "Curly," because he had curly red hair. I know Dad loved him because he often told me endearing stories about him.

Mom always described him as "the most honest man who ever lived." She once told me a story of when he walked her home from school one day. It was snowing hard and was very cold, and he could not afford a new pair of gloves. He told her to go ahead and head home, because he had to walk a mile in the other direction to pay back a loan to a friend.

When she asked how much he owed, he answered, "A nickel."

"Dad, it's only a nickel, you can pay him later . . . it's cold and snowing!" she told him. "Your hands are cold."

"No, I owe him, and I told him I would pay him back today . . ." he said, before walking off in the other direction.

After all, this was during the Great Depression, but that is the type of man he was.

Grandpa Biddinger, as I understand it, loved fish. Not the act of fishing but eating fish. Any kind of fish. Mom and Dad told me whenever they drove anywhere, if her father ever noticed a restaurant sign advertising fish or a fish fry, he would instruct them, "Pull over and let me out and come back and get me later!"

"And at times, if he saw a sign for an all-you-could-eat fish fry, which were much more common back then, Dad would jump out of the car while it was still moving," Mom said.

He died of a heart attack on July 11, 1960, two weeks before his 73rd birthday, and on the very morning on which he and Grandma were supposed to babysit me when I was just four months old.

Anyway, the Biddinger family just didn't have much. And that surely shaped her views on just about everything when we three children were growing up.

"We were poor," Mom recalled. "We didn't waste a penny."

I remember her telling me that sometimes at Christmas, her present was a bag containing an apple, a popcorn ball, an orange and maybe a piece of candy. Her parents didn't have enough money to buy more expensive presents such as toys or new clothes.

Neither of her parents ever had a driver's license or owned a car. They had a house, clothes on their backs, enough food to eat and that was about it. Also, they never took a vacation or left the state of Ohio until after Mom married Dad, and they often took her parents with them to Florida for a week each winter.

Mina, my grandmother, was one of my favorite people in the whole world. To me, she was the perfect grandma: She loved watching her "stories" on television, her term for soap operas; she loved watching sports, especially the Cleveland Indians; she loved knitting or crochet; and she loved baking.

And I know she loved me, my sister and my brother.

Simply put, she was just a wonderful grandma, a laid-back, mild-mannered, lovable person.

She was born June 11, 1893, as Mina McBride.

While we were growing up, Grandma lived with Mom's only sister, our Aunt Florence, whom we all called "Aunty." In many ways, she really was like a second mother to all of us. She never had children of her own, but she treated me and my siblings as her own children.

She had married a former railroad worker from Scranton, Pennsylvania, a man by the name of Daniel John Richards, another World War II veteran. Uncle Dan was something else. I really have a hard time trying to describe him. He was strange at times, eccentric at others. Mom once told me that he had a drinking problem in his

Mina McBride, our grandma on my mother's side, pictured in 1911 at the age of 18.

early years, but by the time I was growing up and staying with them often on weekends, Uncle Dan never touched a drop.

We all learned over time that he had a big heart and truly cared about all of us, probably because his wife loved us and treated us as her own children. I can still see him sitting in his recliner while smoking cigars—inside the house, mind you—while watching either the news or sports while barking at the TV.

Anyway, it seemed as if I must have stayed at their house hundreds of nights or more while I was growing up. And we often had our family's Thanksgiving and Christmas dinners there.

Aunty was a natural-born athlete. She had been a great fastpitch softball player when she was younger and could throw and catch as well as any man. Dad had coached her factory team in the late 1940s, and the pictures of that team remind me exactly of the movie *A League of Their Own*.

When I wasn't staying with Becky, once she left the house in 1967, I often stayed at Aunty's home on Westview Avenue on many weekends. She and I played catch with a baseball almost every summer day next to the yellow cherry tree in their backyard. She had an old catcher's mitt which she had saved from her playing days.

We would often take a break, eat a few cherries, then go back to throwing the baseball again. I still love yellow cherries to this day because of those memories.

Aunty and Grandma and I often watched the Cleveland Indians on TV together or we played card games into the night on weekends. Grandma was a huge baseball fan, and she would easily become disgusted with every Indians' loss.

"GOOD GRAMMITY!" she would say. "THEY ARE JUST TERRIBLE TODAY!"

Anyway, the Indians lost a lot in those days, so I heard her use that phrase often. She also loved watching big-time wrestling and if I ever hinted it was fake or staged, she would argue that not only was it real, but it was one of the best sports on TV.

She smiled and laughed often—and I loved doing or saying anything just to make her laugh or see that smile. She spent her days knitting blankets or sweaters for the family while watching TV. She also was a great cook who baked cherry, custard and creme pies. At night, I slept in Grandma's room. After my grandpa had died, my aunt took her into their home and had placed two twin beds in her bedroom. That is where we would lie awake at night and talk about almost everything.

I would lie in a twin bed across from hers and ask all kinds of questions, and she would answer with the wisdom that came with her eight decades of life. When she stopped answering, I knew she had fallen asleep, probably from the exhaustion of listening to me. Or else maybe she was faking it—just to force me to be quiet and fall asleep.

The day Grandma died was terrible, probably the worst of my youth. It was March 15, 1972, and my memory of that morning is very, very vivid. It was six days before my 12th birthday. I woke up to see Mom and Aunty sitting at the breakfast table, sobbing and dabbing their eyes with Kleenex.

I didn't even have to ask, and they didn't have to tell me. I just knew. They never said a word, but I immediately realized that their mother—my favorite grandparent with whom I was so close—was gone. I didn't say a word, either. I made breakfast and walked out to wait for the school bus with tears in my eyes.

Her funeral also was a very sad day, seeing her lying in that casket wearing her silver-rimmed eyeglasses. She looked so peaceful, just as she did whenever she fell asleep before me.

This time, however, I knew she wasn't sleeping, and I was old enough to realize she was never coming back to play cards or watch the Indians lose another game with me, or to stay awake at night to talk about our life.

As far as Dad's side, his father, Grandpa Snook, had died three years earlier, at the age of 98 on May 16, 1969, when I was only nine.

His was the first funeral I ever attended. His mother died five years later, at the age of 83, and all I can remember about her death was lying on the couch in the living room that day with a case of the flu when Dad walked into the room to tell me the bad news. He asked me if I felt well enough to attend her funeral. I had just thrown up at the time and had a fever, and as soon as he felt my forehead, he knew that wasn't possible.

It sounds terrible to admit it, but as a contrast to my other grandma, I don't remember many conversations I ever had with Grandma Snook in those 14 years of my life. I do remember being very sad for Dad, because I could tell that day he was emotional about losing his mother.

As far as Mom's other siblings, her oldest brother, Paul, was one of my two favorite uncles, along with Dad's brother George.

Paul was the only one in our extended family of his generation to attend college. He graduated from Findlay College, about 80 miles northwest of our hometown.

Mom told me how she had made the cheerleading squad as a sophomore, but her parents could not afford to pay the six dollars for a cheerleading uniform. Thus, she couldn't cheer at football and basketball games. But Uncle Paul, who then was working full-time after college, overheard her talk about that disappointment one day. He then gave her money to buy a uniform when she became a junior, so she could become a cheerleader for her final two years at Ashland High School.

As I grew up, Uncle Paul and I became very close even though he and his wife Helen lived 155 miles away in Dayton, and they had their own family of three grown sons. Their oldest, our cousin Dave, graduated from West Point and then became an engineer for General Motors in Detroit. Denny was a Bowling Green State University graduate who made the U.S. Army his career as an officer. He retired as a full colonel. Their youngest son, Larry, graduated from Miami (Ohio) University, where he met and married a girl named Mary, a direct descendant of Henry Ford.

You could say all three boys were high achievers, as was their father.

Anyway, Uncle Paul was largely responsible for my love of Ohio State football, and one of the reasons I ended up as a student there. He was employed by Ohio State as an instructor on the Wright-Patterson campus in Dayton, and he always had access to season tickets to Buckeye home games. He also often took me to several Ohio State basketball games at St. John Arena, where I saw UCLA's Lew Alcindor, before he changed his name to Kareem Abdul-Jabbar, play on December 6, 1968. The John Wooden-coached Bruins beat Ohio State that night and went on to win the NCAA championship four months later.

Even while I was growing up in the 1970s, access to Ohio State football tickets was like having access to Fort Knox—they were gold. Paul always had four season tickets and would take Dad and me to at least one game each season. I had fallen in love with that giant horseshoe-shaped stadium, the football team, the scarlet-and-gray uniforms, and the university in general, years before I attended my first game in person on September 29, 1972. (On that day, I would have been 12 when an unknown freshman by the name of Archie Griffin rushed for a school-record 239 yards against North Carolina.)

I remember Archie once came to our hometown and spoke at a church and Dad took me to hear him speak. That day was the only time I ever asked for an autograph, but I couldn't tell you where that piece of paper is today.

And to think if you had told me I would grow up and someday become friends with Archie, a college football legend and the only player to ever win two Heisman Trophies, as well as the quarterback at the time, Cornelius Green, it would have blown my mind when I was sitting there rooting for them as a kid.

Those players were legends to me, larger than life football stars, and I had posters of them on the covers of *Sports Illustrated* and *The Sporting News* on my bedroom wall.

By the time I was 15, Paul soon realized just how much I loved and followed the Buckeyes, so he increased my invitations to two games per season. He, Dad and I and another lucky invitee would tailgate on South campus and eat Aunt Helen's homemade fried chicken before the games. She always made fried chicken for Paul to take to the games. It was a tradition.

Mom's other brother, Neil, also was a great guy. He married a woman named Martha and they eventually settled in Cleveland. We took some weekend trips to stay in their house, too, over the years.

Mom's side of the family in 1982: From left, she and Dad, Neil and Martha Biddinger, Florence and Dan Richards, and Paul and Helen Biddinger.

Neil also served in World War II in H Company of the 37th Infantry Division.

Neil, too, was what you would call "a fun uncle." He stood about 6'3", had a deep voice and looked a bit like actor Robert Mitchum. He also could drink beer like nobody's business. He worked at a company which printed all the horseracing programs for the local racetracks, Thistledown and Northfield Park, and he and all of his buddies would hit their favorite bars around Cleveland on their way home. On weekends, when we visited, he often took Dad with him.

Neil always seemed to be in a good mood. I never saw him angry or unhappy. That is, until much later in life. After Martha died in 1982, the first of any of my aunts and uncles to pass away, he settled into life as a widower.

Eventually, after a bout with cancer, he was forced to wear a colostomy bag and when he visited, I would hear him cussing that thing and his condition.

One day in the 1990s, I was at Mom and Dad's house while visiting from Florida and he emerged from the bathroom, totally frustrated.

"Jeff, I hope you never have to have one of these things," he uttered. "I am about ready to give up . . . it's just awful."

I felt so bad for him.

Like me and Dad and most people who grew up in my hometown, Neil loved every Cleveland sports team—the Browns, Indians and later, the Cavaliers. And by living in Cleveland, he often attended games and invited us when he had extra tickets.

The bottom line was that Mom's family was made up of great people, with big hearts and great stories. Of course, I always believed she was the jewel of the Biddinger family. I also loved her mother as much as a kid could love his grandmother. And I loved her three siblings as much as a kid could love his aunts and uncles.

They were each so good to us.

FROM OHIO TO OKINAWA . . .

Mom earned our love with her caring and devotion to all of her kids and grandkids.

I could describe her with a hundred adjectives, but the best one would be "selfless."

I always knew the way Mom had grown up had shaped her feelings on just about any subject. Especially money. Since her family had none, she hated wasting a penny even after she married Dad and raised a family. She would pay all the family bills in cash immediately when they came due. She would skimp and save every nickel as my parents slowly built a decent nest egg, even though Dad never made much money by today's standards.

One thing my parents always did was give back to our church, First Christian Church, where they had been married. They were faithful in their belief and faithful in their tithing. Dad also served on the church's board of trustees for several years and often taught adult Sunday school classes before the main service.

If they had enough money saved, they would take vacations, but they never were extravagant in the hotel they booked when I was a child. As I said, we traveled to Florida each March or April by car when I was a kid. Once they had saved some money, they later often vacationed in Hawaii since Dad had fallen in love with the islands during the war. He knew so many locals on the Big Island through his "Hawaiian Mom," Elizabeth, and then Mom grew to love everything about the islands as well.

Mom always sacrificed for those around her. If we had eight slices of pizza, she would make sure we were full before she would even take one. If we had eight pieces of chicken on the table, she always made sure we had had enough before she took one. That's just the way she was—and that is how she was until the day she died.

She had grown up poor, but still, material possessions didn't mean much to her. She didn't care about wearing a big diamond ring or having a new car to drive. She never forgot her parents never owned a car at all. None of that mattered to her. What mattered was that her husband and three kids were happy, healthy, had clothes on their backs and food in their stomachs.

Mom could cook, too. I considered her a good cook, but we ate mostly "comfort" foods for dinner and deli meat, bologna, tuna or ham salad sandwiches for lunches.

She would drive downtown to the meat market, where her best friend Martha Gusan worked, each Friday and buy enough meat for the following week. That is why we usually had hamburgers on most Friday nights, maybe meat loaf on the weekends and spaghetti on Mondays. Always on Mondays. She explained that she had to use the leftover ground beef by Monday, or it would go bad. Then by Tuesday she would get to the ham or chicken, etc.

I think we only had steak during the summers when Dad would light the charcoal grill. It was too unpleasant to do that outside during the Ohio winters.

To this day, I like spaghetti on Mondays just as most people eat tacos on Tuesdays or fish on Fridays. It's strange how those things stay with you.

As I said, Mom was a giver, not a taker. She had the biggest heart of any person I ever knew. Nothing bothered her like seeing a homeless person. I know that originated with seeing a lot of them during the Depression. But once I moved to Florida, it was very common to see people begging for money on the side of the street. If they held signs that read "homeless" or "hungry," my mother would almost cry at the sight.

She would ask, "I wonder where they are sleeping tonight?" Or "Do you think they have blankets or sleeping bags to keep them warm?"

I would have to explain that often, many may have exaggerated their state of homelessness in order to receive donations, in order to make her feel better.

FROM OHIO TO OKINAWA . . .

She wasn't all talk, either. She always gave back to the Ashland community throughout her life. Mom volunteered as a patient receptionist at the local hospital for more than 50 years, which earned her a special volunteer award. That stretched to 60 years. And then to 70 years, for which she was honored for setting the hospital's volunteer record.

She also was the chairman of the Red Cross' annual blood drive in town for several decades. When I was a kid, I would walk downtown to the Red Cross headquarters, and she always handed me an egg salad or ham sandwich which they fed the donors. I loved those sandwiches.

She also volunteered at the local elections office and at our hometown voting site. I believe the only real pay she received was while working in a ticket booth for the Ashland County Fair, during each September.

I often would visit her tiny booth and see her sitting in there, either shivering if it was a cold day or sweating if it was a warm one. September in Ohio is one month when the temperature could be 40 degrees one week and 80 degrees the next. Whatever it was, she did her job and never complained—and the fair board eventually honored her for her service as well, after she set some sort of longevity record as a ticket taker.

I really believe everybody in town who knew her loved her. She was extremely polite to everyone and had hundreds of friends. She played in bridge clubs and various other card clubs during the days and bowled on a team for many years on Thursday nights.

I am biased, and I know my brother and sister would have agreed, but she was the perfect mother.

And I know Dad always considered her the perfect wife for him. He knew that within a few dates with her near the end of 1945, just months after experiencing the horrors of Okinawa, and he told me that often.

"I guess you would never know we were eight years apart," Dad once told me. "We think a lot alike on most things. I knew she was one-in-a-million almost from the time I met her. And meeting her and raising our family made surviving the war even more than worth it . . ."

CHAPTER FIFTEEN

DAD, ME AND OUR LOVE OF SPORTS

When I was 10, one of my Christmas presents from my parents was a small transistor radio. I didn't realize it then, but it would become my lifeline to the outside world while lying in bed almost every night.

Remember, there were no cell phones. There was no Internet or video games. I didn't have a television in my bedroom, at least not until I was in high school. So, while Mom and Dad watched TV in the living room on most nights, that outside world—the sports world specifically—came to me through that tiny radio, which was no bigger than a pack of cigarettes.

During the summers, I listened to the broadcasts of the Cleveland Indians' baseball games, and during the winter, I listened to the Cleveland Cavaliers' basketball games.

I wasn't just a passive listener. I actually kept box scores. I envisioned every home run, double-play or made basket. I wrote notes during the game and turned them into my own short stories as soon as they had finished.

I never realized it then, but I realize now that I was essentially training myself to become a sportswriter.

Dad and a few members of our undefeated T-Ball team of 1968. I am on the left.

While I loved all the Cleveland sports teams, just as Dad did, Ohio State football surpassed them all.

I really don't know if loving sports is a learned behavior, or it is genetic, but either would have applied to me. Maybe they both applied, because Dad was a sports nut, and I too became one at an early age.

Although, as I said, I regarded him as a very tough disciplinarian at times, when we bonded it was over our love of sports, later over having a cold beer or two at the end of the day, and throughout our lives, watching Clint Eastwood movies, among other things.

And he was very supportive, coaching my T-ball team when I was eight years old. We never lost a game. Then he started catching me as I developed into a pitcher in Little League. He also coached that team for one season, too.

Dad had played fastpitch softball after the war, and he been a wonderful basketball player when he was younger as he recounted earlier. He actually played basketball at the YMCA until the age of 85 when his knees finally gave out.

In fact, he rarely ate lunch while working all those years—from the end of 1945 through 1985 when he finally retired. He spent most of those lunch hours at the YMCA either playing basketball or volleyball, swimming, jogging around the indoor track, or lifting a few weights. Eventually, the YMCA awarded him a free lifetime membership.

When I was growing up, even playing outdoors in the Ohio winters, he and I would engage in intense games of one-on-one. And when he won, which he usually did, at least until I was 16 and he was 57 when things evened out because of our ages, he always jokingly rubbed it in.

"Still can't beat the old man, huh?" he would say.

Or "Still can't stop my hook shot?"

And that went for the game of ping-pong, too. We had a table in our basement, and Dad was one of the finest table tennis players

I ever saw. He would kick my butt in a match before dinner, until I caught up with him in talent about the time I went to college. Then he would bound up the stairs with his bad knees and tell Mom all about his dominance, sit down, have a beer and read the newspaper. It was almost a daily routine.

Dad was that way when playing cards as well. He basically was an amateur card shark who had an uncanny knack for remembering every card played in about any card game he played. He would usually win in whatever card game he played—Gin against Mom or in Euchre or Bridge, and then he would recount how he did it like an athlete being interviewed in the locker room after a big game. But he did it all with a smile on his face, in a lovable joking manner. (He and Mom often played together in Bridge clubs around town).

Playing basketball outdoors in the winter, with holes cut into my gloves, strange as it seems now, will always result in one of my best deeds, accidental as it was.

A neighbor, Mike McCuen, and his family farmed a large area off of King Road, with large cornfields extending from the edge of town more than a mile all the way behind the lane that ran next to our house, which led to the four houses behind us. At the very end of the lane stood one basketball hoop, which a neighbor, Charlie Ferrell, had constructed in front of his house. He never seemed to care if we played basketball there since the lane served all the other houses as well as his.

Anyway, on one winter day, in 1975 when I was 15, I was at that spot shooting baskets alone before Dad had gotten off work, and I was just about to walk back home since the sun was setting and it was almost time for dinner. It was bitter cold.

I then heard a faint voice, as I turned to see Mike waving at me with one arm from a few hundred yards away in the cornfield. I ran out to him and he was screaming in pain. His left hand had gotten stuck in the corn-picker, a large piece of farming equipment which automatically picks corn while husking it.

FROM OHIO TO OKINAWA . . .

"JEFF, CLIMB UP THERE AND TURN IT OFF!" he shouted. "MY HAND IS STUCK!"

Mike had reached into the giant machine's blades to remove an obstruction, and it had snagged his glove, pulling his hand in with it. After I turned off the machine, I ran home and rushed into the house, yelling at Mom, "Call the emergency squad now! Mike McCuen is stuck in his corn-picker in the field behind Ferrell's house!"

There was no 911 system in my hometown back then. If you needed the police, you called the police station. And if you needed emergency medical care, you called the "emergency squad" at our local hospital, where Mom volunteered so she knew the number by heart. I ran back to Mike and in about 10 minutes, the paramedics and a large fire truck arrived. It took them about an hour to remove his hand from the picker, and when it emerged it was a flattened, bloody mess. Then they rushed him off to the hospital.

About two weeks later, Mike showed up at the house with his hand in a cast to see me. I remember his first words as he walked into our kitchen: "Young man, you saved my life!"

Mike explained that the doctors told him he would have either bled to death within hours or froze to death overnight if nobody had discovered him.

By pure happenstance, and from something so simple as being outside shooting a basketball on a cold winter day, I stumbled into the right place at the right time to save a life.

Anyway, I had hoped that sports somehow would provide a way for me to make a living someday, and I soon believed the luckiest people on earth could claim that they never really worked a day in their life.

By that, of course, I mean to find a career that doesn't seem like real work.

Anyway, as I had planned, after receiving my degree in journalism from Ohio State in 1982, I started my career as a sportswriter.

First, it was for a small newspaper in Baytown, Texas. For two years, I wrote about the old Southwest Conference, high school football, the Houston Oilers and Astros and even spent a week in nearby Huntsville writing stories of a condemned killer, Ronald Clark O'Bryan, who was on death row at the state prison. (He was executed March 31, 1984, for poisoning his son Timmy on Halloween night 10 years earlier.)

And I learned about hurricanes. As the intense winds of Hurricane Alicia shook the apartment building in which I lived, and once the windows were blown out and it became downright frightening on the morning of August 16, 1983, I retreated to the kitchen. There, I stayed on the floor and covered myself in couch cushions. I pulled the phone receiver from the wall and called Dad at his office in Lexington, Ohio.

With the roaring hurricane and Dad's hearing impairment, I screamed into the phone that morning, letting him know how dire the situation appeared.

He tried to reassure me the thing would pass and I would be okay, telling me, "Just keep your head down!"

He had experienced the devastating results of raising one's head prematurely, out of curiosity, during war. It was good advice.

After two years living in Texas, I moved to West Palm Beach, Florida, to seek a better job at a larger newspaper. I always wanted to live in Florida, which offered year-round warm weather and also was considered the newspaper mecca of the country. It especially offered the best sports pages of some of America's best newspapers.

But first, before I had one interview, I took a job as a lifeguard at a place called the Rapids Water Park just to make some spending money while I looked for a sports writing job I always desired.

I had never life-guarded before.

It was a fun job, where I met some great people, such as the owner, Tommy Lumbra, a fellow Buckeye. Admission to the tiny waterpark then cost only eight dollars. My boss and I became very close within weeks of taking that job and he once told me his dream was to build the place into one of Florida's premiere water park attractions.

One day, I was working at the small receiving pool at the bottom of the water slides, when a young kid came barreling down headfirst, only to go under the water and not pop back up. I jumped into the pool, swam over to the area where I last saw him and tried to find him among a large crowd of kids splashing around. I dived underwater and saw him in the corner of the pool, not moving. I swam to him and reached for the top of his head, grabbing a handful of hair to pull him above the surface.

With the help of a more experienced guard, we then laid him on the cement, where the guard performed CPR. The kid soon spit up about a pint of water and started breathing again.

In addition to Mike McCuen, my farmer friend who lost the battle with his corn picker, I now had two lives in the save column.

The following week, I took a CPR course.

(Tommy Lumbra's dream came true: The Rapids now is one of the largest waterparks in the Southern United States.)

Within one month, I was offered a job from my first interview: At the *Palm Beach Post*, where I worked my way up from being the tennis writer (a low-level beat) to soon traveling the country covering many major sporting events.

I know it was a career Dad greatly admired and approved of, because he once told me that when I was covering a college football game in Oxford, Mississippi.

In the fall of 1985, I began arranging for flights for him to wherever I covered an event, once or twice per year, just so we could be together and he could experience some big-time sporting events with me.

Over the years, Dad attended several Daytona 500s, Indianapolis 500s, a George Foreman fight in Las Vegas, and several college football games with me and I always arranged for him to have a good seat, if I couldn't sneak him into the press box.

I was fortunate that one of my early passions—the game of college football—became the primary manner by which I made a living for most of my working life. Even though I put a ton of effort into reporting and writing about the game for newspapers, magazines and eventually for my books, it never seemed like real work to me.

I simply loved watching a college football game and then writing about it; or researching and interviewing former players and coaches for a history book or a biography.

Along the way, I wrote 13 books on the game, collaborating with such notable coaches as Ohio State's Jim Tressel and Urban Meyer, Nebraska's Tom Osborne, Florida's Steve Spurrier, Virginia Tech's Frank Beamer and Oklahoma's Barry Switzer.

I have so many memories of the great players, great games, great times and great people, and I was fortunate to get to know some real legends of the game. And I tried to include my father in many of them.

Of all the players or coaches whom I ever covered, however, nobody will ever top Florida State's legendary coach, Bobby Bowden, in my book. He never, ever refused to give me five minutes of his time, which usually evolved into 30 or 60. Even after difficult losses. Even on Friday afternoons before big games. Even on New Year's Eve from his hotel suite before a bowl game. And even after the tragic death of one of his star players when he was murdered on campus, Bobby always took or returned my call or sat down to talk with me. There wasn't one circumstance I can recall in which he ever said something like "not now" or "catch me later."

Over the years, he became somewhat of a second father-figure to me and often advised me when I came to him with a personal question. I am positive that hundreds of his former players and coaches could make the same claim, too. Bobby was full of good, old-fashioned wisdom.

A few times, the schools' sports information directors even let me sneak Dad into the press box to watch a game, but I first had to teach him the "no cheering rule." Over the years, he joined me at such places as LSU, Florida, Florida State, Ole Miss, Mississippi State, the New Orleans Superdome, the Sugar Bowl and the Gator Bowl—and he always fit right in with my sportswriter buddies.

I guess it was sort of my way of repaying him for first taking me to Ohio State games when I was only 12 years old. And since I lived in Florida and he was still in our hometown in Ohio, I wanted any chance to spend time with him and Mom.

It just seemed natural to have Dad come along for the ride when I covered college football. I remember one day before a game at LSU in Baton Rouge in the early 1990s, Dad and I met in New Orleans when his plane landed. We boarded a riverboat, then enjoyed raw oysters and a few beers, as it cruised up and down the Mississippi River for a few hours.

"I first saw this place in 1941 with Ted, Cockey and Buck on our motorcycle trip," he said. "But I never saw it from the river . . . Wow! It sure has grown!"

We had so many fun times like that one over the final three decades of his life.

And Dad naturally became friends with my friends, both the coaches I covered as well as fellow sports writers.

When Coach Bowden was 13 years old in 1942, he was diagnosed with rheumatic fever and was bedridden at his childhood home in Birmingham for more than a year. He passed the time listening to news reports of the war on the radio, which sparked his deep interest in World War II, something that would last his lifetime. Bobby was an avid reader and devoured books on the war.

Thus, when he heard me once describe Dad's history, he immediately wanted to pick up the phone to call him. Then I told him that he couldn't hear very well over the telephone.

Before the game against Miami in 1985, after Dad arrived for the first time in Tallahassee, I picked him up at the airport and I drove directly to the Florida capitol building where Governor Bob Graham was hosting a cocktail party. We, along with two other sports writers, walked out of the elevator, and I noticed Graham, along with his personal security detail, engaged in a conversation with Bobby, who was holding a Coke, in the middle of the room.

Earlier that week, I had told Bobby that Dad was coming into town for the weekend.

As we waited for their conversation to finish, Bobby noticed me and waved for us to come over. I made the introductions, and we all made small talk with Governor Graham. Then for about the next 15 minutes, Bobby peppered Dad with several questions—not all of which he heard clearly—about where he served during World War II and then offered his own recollections of those battles from his own research and childhood memories. Bobby knew all of the details of Saipan and Okinawa, two of Dad's fiercest battles.

For me, it was a conversation I will never forget, seeing my two favorite men finally meet and have so much in common.

About an hour later, we departed for dinner and as Dad climbed into the car with me and my buddies, he said, "Bobby is such a great guy! He is just like I expected him to be! He knew as much about the war as I do! What a great guy . . . what a great guy!"

He went on and on for a few minutes, telling us what we already knew. Then he added, ". . . But who was that guy with the bodyguard who kept interrupting us?"

All of us inside that car erupted in laughter. One of my buddies had just taken a sip of beer and spit it all over the dashboard. Dad's hearing issue and being from Ohio prevented him from realizing he had been talking to the governor of Florida.

FROM OHIO TO OKINAWA...

Another night a few years later, Dad and I were dining at the Silver Slipper Steakhouse in Tallahassee before another big game when I noticed Bobby sitting with CBS' Brent Musburger and Pat Haden in a corner booth. I pointed him out to Dad, and five minutes later, there was Bobby, standing over our table.

"Ed, it is so good to see you again!" he said.

He then sat down and dined with us. And that was the type of guy he was, leaving the well-known broadcasters who would call his game the following day in order to talk to a World War II soldier again.

In the following years, I took Dad to several more Florida State games and it was always the same: He and Bobby bonded like long-lost childhood buddies.

Two of my all-time favorite coaches, and two of the greatest in college football history, Bobby Bowden and Tom Osborne. Over the years, Bobby became a father-figure to me, and I once co-authored a book with Osborne, the Nebraska legend.

Like Dad, Bobby Bowden was a devout Christian and a man of faith. He also didn't believe in that separation of church and state thing. If he could guide one or more of his players toward God, he did, and he didn't care much if any outside criticism came his way.

"Because that's what I believe," he said. "If I can have one of my boys saved and go to Heaven for all eternity, don't you think that is the right thing to do? Because I do."

That was never more evident than in the aftermath of when one of his players was murdered on campus during the 1986 football season. It was an incident that also affected me deeply and consumed me for years.

Let me start at the beginning of this story and set the backdrop:

I spent one Thursday night in September of 1985, on a barstool at the American Legion in Lincoln, Nebraska, the town where Dad had lost eight buddies from the troop train when returning home from World War II exactly 40 years earlier.

I was a guest of the great Bob Devaney, then the Nebraska athletic director and the former head coach who had built the Cornhuskers' dynasty before handing it off to Osborne. I realized I was sitting next to football royalty that night, although his Legion buddies knew him as a beloved, modest and humble legend.

Florida State's team was flying into town the following day to play his Cornhuskers that Saturday. I had called ahead earlier in the week to interview Devaney, but my flight had been delayed, so by the time I arrived, he was walking out of his office. I introduced myself, apologized for being late, before he suggested we have a few drinks at the Legion. A few turned into a four-hour extravaganza of listening to a living legend deliver hilarious stories which had everyone inside the bar falling off their stools.

That Saturday, the temperature reached 133 degrees on the artificial turf at Memorial Stadium as the Seminoles shocked fourth-ranked Nebraska 17-13. Bowden's underdog team had pulled off another huge upset of a football powerhouse on the road, for which he was becoming well known.

A year later, Florida State returned to Lincoln, but the weather was much different. Temperatures hovered in the 40s and it was raining on that Friday before the game. Not being able to do much outside, I swam some laps in the indoor pool at the Holiday Inn, the team's hotel, when two offensive linemen sat down on the edge of it.

One was a hulking junior offensive tackle by the name of Pablo Lopez, who had an NFL future ahead of him. We made small talk that day, and I remember Pablo saying, "Catch you after the game tomorrow night."

The next night, Nebraska got its revenge, beating Bowden's Seminoles easily 34-17. But Lopez had sustained a minor shoulder injury, an event that would set off a chain of events that would become tragic and ultimately change many lives.

The following Saturday happened to be an off weekend for the team, and many players traveled to their hometowns. Lopez, however, was required to remain on campus to receive medical treatment on his shoulder, a team rule for all injured players.

On that Sunday, September 14, 1986, my telephone rang at 7 a.m. It was my sports editor Steve Moore, informing me of the horrible news: Pablo had been shot and killed outside a dance on campus just a few hours earlier. He ordered me to catch a flight to Tallahassee as soon as I could pack a bag and get to the airport. After my flight landed, I hurried to the crime scene to get a mental picture of what had happened, only to see a large bloodstain in the parking lot.

Some images you just never forget, and I will always remember standing there staring at it in shock, thinking of talking to Pablo on the edge of that hotel pool just nine days earlier. It was eerie, morbid and terribly sad. I was heartbroken that his young life and bright future had been snuffed out just like that.

Pablo Lopez was 21 years old when he was shot to death on the Florida State campus September 14, 1986.

FROM OHIO TO OKINAWA...

I had no idea then, but for the next two years or more, I would become consumed with the case of Pablo's death. From covering his funeral a few days later and watching his young teammates overcome with emotion, I wrote story after story about Pablo and the emotional and legal aftermath of that terrible night. I interviewed the Florida State police chief, and slowly uncovered details of what led to the shooting.

The shooter, a local 19-year-old kid by the name of Byron Johnson, a part-time cook who worked at Church's Chicken just down the street from the shooting, had felt insulted by Florida State linebacker Ed Clark earlier in the evening outside the entrance to the gymnasium. So, he and a friend drove to his house to retrieve a 12-gauge shotgun. They loaded it and placed it in their car trunk, then drove back to the dance, parking behind the gym. They then left the trunk ajar.

Within an hour or so, Johnson purposely started an altercation with another football player, leading to another teammate running inside to grab Pablo off the dance floor for protection. After all, he was 6'4" and 280 pounds.

Naturally, even though it wasn't his fight to begin with, Pablo walked outside to help his teammates, confronting Johnson who stood behind his car. Words were exchanged when suddenly, Johnson lifted the trunk, grabbed the gun and pointed it at Pablo.

"You don't have the guts to pull that trigger . . ." were Pablo's final fateful words.

Johnson shot him in the chest from about three feet away and Pablo had no chance to survive. Within two hours, as Bowden and dozens of teammates gathered in the hospital's emergency room, a doctor emerged to deliver the awful news. Pablo was gone. Football players fell to their knees in tears and screamed in agony.

It was now Bowden's job to pick up the pieces.

That Monday, two days later, as his heartbroken players sat in their assigned seats in the team's main meeting room, Bowden walked in and immediately pointed to Pablo's empty seat and asked, "Does anyone here know where Pablo is?"

The players were dumbfounded, wondering why their beloved coach would ever utter such a question.

"Pablo used to sit right there in that chair, but now he is gone. But gone where? Where is he? I will tell you where he is . . . ," he said. He then pointed upward.

"Pablo is in Heaven. He is with God. How do I know? Because Pablo came to me to be saved last year. He was a believer. You are 18 to 22 years old, and you think you will live forever. But if you die tomorrow, where will you spend eternity? What will happen to your soul? If you want to know how to accept Jesus Christ into your life and be saved for all eternity, my door is open to you. Come see me anytime . . ."

Pablo Lopez was 21 years old when he was shot to death on the Florida State campus September 14, 1986.

The next day, a little-known graduate assistant coach by the name of Mark Richt arrived at Bowden's office door to accept his invitation. That talk changed Mark's life. "I was a real hell-raiser before that day," Mark once told me. "Pablo's death hit me like a ton of bricks. I know where I would have spent eternity, and it wasn't a very nice place. That changed my life."

Mark later became the head coach at Georgia and then at his alma mater, Miami.

Clark, the troubled linebacker from Miami who first argued with the would-be shooter before the dance started, changed, too. He cleaned up his act, graduated and then earned a master's degree. He became a teacher.

I was about to cover Johnson's trial the following year, when suddenly, the state attorney announced a plea deal in which the shooter would serve 10 years in prison for first-degree manslaughter. Wow, I thought, only 10 years for retrieving a gun, driving to the scene, starting an altercation, and then shooting a man at point blank range in front of more than 100 witnesses. Anyway, investigators interviewed one witness who said Pablo had threatened the shooter. And it was the matter of his intimidating size, too, while Johnson was much smaller.

On one trip to Tallahassee, the university police chief took me to the evidence room and handed me the shotgun involved in the shooting. "We will destroy it now that the case has been resolved," he told me.

I had always wanted to interview the killer and ask the question: "Why?"

Two years later, I called the state department of corrections' media relations office to inquire about Johnson's whereabouts in prison. I wanted to visit him, just as I had "The Candyman" four years earlier in Texas.

I was completely shocked at what I had discovered: He had been released from prison after serving only 18 months. It turned out the state of Florida had something called "prison gain time," in which inmates who exhibited good behavior were eligible to serve only a certain percentage of their original sentence due to prison overcrowding—if they were determined to be "non-violent."

It was a law I had never heard of, and as it turned out, neither had many others. The bottom line: Pablo's killer, who left the scene of an earlier argument to retrieve a weapon, served 18 months for a crime many, like I had, believed should have been tried as first-degree murder.

I promptly called coach Bowden.

"Nobody notified me of this!" he said. "That's unbelievable!"

I then asked another writer in our newsroom who spoke fluent Spanish to act as my interpreter. The two of us drove to Miami, where I talked to Pablo's Puerto Rican mother. She had not been informed, either. She turned very, very angry.

"I thought 10 years meant 10 years!" she screamed in Spanish. She soon fell to the floor while crying uncontrollably, and I felt awful for her. And I felt worse that I was the one who broke the horrible news.

That night, I returned to the newsroom and began to write a long story about her grief, as well as the obviously flawed penal system which set a convicted killer loose after such a short time behind bars. I also had learned Pablo had been married a short time before his death, and a son, Pablo Jr., had been born just months after it. None of his teammates or Bowden knew that, either.

I wasn't done, however. In the coming months, I tracked the shooter to a small house his sister owned across the state line in Georgia. And remember, there was no Internet then. There were no cell phones. Working as a reporter involved making a ton of phone calls from the office and often following up by using pay phones along the road. I had found the phone number to the house where he lived, but no one ever returned my messages.

Thus, my next step was to show up on his doorstep. I flew into Tallahassee, rented a car and drove across the state line to Georgia, locating the house far out in the country. A woman opened the door and identified herself as his sister. She also was in a foul mood. I immediately noticed she also was holding a silver revolver at her side. I knew then this wouldn't be an easy interview.

I knew guns and it looked like a .38 caliber to me. I identified myself as a sportswriter and told her I simply wanted to talk to her younger brother for five minutes. It turned out she had been expecting me after all of my phone calls, and she knew exactly who I was and what I wanted. She wouldn't budge, however, claiming he was not home.

I had no idea if itchy trigger fingers ran in the family, so I had no choice but to slowly back away toward my rental car.

Eventually, my story of the shooter's brief incarceration sparked outrage across the state, and fortunately, gained some attention from state lawmakers. (Florida later modified "prison gain time" so prisoners could not be released until they had served at least 65 percent of their imposed sentences.)

For several years, I chipped away researching a book on the murder, interviewing Richt at his Georgia office for several hours, Ed Clark in Tallahassee and Pablo Jr., who loved the idea as way to honor his late father whom he never knew, as well as Bowden at length, and even Deion Sanders, who was the star of the team at the time. I met with Deion in Miami when he was with the Atlanta Braves, and he consistently steered the result of the plea deal to be about race, when it had nothing to do with race at all. After all, the shooter was Black while Pablo was Puerto Rican.

I still believed the subject was very book-worthy because it changed so many lives in positive ways, such as Richt's and Clark's. However, the project hit a big roadblock when Pablo's widow, who became a police officer in North Miami Beach largely because of what happened to Pablo, sternly instructed her son not to cooperate with me. And Clark, too, grew very angry with me when I delved into his role of starting the fight on that fateful night. He had to be living with extreme guilt.

Anyway, I eventually dropped the idea, but that horrible crime, the legal case, the sentence of injustice, Richt's and Clark's change of direction in their lives, Johnson's sister flashing a handgun, and Bowden's handling of his heartbroken players will always remain with me.

My time covering Florida State came to an end in 1991, when my sports editor assigned me to cover its main rival, the Florida Gators.

Bobby would go on to win another 177 games, finishing as the second-winningest coach in college history, with 377 career wins, behind only Joe Paterno's 409. And over the next two decades, I often received short notes from him, asking how I was and how Dad was doing.

I would always write him back telling him the good news: He was still alive and telling war stories.

I just had no idea it was something Bobby already knew, which I would learn many years later.

CHAPTER SIXTEEN

LIKE DAD, I DODGED A FEW "BULLETS"

That time in which Dad almost accidentally backed over me with his company van when I was a kid was just the first of many occasions in which I almost departed this earth prematurely.

Many other close calls and near-death experiences would follow over the years, in a variety of ways, from the usual car crashes to the unusual, like falling off a cliff and stepping on a poisonous snake in an extremely remote area.

Was I just lucky, just as Dad had been to survive World War II? Or was there some sort of divine intervention which allowed me to live to tell about them, or in this case, write about them?

I think there was a little of both, just like Dad had believed.

Looking back on all of them, maybe God did have a plan for me like he had one for Dad. I always wondered about that. And as I have grown older, it is one of the reasons my faith in Him has grown stronger.

A high school buddy, Randy Allen, talked me into hiking the Appalachian Trail during the summer after we graduated in 1978. It was the final week of July, and I remember that date because it was the final week of Pete Rose's National League record 44-game hitting streak.

I had taken my beloved small transistor radio for our hike, which began in the mountains of southern Pennsylvania and ended one week later in the mountains of Maryland. Each night I would listen to updates of whether Rose, then still with the Cincinnati Reds, had continued his streak (which began June 14).

It was brutally hot that week, so by most afternoons I had an empty canteen, was dying of thirst and dragging along behind Randy, an experienced hiker.

One day I was walking far behind him when I stepped on something squishy. After taking another step or two, I turned to see a Timber rattlesnake, now all curled up and ready to strike. And it was shaking its rattle. However, I was shaking more.

That thing was no less than four feet long and about as thick as my bicep. It was a frightening sight to see. I stood at a safe distance and just watched it for a few minutes, until it uncurled and slithered away from me.

When we saw a park ranger later, I described the snake's length and size and described my encounter with it. He told me, "You are so damn lucky! It probably had just eaten something and wasn't aggressive—or it surely would have bitten you."

At the time, we were several miles from any road, and I always wondered if I would have made it to a hospital in time to receive the necessary antidote for a poisonous snake bite. I read later that a Timber's venom can be lethal if not treated immediately.

For the remainder of that hike, I always double-checked each night to make sure our tent was zipped tight.

If that wasn't rare enough encounter with the animal kingdom, just three years later, I was almost gored by a raging bull on Ohio State's campus.

It was a cold, rainy day in November, 1981. and I was walking from campus to the football facility (now named the Woody Hayes Athletic Center). Where the Schottenstein Center and Jack Nicklaus

Museum are located now had been a large fenced-in field in which the university raised livestock.

Since the weather was poor, I decided to take a shortcut to practice, so I climbed that fence and began walking. I must have been three-quarters of the way across the field when I heard the hoof stomps behind me. I turned to see two large horns, seemingly about six feet apart, bearing down on me. They were atop a giant black bull, and he was charging at me in full gallop.

What could I do? I wasn't a matador, so I just took off running as fast as I could. I could hear he was closing in on me by the time I reached the fence on the other side, and I had no choice but to dive head-first over it. I made it, but I landed face-first in mud.

The giant animal stopped at the fence, stared at me, snorted loudly and turned away in frustration. I laid there covered in mud, thinking the headline in my newspaper the following day was almost, "STAFF WRITER GORED TO DEATH ON CAMPUS."

A few minutes later, I walked inside and the first person I saw was Ohio State Coach Earle Bruce.

"What the hell happened to you?" he asked.

As I tried to explain about the rain, the field and my shortcut, he quickly interrupted me . . .

"There are no shortcuts in life, son!" he said.

Then he turned away in disgust, and I swear if he had snorted, it would have been just like the bull had treated me moments earlier. However, it was good advice. It was the last shortcut I ever took to practice.

By my junior year at Ohio State, Mom and Dad let me drive a black 1975 Ford LTD. I have to say, and I am convinced of it to this day, but that huge car saved my life one Friday night in the spring of 1982.

I had been to a fraternity party near campus before I started driving back to my apartment off campus in northwest Columbus. I was headed north on Olentangy River Road, approaching the intersection of Ackerman Road, but I admit I was probably traveling about 55 mph, too fast for that road.

I saw a green light in front of me, but as I crossed the intersection, all I remembered was seeing my headlights suddenly shining on the passenger's side door of another car, which was speeding through the intersection from my left. The driver obviously had run a red light. That big LTD smashed into the other car and the next thing I remember were paramedics shining a flashlight at my face. Somehow, I ended up on the passenger's side floor and my right knee had been sliced open.

I was dazed, but heard a voice asking, "Young man, can you hear me? Are you okay?"

Remarkably, the crash happened right in front of Riverside Hospital, so it took only a 30-second ambulance ride to reach the emergency room, where doctors told me I had a concussion. Sadly, they also let me know a lady driving the other car had been thrown onto the street and was not likely to survive.

Anyway, what remained of the LTD was impounded and it took a few days before someone could drive me to the impound lot. I had to get inside to retrieve my psychology book, because I had an upcoming exam in that class. When I got my first look at that mangled car, I absolutely could not believe what I saw.

To label it simply as "totaled" would not do it justice. The entire front end of that huge vehicle was gone. I mean, it was gone! It was as if the car had been sawed off to the front windshield. The giant front end and huge engine had acted as a buffer and saved my life. If I had been in a smaller car, surviving that violent collision would have been highly unlikely. From that day on, I became a big believer in owning a bigger car.

(Not to mention, I grew quite tall, so I needed the headroom and legroom. I stood 5'6" and was very thin in ninth grade, then graduated high school at 6'2" and college at 6'5".)

FROM OHIO TO OKINAWA...

If not for that big LTD, I would have never lived to even graduate a few months later. Besides my concussion, I had nine stitches in my knee.

Fortunately, I learned later through the insurance company investigators that the lady who was driving the other car, who had been in critical condition for that first week, pulled through and gradually recovered.

As I write this, it seems I have taken almost a thousand flights in my life, but only once did I think my time had come while in an airplane. I have recounted this story many times before, both to my friends and also written about it, but when I think of Notre Dame football, or South Bend, Indiana, I sometimes endure a tiny bit of post-traumatic stress syndrome.

Of all my close calls, none of them—NONE—were as frightening as what happened on one snowy day during the first week in December of 1988. My assignment that week for the *Palm Beach Post* was to travel to South Bend and spend two days with No. 1-ranked and undefeated Notre Dame and then fly from South Bend to Chicago to Pittsburgh, before driving south to Morgantown, West Virginia, to spend two days with the No. 2 West Virginia Mountaineers.

This was a prelude to the two teams meeting in the Fiesta Bowl three weeks later to play for the national championship. I had to write several stories on each team, previewing the game in Tempe, Arizona. On my final day in South Bend, I had finished talking to Notre Dame coach Lou Holtz at a round-table session and was sitting with his quarterback, Tony Rice. I glanced outside and noticed it had started to snow—and snow heavily. Then it started to blow—and blow heavily.

I looked at my watch—people wore wristwatches then—and realized I had to hurry to catch my flight. I walked outside, and it seemed as if I had stepped onto the North Pole. The wind was whipping and by the time I reached my rental car, snow was caked all over my mustache (yes, they were in back then, too).

I drove to the South Bend airport and boarded a tiny commuter plane from the now-defunct Midway Airlines for the short flight to Chicago, where I would catch my connection on U.S. Airways to Pittsburgh. I grabbed an empty seat in the last row. Once boarding finished, I noticed I was the only male aboard. The other seats were taken by co-eds from nearby St. Mary's College who had just finished their final exams and were headed home for the Christmas break.

I also noticed the two pilots looked like Richie Cunningham and his buddy Potsie Weber from the sitcom *Happy Days*. I really don't think either one of them had shaved yet, but here they were, about to fly a commercial airplane with me in it. I never had been nervous for flights before, but with the nasty weather and the airplane appearing no longer than a first-down marker, I admit I was a bit edgy before takeoff.

I just had a bad feeling.

Sure enough, we were no more than 10 minutes into the short flight, somewhere over Lake Michigan when it happened. Without warning, the two pilots, who had left the cockpit curtain open, lost control of the tiny plane.

It wasn't your average turbulence, either. This was much worse. We started to fall, losing altitude rapidly. I could see into the cockpit and noticed the young pilots struggling with the controls. Damn, I wondered, why hadn't they closed that curtain? It was like watching a surgeon about to operate on you with his hands shaking so badly that he drops the scalpel. It was at about this time when the co-eds started crossing themselves and loudly reciting Hail Mary's.

Now, I was not raised Catholic, but I was about to convert right then and there and do the same. One of them even started to scream that we were all about to die.

And I'll be honest: I believed her.

FROM OHIO TO OKINAWA . . .

The thoughts that race through your mind when you think the end is near. I would never see my family again. I would never get married. I would never have children. And I wouldn't live to see which team would win the Fiesta Bowl which I had already written so much about. I even wondered if they would hold a moment of silence before the game, honoring the memory of the 11 people who died in a plane crash which had departed South Bend three weeks earlier and crashed into Lake Michigan.

I really couldn't tell you how long our freefall lasted, but it seemed like more than two minutes. I am sure it had to be less, or we likely would have been beneath the surface of the water by then. I stopped watching the pilots' struggles, bowed my head in silent prayer, as the girls continued loudly repeating theirs.

Just as I thought for certain we were about to crash into the water, the pilots somehow regained control, and I felt that sudden updraft. It was like a wild rollercoaster ride at Cedar Point, but I have to admit that going up never felt so good.

The girls' screaming suddenly stopped, too, but I could see the wings still wobbling up and down as snowflakes flew by their blinking red lights. That plane rocked side to side, and we were not out of the proverbial woods yet. With the strong winds bouncing us as we approached Midway Airport, I looked through the cockpit window to see the runway lined with emergency vehicles' lights flashing—not a reassuring sight by any means.

I anticipated it would be a rough landing. I just hoped it wouldn't be a rough CRASH landing. To their credit, however, the young pilots leveled it out and hit the runway, albeit a tad late, skidding the airplane to a stop at the end of it, directly in front of a large snow drift.

All the girls were thanking God aloud, while I bowed my head and did the same in silence. I allowed them to deplane as I slowly gathered my computer and made my way up the aisle. The two pilots were slumped over the controls, both sweating profusely even though it was about 20 degrees outside.

I really wanted to ask what had gone so wrong, but I couldn't muster any words. I walked down the steps, starting to walk toward the terminal, then kneeled down and kissed the icy pavement (there was no jetway in those days for commuters).

I soon caught my flight to Pittsburgh and was relieved to see it was on a larger jet. Once we reached cruising altitude, I ordered a cocktail to either calm my nerves or celebrate being alive, I am not sure which. After we landed, I discovered U.S. Airways had somehow lost my luggage. I really didn't care. I had no clothes and no toiletries, but I had a future.

A Midway Airlines EMB-120, which gave me the ride of my life over Lake Michigan in December of 1988.

Once I rented a car, I headed directly to K-Mart and bought a few sweatshirts, some underwear and socks, a pair of jeans and a pair of gloves. I showed up in Morgantown the following day, realizing I had to be the worst-dressed sportswriter there.

Which is really saying something.

From that day, I usually flew on jets while covering college games, landing in major cities before I rented cars to drive hours to college towns like Hattiesburg, Oxford, Auburn, Starkville, or Clemson. I officially had sworn off commuter flights, unless it was completely unavoidable.

Anyway, more than three weeks after that frightening flight, Notre Dame beat West Virginia 34-21 in a rainy, muddy Fiesta

Bowl, and Tony Rice was named the MVP of the game. It was the Fighting Irish's last national championship.

Over the years, I often have wondered what happened to those St. Mary's co-eds who would be in their late 50s by now. I also have thought about the two baby-faced pilots and whether they still are flying today.

Years later, I recounted the ordeal to Holtz and told him he would have been one of the final people I ever spoke to on this earth. Bear in mind that he is a Catholic who rarely ever missed Mass. He didn't miss a beat, joking through his well-known lisp, "You know why that plane didn't crash, don't you? . . . Those devout Catholic girls saved your ass!"

Yes, perhaps they did.

Anyway, wherever they are today, here's to the girls of St. Mary's College. I am guessing most of them got married, had children and told the same story many times. I am also sure they, like me, never forgot that windy, snowy December day over Lake Michigan when we had only one common goal: To live to see another day.

On April 19, 1995, my wife and I flew to San Francisco for a week's vacation, because we had always wanted to see the famous Fisherman's Wharf and also Big Sur, which was more than 100 miles away. After we landed, we rented a car and drove to the Wharf and ordered lunch. While we were eating, the television above us showed the horror of the Oklahoma City bombing, which had occurred while we were in the air, killing 168 people.

After lunch we drove south, first to stay in Carmel-by-the-Sea and finally, to Big Sur. Three days later, on a Saturday morning, we walked into the Big Sur River Inn. I wanted to get there early to watch the NFL draft, since we did not have a TV in our cabin, and there was the matter of the three-hour time difference. The draft was starting at 9 a.m. PST.

However, the bartender was just setting up the bar, and when I asked him to turn on ESPN for me, he said, "I have to go down the street to flip a switch to turn on our cable system."

I thought he was joking about being in such a rural area.

"But if you watch the bar for me, I will be back in a few minutes," he told me, before walking out the front door.

Fortunately, I had three years of bartending experience at a place called the Black Forest Inn on the Ohio State campus when I was in college, because two patrons were soon sitting next to us, ready to order drinks. Then there were four. Then six. The bartender still had not returned, so I filled drink orders and wrote them on bar napkins to keep track of who ordered what.

After about 30 minutes, he returned to the bar, and I handed him four or five napkins so he could calculate the tabs. Most of the customers were regulars and trustworthy enough not to leave before paying, because I had no idea what to charge them.

As the day wore on, and we watched the draft, another couple sat down next to us. They were outgoing and very friendly. He said he owned a landscaping company, and his girlfriend was a wine wholesaler. A few hours later, we had plenty to drink, and as we got up to leave, they invited us to dinner at their home. They explained they were building a house and told us they were living in a mobile home atop Big Sur, about two or three miles to the south off the Pacific Coast Highway.

We accepted their invitation, so the guy wrote directions and a makeshift map on a bar napkin. We went back to our cabin, took a nap, showered and then headed out to find their place. When I located their driveway, I noticed it appeared to be a straight-up-a-mountain trek with no guardrails. It was downright scary. I had rented a Lexus sedan, and I slowly inched that car up the mountain. It was so frightening that I would have turned around several times if it had been wide enough to do so.

When we reached the top, there was nothing but a small mobile home, an outdoor shower, and dozens of pink-flagged stakes marking the spots where this couple was building a permanent home. We enjoyed a wonderful dinner of venison and consumed several bottles of great wine the woman had collected from her job. It was like a scene out of one of my favorite movies, *Sideways*.

At one point after sunset, I asked the guy to direct me to the bathroom. He responded, "We have one back there toward the bedroom, or you can just go in our backyard and pee out under the stars, like I do every night."

That was fine with me, since I did that as a kid so often, so I went outside and made it a point to walk far enough away from their mobile home. The stars were so spectacular in that night sky, without any competing city lights. I remember standing there, looking up in amazement. It had been a long time, many years probably, since I had been to such a remote area to fully appreciate a sky full of stars with no city lights obscuring them.

After I finished, I turned to walk back to the mobile home, but I had taken a few steps in the wrong direction. Then I started to fall. It was as if I stepped onto nothing but air and I landed hard on my left arm. I really could not see where I was and had figured I just had fallen down a small hill.

I then grabbed the dirt on the side of the hill and stepped on some outcropping of rocks to climb up to the backyard. When I walked inside, everyone noticed my clothes were covered in dirt and my arm was bleeding. The guy took me back to the bathroom to wash off the blood and clean up a bit. We still stayed a while more, then thanked them before I slowly drove the car back down the mountain, pumping the brakes constantly, relying on the headlights to show the way. I never should have been driving down that guardrail-less, winding mountain road after drinking all that wine.

The next morning, my left arm was throbbing, as was my head. I had a long scrape and a line of dried blood from the inside of my palm all the way to my elbow. Then it dawned on me: Where is my gold watch?

"We have to go back up there!" I told my wife. "We have to go find my watch!"

We ate breakfast before I slowly drove back up that mountain a second time. When we arrived, the guy was walking naked from the outside shower into the mobile home. He stopped when he saw us. As my wife covered her eyes, I got out of the car and explained I must have lost my watch during my fall, so I walked over to the spot where I thought I had relieved myself and fallen.

I couldn't believe my eyes. I was standing on a cliff about 1,200 feet above a rocky shoreline of the Pacific. I looked down to see the waves crashing upon the rocks. Then I looked to my left to see a tiny ledge, about eight-by-eight feet, at least 15 feet below us.

And there, glistening in the morning sun, rested my gold watch. Seeing that tiny ledge, I suddenly realized if I had taken a step in any other direction or had fallen a few feet one way or the other, I would have plunged off that cliff to my death.

"THAT IS WHERE YOU FELL?" the guy asked me. "YOU LANDED ON THAT?"

I had. I could not believe it, and neither could he.

My watch was nestled in the dirt on that ledge, illustrating just how close I came to my demise. He then rigged a long-handled instrument from his landscaping business to retrieve it for me.

I had come so close to dying, just a month after my 35th birthday, out of simple carelessness of drinking too much wine while trying to find a spot to relieve myself under the stars.

It was a night, a trip and another close call I will never forget.

Two years later, in 1997, I began to notice that same watch was becoming loose on my left wrist. I also could wrap my right hand completely around my left wrist. It was noticeably thinner than it had been. So too was my right wrist and also both of my forearms.

FROM OHIO TO OKINAWA...

It was obvious I was losing muscle mass from the elbows down to my fingers.

I went to the doctor, who promptly ordered an MRI of my spinal column. Sure enough, it revealed that I had a small cyst or fluid mass—a syrinx as it was called—in my spinal cord at C-5/C-6, the base of my neck.

I then received a recommendation from my brother-in-law, a doctor at Miami Jackson Hospital, to be seen by Dr. Barth Green, one of the foremost spinal surgeons in the United States. Dr. Green read my MRI and said it appeared a blunt-force trauma in the past had caused it. He also said it should be consistently monitored by a series of MRIs every few months to discover if the syrinx was increasing in size. So, for the next several months, I would drive 70 miles to Miami Jackson, where they would load me onto a gurney, inject dye into my right arm and slide me back into the dark hole in the wall.

That is what an MRI was like then, before the open-ended MRIs came along, and it was terrifying. I always have been a touch claustrophobic. Not to mention, the pounding of the imagining machine was quite loud. I dreaded those sessions, which lasted from 45 minutes to one hour, and I had six or seven of them before Dr. Green made his final determination.

He had seen enough to know that my syrinx was increasing in size and had to be surgically repaired. In October of 1998, I had no choice but to undergo spinal surgery. Dr. Green explained he would insert a tiny tube into syrinx, remove the fluid, thus eliminating it and drawing my spinal cord back together. During one of the final pre-op checkups, I noticed the chart Dr. Green was examining had someone else's name listed at the top of it. It was for Barbara somebody.

"Doctor Green, is that my chart?" I asked.

He looked at it again, tilted his head, and said, "Oh, no, no, I grabbed some other patient's chart by mistake."

That is the first moment I realized, along with several nurses' accounts, that Dr. Green was the absent-minded professor type. They told me stories of how he would drive to the hospital, forget that he drove there, then take a taxi back home after work. These were not exactly encouraging anecdotes of a guy who was about to take a knife to my spinal column.

After surgery, I woke up in the intensive care unit, sore as could be. I could barely move. The back of my neck burned like fire, and I felt partially paralyzed. I could not feel anything below my waist, and I could move only my fingers and arms. I was bedridden at the hospital for the following week, but the pain would not subside. Dr. Green was baffled. He actually accused me once of exaggerating the pain.

Finally, on about the seventh day post-op, an orderly said, "I have an idea."

He left my hospital room but returned with a massive ice bag. He gently raised my head and placed it underneath my neck. Within two hours, my pain was gone. It turned out I had massive swelling from the surgery, something that should have been diagnosed and solved easily. But my highly paid, nationally acclaimed surgeon who had founded the Miami Project to Cure Paralysis and was the surgeon who had operated on Superman, actor Christopher Reeve, after his horse-jumping accident left him paralyzed, couldn't solve the mystery.

I eventually was discharged, had lost about 20 pounds, and it took about six months to regain any strength. My neck, however, has never been the same. There was one other aspect of the surgery that I did not realize before it took place—Dr. Green removed the lamina in my neck from C-5 to the base of my skull. Thus, my spinal cord now has virtually no protection.

"You shouldn't play any more basketball," Dr. Green told me. "You can't do anything risky."

FROM OHIO TO OKINAWA . . .

At least I was not in a wheelchair, which is where Dr. Green told me I was headed if I had not undergone the surgery.

The bad car crash in college wasn't my final one.

I always had loved Jeeps, so I bought a used green Jeep Wrangler, which came with a large black tubular front bumper, in 2010. Two years later, I was driving to one of my rental properties in Lake Worth, on a rainy day, when once again, another driver made a mistake.

A car headed from my left darted through a stop sign and pulled directly into my path. This time, however, I hit the brakes and steered to the right, my tires sliding on the wet pavement before I crashed head-on into a wooden telephone pole, which didn't budge an inch. The airbag exploded into my face, pushing me out of the open driver's side onto the street. As I laid on the pavement, I was dizzy and fading in and out.

I looked over to my left to see the other driver getting back into his car, before speeding away. I had missed hitting his car, and he didn't have a scratch on it, so he obviously figured he could just drive off—even though he had caused my crash. Fortunately, a witness saw his license tag number and gave it to a Palm Beach County's sheriff deputy who soon arrived.

Here's the interesting part of the story. The deputy tracked down the culprit, a man by the name of George Michael (just like the singer) and issued him a citation for leaving the scene of an accident involving injury. Then when the man refused to notify his insurance company (since he had no damage to his car and hoped the incident would fade away), I was forced to hire an attorney in order to have my Jeep and my emergency room costs covered.

Once again, I had escaped with only a concussion, but another car of mine had been totaled.

Anyway, my lawyer soon filled me in on the details of the other driver. He had served several years in prison on a racketeering conviction. My lawyer inferred the guy had connections, if you know what I mean. I didn't think much of it until a few days later, when the case became really tragic: That deputy who responded to my crash was driving to work when he lost control of his patrol car, which flipped upside down into a canal on Southern Boulevard in West Palm Beach. He drowned inside of it.

Anyway, the culprit of my crash obviously discovered it, because he showed up to the court hearing in Delray Beach with a high-priced attorney and pled not guilty. He had figured he would walk out of court scot-free without a witness there to testify against him.

But I had showed up. When the judge asked for any witnesses to the case to step forward, I approached, placed my right hand on the Bible for the second time in my life on the witness stand, which surprised both Mr. Michael and his attorney. I testified to what happened, before the judge pounded his gavel and announced, "Guilty as charged!"

He also levied a heavy fine and instructed Mr. Michael's attorney to guarantee I would be reimbursed for my losses. As I left the courtroom, my lawyer grabbed me.

"Watch yourself!" he said. "Be careful because he's a bad guy and he may not let this go."

He then handed me a thick dossier on the guy's background: It contained every bit of information you could imagine, from what cars he drove to where he worked, and all the details of the crime that once sent him to prison. And sure enough, a week or so later, I looked in my rearview mirror near one of my rental properties to notice him following me. I figured a confrontation was coming as I pulled into my parking lot.

Instead, he sped past me. Maybe he was just learning my routine, I figured, and I thought there was no way that would be the end of it. I surely would see him again, if I saw him coming that is. I carried a gun in my pocket everywhere in those days because the area had so much crime.

Surprisingly, however, I never saw or heard from George Michael again.

The next two times I almost bought it, as they say, were eerily identical.

On December 8, 2007, I headed to the Ace Hardware in Lantana. I shopped at that store so often that the clerks knew me by name. This day, as soon as the glass entrance door closed behind me, it was as if a cannon had been fired from behind my head. The explosion was deafening. I turned to see a yellow blur coming at me. I ran straight ahead to get out of the way of whatever it was.

That blur was a small Chevy, driven by a 72-year-old woman who had mistaken the brake pedal for the gas pedal.

The car was only about a foot behind me as it entered the store, the cashier told me later. It finally came to a rest when it made contact with the paint aisle and could not progress any further. The lady then panicked even more, trying to reverse the car, with large shards of glass on top of it, to back out of the store until an employee reached in to turn off the ignition.

For the next several years, a picture of the yellow car resting inside the store was taped to the door's entrance, and every time I saw it, I flashed back to that day.

Five years later, almost to the day, on November 30, 2012, it happened yet again. This time, however, it was tragic.

I was walking out of a CVS store and had taken a few steps toward the grocery store next door on South Congress Avenue in Boynton Beach, when I saw something large to my right and then heard another large explosion behind me. I turned around to see a van had crashed through the glass doors of the CVS, just a few feet from me.

If it had happened a split-second earlier, it would have hit me.

I walked around behind the van to the driver's side to help another confused elderly woman, who was slumped over the wheel. I opened her door, turned off the ignition, and told her to remain seated. I closed her door and then noticed the worst possible sight: An arm was bent backward extending from under the left front tire. The lady had run over someone who had been walking directly behind me. I reached down and felt the person's wrist, not being able to tell if it was a male or a female.

Sadly, there was no pulse.

The arm appeared to belong to a younger person, perhaps a teenager. Whoever it was had been killed instantly, but I could not see the body which was crumpled under the van. Again, it was the same cause—an elderly driver had mistaken the gas pedal for the brake pedal. A police officer was on the scene immediately. I did not want to look under the van, so I gave a statement to him and then left quickly without buying groceries.

"You're a lucky guy," the officer said. "Another witness told me that the car just missed you."

It happened so fast, and since it had been behind me, I wouldn't have had a chance to jump out of the way as I had at Ace Hardware. I didn't sleep much that night because I had gone to bed believing the person who died was a young child or a teenager.

Then I read in the *Palm Beach Post* the following day that the victim was a 76-year-old woman named Mary Elizabeth Bonnel. The driver of the van was 78.

The van which killed a 76-year-old woman who was walking behind me, resting inside the entrance to a CVS store in Boynton Beach, Florida, on November 30, 2012.

I was absolutely shocked. Her arm appeared to be of someone so much younger. I remember her skin was so soft. I don't want to claim that I was relieved, but I was somewhat comforted because I had believed a younger person with their entire life in front of them had died so needlessly.

Still, as it was, someone had lost a mother and a grandmother and perhaps a wife.

I realized that this type of accident was so common in a state like Florida for one simple reason: The state has more than its share of elderly drivers who often confuse the brake pedal with the gas pedal. It is what makes the parking lots in Florida almost as dangerous as the roads.

And it almost cost me my life, not once, but twice.

It really was as if I was carrying a rabbit's foot or horseshoe in my pocket all these years. I was lucky after Dad's foot slipped in the van on a snowy Saturday when I was a kid. I was lucky that neither one of those store-crashing vehicles hit me. I was lucky I landed on a tiny ledge one night in Big Sur. I was lucky I had been driving big, sturdy cars when I needed them most. And I was lucky the sister of Pablo Lopez' killer didn't shoot me.

I have discovered over the years that there is one thing that comes with almost dying: It changed my approach to living. Little problems didn't bother me as much.

What's more, I will always believe Someone up there was looking out for me—and the line between living and dying sometimes is very thin.

CHAPTER SEVENTEEN

~

HAWAII: OUR MUTUAL PARADISE

When I was a kid, Mom and Dad often took us on a Spring Break vacation to Florida, specifically to Hollywood Beach, just north of Miami. From the time I first saw it, when I was seven years old, I instantly fell in love with the beach, the Atlantic Ocean and the well-known Hollywood boardwalk.

There happened to be an arcade on the north side of the main beach road, Johnson Street, and behind it were several ground-level trampolines next to the beach. There was the famous Hollywood Bandshell, where several movies have been filmed, such as *Body Heat* with William Hurt and Kathleen Turner. I would sit in front of that bandshell as a kid, listening to the bands play into the night under the stars.

We always stayed at the same place, a small motel called the "Swim 'n' Play," located directly behind the trampolines. When I wasn't running on that beach, or swimming in the Atlantic, I was playing in that arcade or constantly jumping on those pay-by-the-hour trampolines.

Anyway, I loved the brown sandy beach, greenish-blue ocean and coconut palm trees which lined the boardwalk. Those trips were the impetus for my desire to reside in Florida, or at least some place warm, when I grew up.

At that point in my young life, I had only seen a beach at Lake Erie, so I didn't realize white sandy beaches and clear blue oceans existed.

That is, until March of 1979.

Mom and Dad had planned a two-week family trip to Hawaii, taking us three kids and Becky and Bill's spouses. I was in college then and could only go for one week during Spring Break.

As Dad said so many times over the years, from the first time the USS *Lurline* pulled into the port of Honolulu in early 1942, just after Pearl Harbor was bombed, he had fallen in love with the Hawaiian Islands at first sight.

For our first two days and nights in Waikiki, we stayed at the famous Rainbow Tower in the Hilton Hawaiian Village, we visited Pearl Harbor and the National Memorial Cemetery of the Pacific. After that, we didn't stay at a hotel like normal tourists. We flew to the Big Island to stay with Dad's "Hawaiian Mom," Elizabeth.

Her first husband Henry Kailikole, the man whose truck had broken down in 1942 when Dad first met him, had died several years earlier. Elizabeth had remarried—to a man named Richard Kamai, a tiny guy who was half-Hawaiian and half-German. Everyone called him "Dickie."

"Dickie once told me he never even met his father," Dad explained. "His father was a German sailor, and he come into Hawaii on a ship, met his mom one night, impregnated her and then shipped back out . . ."

They still lived in the same ranch house high above the Pacific in the small town of Captain Cook, where she and Henry had hosted Dad on many weekends 37 years earlier. She was now 75 years old. She loved children and taking care of people. And she took care of all of us, just like she did to Dad almost four decades earlier.

Elizabeth's property included a guest house behind the main house, and it was surrounded by banana trees and pineapple plants.

Dad had first returned to the islands after the war in 1968, taking Mom, some 24 years after he last sailed out of Hawaii on a troop ship headed toward Saipan. They had corresponded with Elizabeth frequently and even talked over the telephone on birthdays and Christmas. And Mom instantly fell in love with the islands on that trip as well, when they stayed with Elizabeth and Dickie.

Naturally, Elizabeth took to Mom immediately as well, as the two became very, very close over the years. She called Mom "Girlie."

Three years after their trip, in 1971, when I was 11, Elizabeth—she insisted that we children also call her "Mom"—and Dickie made the long trip to Ohio and stayed with us for two weeks that summer. Elizabeth was just as I pictured her: A sweet, wonderful woman, who laughed often and enjoyed a good time. She spoke broken English, with a thick Hawaiian accent. Dickie, a tiny man who stood no more than five-foot-three, was always the life of the party. He also was a practical joker who drank beers one after the other and broke into song when they took effect.

Elizabeth had been a trained singer with a wonderful voice and Dickie played several instruments, specializing in the Ukulele, as they performed Hawaiian music in packed bars and restaurants all over the Big Island. They were local celebrities of sort with hundreds of friends, who of course became Mom and Dad's friends. That was just the Hawaiian way.

In 1973, Mom and Dad returned to Hawaii again and continued going back every few years.

It took me only a week to fall in love with Hawaii, just as Dad had when he first saw it.

That week on Spring Break in 1979, Elizabeth took the time to teach all of us so much about their culture, the natives and the special language and phrasing they utilize. Besides the Islands' pure natural beauty, that culture was especially attractive to all of us. It seemed she and Dickie knew everyone on the Big Island and everyone knew them. And when we went out to dinner or to a bar to watch them perform, we were treated like royalty, too, just because we were with them.

Elizabeth had a heart of gold. On that first visit, she and Dickie hosted a luau in Mom and Dad's honor. Now this wasn't one of those tourist luaus for $50 per person at the beachfront hotels. This was the real thing with real Hawaiian food.

With Elizabeth and Dickie Kamai (two days after my 19th birthday) March 23, 1979, in front of their home in Captain Cook, Hawaii.

There must have been 50 or more locals and her extended family there, and local dishes were lined up on several tables in Elizabeth's backyard. She quickly noticed that none of us were trying the fish-head soup, in which fish eyeballs actually floated freely in the broth, or the many kinds of Poi she loved so much and ate three times daily. I tried it, but it tasted like paste to me.

I saw her whisper to one of her nephews and then she handed him a few bills. He left and returned minutes later with several buckets of Kentucky Fried Chicken for the so-called Haoles (us) who were still hungry. She was always thinking of others.

That week was the last time we saw her. She died less than a year later, on March 3, 1980, a month before her 76th birthday, of heart failure. I remember her death really hit Dad hard, because she really

On my last trip to the Big Island in 2021, I found her gravesite behind the "Painted Church," where she had played the organ during Mass every Sunday. It was the same church Dad had attended most Sundays with her in 1942.

was like a second mother to him, taking care of him when he was in Hawaii in 1942.

Once she was gone, we often re-connected with many of Elizabeth's friends and extended relatives over the years.

In the winter of 2001, Mom, Dad and I spent an extended vacation on the Big Island for three months and during that visit, we frequently hung out with two brothers who were retired from the U.S. Army. Their names were Eddie and Harold Awa. Their mother Mae was Hawaiian and was a coffee picker Dad knew during the war. She was one of Elizabeth's childhood friends who remained close their entire lives.

Dad also had known Mae's husband, who was half-Japanese, half-Hawaiian, in 1942.

He told me that one night in the 1950s her husband was walking to a nearby store and had told Mae he would be back within the hour. He never returned—and the police never found his body, either. Dad always suspected that someone probably hit him while driving drunk on the rural road where they lived and then placed his body in their trunk and disposed of it in the ocean to cover up the crime.

Anyway, their two sons served overseas in the army and had recently retired, moving back to Captain Cook. They raised children and grandchildren of their own by the time I got to know them. One Sunday, which is the day Hawaiians usually gather their extended family somewhere to hear the elders "Talk Story" as they call it, we were invited to join the Awas' extended family at a remote beach, within a few hundred yards of the Captain James Cook Monument.

They had lined up about seven or eight picnic tables, started the barbeque grills, unloaded several coolers of beer, wine and wine coolers—most of the elderly Hawaiian women love their wine coolers—and threw one day-long party. I had attended several over the years and it was always a "more the merrier" type of atmosphere.

Within minutes, Harold and Eddie and their sons were diving at the local reef using spear guns. They soon came ashore holding large nets full of Ahi, Yellowfin Tuna and Ono—a local fish which is delicious. They then sliced it up, rolled it in rice, pulled out the soy sauce and served up mounds of sushi that couldn't have been any fresher, since the fish had been swimming offshore just moments earlier.

"Eddie," I asked, "Do you have any idea what this would cost on the mainland?"

"How much?" he asked me.

"At a nice restaurant, you are looking at one-thousand dollars or more worth of sushi here!" I told him.

"No, brudda!" he said in his thick Hawaiian accent. "No way brudda!!"

Dad at Pearl Harbor in 1993, some 51 years after he saw it for the first time, when the harbor still reeked of burning oil.

FROM OHIO TO OKINAWA...

Then he smiled and chugged a beer. Most native Islanders I knew were often big drinkers. And when I say big, I mean they started early and didn't stop until late, at least on the weekends. The Hawaiian term for that is, "Suck 'em up!"

That was a phrase Dad used often over the years as he threw back a cold one, mostly when he was in Hawaii. It was almost as common and popular as "Hang Loose."

Mom and Dad both loved nothing better than a good Hawaiian luau and they threw a few during the summers in our backyard. Dad, who must have owned 40 or more Hawaiian shirts, often would get that silly look on his face, throw on a grass skirt and start dancing the Hula.

Anyway, we enjoyed many Saturdays and Sundays like that day throughout the years.

It was in Hawaii the only time I felt the earth shake. It happened on October 15, 2006, when we were jolted awake at 7 a.m. at our oceanfront condo on the Big Island. Paintings flew off the walls, glasses and dishes fell out of the cupboards, and my bed frame actually left the floor.

I initially thought I was having a nightmare, but I was wide awake.

An earthquake which measured 6.7 on the Richter Scale had hit just offshore.

I rushed to Mom and Dad's bedroom, screaming, "We have to get out of here! We can't risk staying because a tsunami might be coming!"

Dad couldn't hear a thing I said and turned over to try to go back to sleep, so I had to physically grab him and lift him up to get him dressed. I continued to look at the ocean, as we drove along the beach road, headed for a coffee shop at a higher elevation. We remained there in the parking lot for two hours with hundreds of others, just sipping coffee, eating donuts and staring at the Pacific until the tsunami warnings were lifted. Then we spent the next several hours sweeping up the broken glass and dishes and placing the paintings back on the walls.

I admit that damn thing was very frightening.

On my parents' final trip to Hawaii, in April of 2010, we stopped by Fort DeRussy on Waikiki Beach, to tour the exhibit dedicated to World War II veterans.

Since 1976, the U.S. Army Museum of Hawaii is housed inside DeRussy, a former coast artillery fortification that had two mounted 14-inch guns. It originally was built to serve as the first line of defense against an enemy naval attack on the south shore of Oahu. When the massive guns were mounted, they were the largest guns in the entire Pacific—from California to the Philippines. However, they never had to be fired except for a few tests over the years.

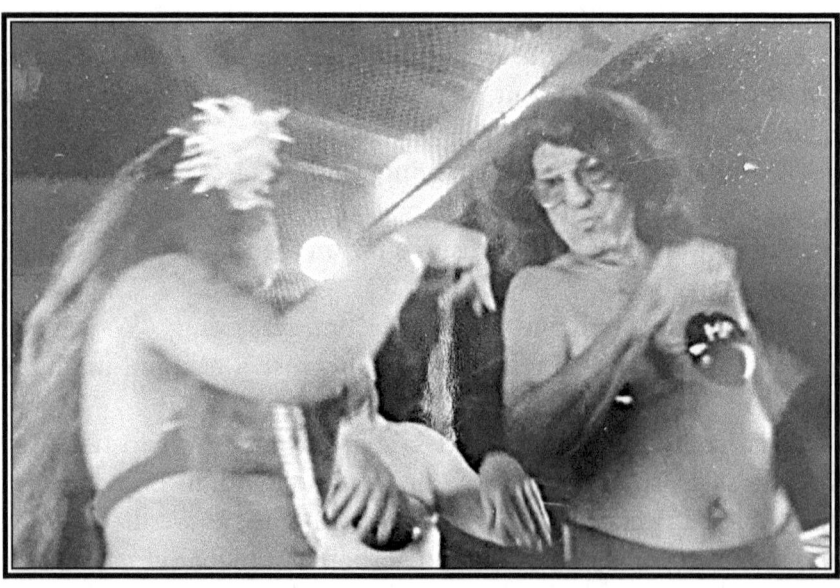

On a sunset cruise in Kona, Hawaii, in 2001, Dad was picked from the audience to perform the Hula, complete with a wig, coconut bra and grass skirt. He never passed up a chance to ham it up in front of an audience.

FROM OHIO TO OKINAWA...

The tour guide that day noticed Dad's World War II hat and asked him if he would share his memories with the others in the tour. That was like asking a fish if it wanted to swim.

Dad grabbed the microphone and started, "I stayed here for about $2 a night a few times over the years in the 1940s. We could get beer back then for five cents a can and we had a nice few of the Pacific. What more could you want? . . ."

For the next 15 minutes, he entertained the tour with stories of the war, the battlefield, and what Waikiki was like in the 1940s.

Over the years, I have heard friends complain about their visits to Waikiki, labeling it "too touristy," or just "Miami Beach with mountains." It was always obvious to me that they flew into Honolulu, spent a week at the beach, saw the high-rise hotels or condos, were turned off quickly and then flew back home.

I would guess they never took the time to explore the north or east shores of Oahu, or the other more remote islands, or any of the tiny beach towns on Maui, or Kauai, or Hawaii (the Big Island). If they had, they would see the Islands' natural beauty—as well as a taste of all the culture of what the locals have lived and provided.

In fact, many tourists don't realize that there is a massive cattle ranch (Parker Ranch), where Dad was stationed throughout 1942, or snow on the top of volcanoes, or rain forests, or waterfalls, let alone the beauty of all the pineapple (Oahu and Maui) and coffee plantations (Hawaii) as far as the eye can see, or the green and black sand beaches on the Big Island. Walking across natural green or black sand is a wonderful experience.

At the only active volcano, Kilauea, hot lava still flows down the mountain to the ocean when it erupts. I have visited Volcano National Park several times and it is an awesome experience. Believe it or not, you can snow ski on the Big Island.

For me, nothing beats a walk on Waikiki Beach, even at night when the lights from the hotels reflect off the Pacific. If a full moon appears over Diamond Head, it is nearly perfect. When I walk that

My first trip to the National Memorial Cemetery of the Pacific, aka "The Punchbowl," March of 1979, with Bill and Dad. The map of Okinawa, where he almost died 34 years earlier, is in the background.

beach at night, I often wonder what it must have been like during the 1940s. I make it a point to have at least one drink or breakfast at the famous Royal Hawaiian, the original plush resort on Waikiki, known worldwide as "The Pink Palace."

My favorite Elks Club sits at the base of Diamond Head on the rocks of the Pacific, about a mile from Waikiki. That club doubled as the original King Kamehameha Club for the first two seasons of the original *Magnum P.I.* series in 1980 and '81. It was one of Dad's favorite places to enjoy a cold beer and watch the sunset. By the end of most visits, he knew everyone in the bar. It had so much history, and once a few Hawaiian elders told me the millions of dollars they had been offered over the years to sell it to condo or hotel developers.

No trip to Hawaii is complete without seeing the historical sites on Oahu, such as Pearl Harbor and the National Memorial Cemetery of the Pacific ("The Punchbowl"). Any patriotic American should see them at least once.

The Punchbowl, which opened in 1949, is a majestic place, built in the crater of an extinct volcano and overlooking downtown Honolulu. Today, it holds more than 61,000 gravesites.

At the very head of it is a large stone memorial, adorned with a large statue of Lady Liberty, which was featured on the opening credits of the original *Hawaii Five-O*. Below her, these words, delivered in 1864 from President Abraham Lincoln to the grieving mother Lydia Bixby, who lost five sons during the Civil War, are inscribed on the wall:

"THE SOLEMN PRIDE THAT MUST BE YOURS TO HAVE LAID SO COSTLY A SACRIFICE UPON THE ALTAR OF FREEDOM."

Underneath the statue, a large circular wall is adorned with several giant mosaic tiles illustrating the various major battles in the Pacific Theater during World War II, starting with the attack on Pearl Harbor.

Three generations of Snooks—with son Dillon, then 15 months old, and Dad—beneath Lady Columbia, or some call her Lady Liberty, at the head of the National Memorial Cemetery of the Pacific, in 2010.

I have visited the Punchbowl often, the first time in 1979 with Dad and my brother Bill, but the one trip I remember most was in 2010, when he and I found the detailed map of gravesites listed in alphabetical order. In earlier trips, that system didn't exist, so Dad had no idea where any of his friends were buried.

We first found Ernie Pyle's grave near a line of trees close to the entrance. Then I pushed him in his wheelchair across the entrance road to the grave of Joe Majernik, the tiny radioman to whom Dad yelled to "stay down!" on Saipan just as a piece of a knee mortar ended his life June 25, 1944.

Just as he was at Pyle's grave, he was ever more emotional seeing Joe's, "I told him to stay down, but I guess I didn't say it in time ... that still hurts me to this day."

Dad has many other friends buried there. Remember his bucket-list motorcycle trip in 1941 before Pearl Harbor was attacked?

Howard "Cockey" Morekel had been killed when the bomber he was flying was lost somewhere over the Pacific in 1942. The airplane

Joe Majernik's headstone. Dad was the last person to speak to him before he was killed on Saipan.

and his body were never located. But we located his headstone, although of course his grave is empty.

"I thought a lot about Cockey over the years," Dad said. "Such a nice guy . . . I was hoping all four of us would make it home to talk about the old days and our motorcycle trip, but only three of us did."

The other two, Ted Deever and Ed "Buck" Bentle, survived the war and returned to Ashland to live long lives. When I was a kid, Buck always sat a row or two behind us in the church and he always called me "Chicky," as in "Hey, Chicky, how are you doing this morning?"

I had no idea why, unless Buck called everyone Chicky.

"Ted served on a destroyer that roamed the Pacific and sunk a lot of Japanese cargo ships. Buck had served in an artillery unit which later invaded the Philippines. When we all returned, we met up in October of 1945, told our war stories, and had a toast to Cockey's memory," Dad said.

(Buck died in 1994 at the age of 77 and Ted died two years later at the age of 78.)

Dad was the final survivor of the four motorcycle adventurers.

He never tired of seeing the Punchbowl and must have visited it eight or more times over the years. I noticed he always grew solemn and sad for a few minutes when we walked among the gravesites. As a soldier who served in the Pacific Theater, he also had the privilege to be buried there, along with Mom, and he once told me he had considered it, but he wanted to be buried in our hometown cemetery.

Of course, Pearl Harbor is awe-inspiring, but there are always thousands of tourists visiting each day and there is a 30-minute limit after taking the ferry to the Arizona Memorial. Visiting the Punchbowl, however, just like Arlington, Virginia, seems to put life and death, war, and especially freedom, into its proper perspective.

Dad, talking to my son Dillon, at the head of the Punchbowl in April 2010. It was Dad's final trip to the place he loved so much.

My memories of my visits to Hawaii will always be with me. Especially the ones with Mom and Dad, where he would walk among those large wall tiles and add his own personal stories to the Pacific battle maps depicted there.

I last returned to the Punchbowl in 2021, my first visit without Dad. It was very different. It was sad and solemn, and I missed him being there with me. As I walked along the mosaic battle depictions, I could actually hear his voice describing them as he had done so many times before.

As usual as during most days there, a gravesite service for a veteran who had just passed was being conducted on the hill in the distance.

I walked over to see Joe Majernik's headstone one more time. His is surrounded by several headstones marked "Unknown," and their dates of death were December 7, 1941. There are more than 70 of those at the Punchbowl.

The truth is that life and death really is determined by inches on the battlefield. Joe was no more than a few feet from Dad when he was killed. Standing there, I couldn't help but think that small distance determined Joe had died that day 77 years earlier while Dad later came home to live a full life, to father three children, which led to seven grandchildren and 11 great grandchildren.

War, as they say, is hell, but it too often presents cruel irony.

Since that initial trip, in 1979 while I was in college, I have returned to Hawaii at least 12 times, and I always visit the Punchbowl to remember those heroes buried there.

Anyway, you can have Paris or London or Rome or the Swiss Alps. I am sure I will never see those places in my lifetime, and I am okay with that. I already found a place I call paradise, just as my father did way back in 1942.

Seeing the islands always seems to bring me closer to my parents because of the memories of them there. Whether I visit Pearl Harbor, or the Punchbowl, or the Royal Hawaiian, or see Diamond Head

FROM OHIO TO OKINAWA . . .

With my daughter Savanna atop Diamond Head, with Waikiki in the background, in 2024.

from Waikiki Beach, or visit Parker Ranch or walk across the black sand beach on the Big Island, it's impossible not to think of those many times I enjoyed there with both of them.

I remember sitting at the Elks Club in Waikiki one night with Dad in 1993, when he took a sip of beer, looked at the sun setting over the Pacific, which was splashing on the rocks behind the lit tiki torches.

He smiled and held his beer glass up to the sun, as if he was toasting it.

"It's just as beautiful as it was when I first saw it in 1942," he said. "They call Hawaii paradise for a reason . . . because it is."

CHAPTER EIGHTEEN

SAYING GOODBYE: THEIR FINAL YEARS

I was always very conscious of the huge age difference between me and my father. When I was born, in 1960, Dad was already 41 years old.

In high school, when most of my friends' fathers were in their 40s, Dad was approaching 60. And then when I got married in 1991, he was 72 years old.

These days, of course, I don't think of that as being that old. But back then, I surely did. I always wondered how much longer we kids would have him around, although he always seemed younger than his actual age since he was so active.

That is one reason, in addition to just how much I admired and respected him, that I chose him to be my best man.

"I would be honored," he told me.

One interesting story about the weekend of my wedding, which took place July 20, 1991, in Indianapolis . . . on the night before, Dad, my brother Bill, brother-in-law Jim, and my groomsmen Keith Imhoff, Jim Mariotti, Gary Long and a few others threw me a small bachelor party in the downtown area. The bar and restaurant I chose was elevated and happened to have large glass windows facing the Omni Hotel.

FROM OHIO TO OKINAWA...

Just as Dad was about to make a toast, I looked out the windows to see contestants from the Miss Black America pageant lined up in front of the hotel wearing evening gowns, posing for a group picture.

In the middle of the group, I noticed a familiar face.

"Look you guys!" I announced. "That's *Mike Tyson!*"

Everybody walked over to the windows to get a closer look, and sure enough, there was the heavyweight champion of the world posing for photos with the contestants.

(Talk about irony: Two years earlier, almost to the day, I had covered Tyson's fight against Carl Williams in Atlantic City.)

And as we would discover later, that would be the very night in which he raped one of the contestants, a young woman named Desiree Washington, for which he would serve six years in prison.

Anyway, as the years passed, all of the aunts and uncles on my mother's side of the family passed away one by one, until Mom and Dad were the final couple remaining.

Also, so did every one of them on my father's side, except for Uncle George, who was going strong into his 90s just as Dad was, often giving public speeches and interviews to the local media about his time serving in the war under Jimmy Stewart's command.

Mom's oldest brother, Uncle Paul, died on April 18, 1990, of kidney failure. He was 77. The man whom everyone, even his wife, had called "Biddy," sure left his impact on the world.

Two years later, in the summer of 1992, Mom called to tell me Aunty had suffered a severe stroke, so I caught a flight out of Florida and drove straight to the hospital in Ashland. I flew home to Ohio to visit her in the hospital for one week.

A month later, on September 12, I was in Gainesville, covering the Florida-Kentucky football game when I got the call I dreaded. Becky reached me at my hotel to tell me she had died earlier that day. Becky barely got the words out before bursting into tears. That's just how much she meant to all of us.

With my father and my best man, on the day I was married, July 20, 1991.

She was only 73.

Uncle Dan, her husband, couldn't attend her funeral because he too had suffered a stroke. He was living in the nursing home just down the hall from her room at the time. He died just three months later, on December 13, 1992, never realizing his wife had passed away earlier. He was 85.

Uncle Neil died May 27, 2004, at the age of 87. I never saw him over the final few years of his life, and the last conversation we had was when he expressed frustration with wearing a colostomy bag.

Paul's widow, Aunt Helen, passed away on June 6, 2017, while Mom and Dad were with me in Florida. After Mom took that call, she sat on the edge of the bed and started sobbing, repeatedly saying, "She didn't want to die yet. We just talked . . . she just wasn't ready to die yet!"

Aunts and uncles, at least the good ones, always leave you with cherished memories and influence you in their own specific ways. I know mine certainly did.

As I had said, I was introduced to Ohio State through Uncle Paul, and the memories of those simple nights sharing a frozen pizza or watching a football game at his house in Dayton were priceless to me. I always loved talking about the Browns and Indians with Uncle Neil at his house in Cleveland. And Aunty . . . she was much more than an aunt to each of us.

With Helen's passing, the only couple which remained on Mom's side were Mom and Dad themselves.

They were the final survivors. The four couples had gone in together to purchase eight burial plots side-by-side with four matching headstones at the Ashland Cemetery, and now six of the eight graves were full.

And I never once took those two empty graves for granted.

We had parents who lived longer than most and much of that was pure luck.

In the winter of 2012, Mom and Dad were staying at our home in Boynton Beach when he became very sick. He told us he had only a bad cold, but then one day he started sweating profusely and couldn't get out of bed. We fed him soup, and took care of his fever, but day after day, his condition grew worse.

"Dad, you have to go to the hospital!" I demanded.

"Nope! You promise me you are not taking me to the hospital!" he would say.

I never made that promise.

He had spent enough time in the hospital over the years to know he hated being there, like most everyone else. He always said he would rather die in his own bed. He had his right hip replaced in 2005 at the age of 86 and that five-day hospital stay at the Delray Beach Medical Center had been very miserable for him.

One day he was hooked up to IVs, and needed help to go to the bathroom, but the nurse was standing against the wall in front of his bed—and she was sound asleep.

"Jeff, she was sleeping just like a horse does—standing up!" he told me.

When he couldn't wake her, he finally tossed a washcloth at her, hitting her, and she woke up. I always got a kick out of that story and how he described it in vivid detail. Every time we drove past the hospital, he would tell it again.

Anyway, another day or two passed and Dad still hadn't been able to sit up in bed, when Mom pleaded with him, "Ed, you have to go to the ER! You haven't been out of bed in five days!"

He had a fever and when I couldn't manage to lift him, so finally I had had enough of his stubbornness, too. I called the hospital and asked them to send paramedics. I told Mom I didn't care if he got mad at us, it was the right thing to do and I would take his wrath for both of us. The fact is that Dad had grown too weak by then to yell at me.

Within an hour, we got the diagnosis: He had severe pneumonia, and at 93 years old, it could have been deadly. The doctors pumped antibiotics into him through an IV, and he slowly improved, until he was healthy enough to return home 10 days later.

"He would have died within a few more days if you had not gotten him in here," a doctor told me. "That was a very severe case, and you shouldn't have let it go that far!"

He was right. I shouldn't have. I had let Dad's declaration about dying in his own bed scare me out of doing the right thing.

The following year, it was Mom's turn.

She was experiencing chest pains, so I drove her to the ER. They performed a scan and discovered she had severe blockage in one artery leading to her heart, so she underwent surgery to have a stent inserted. The heart surgeon walked out of the operating room and asked me, "Did she ever pass out or have a fainting spell recently?"

While she was recovering, I asked her and she told me that months earlier, while at her bridge club in Ashland, she had passed out, placing her head down on the bridge table in front of all her friends. They couldn't get her to respond, when about 30 seconds to a minute later, as her friends told her, she opened her eyes and started playing the hand again as if nothing had happened.

"Well, I will tell you what happened that day," the doctor said. "She was having a massive heart attack while playing bridge. A piece of plaque obviously had blocked the artery to her heart, and she was about to die. Then something broke loose and pushed it through and she came to. She is really lucky to be alive."

For the next five years or so, both were doing well other than some small episodes, such as the time Mom fell backward over the open dishwasher and severely cut her leg on an unwashed steak knife at their condo. That day, she limped into the den with blood running down her leg and told Dad, "Ed, I cut myself pretty bad and have to drive to the hospital. I'll be back later . . ."

He responded, "Yes, a bowl of potato soup will be fine. That's all I want for lunch today."

That was life with Dad as he grew into his 80s and 90s. His hearing problems were so severe, he often just guessed at what we were saying. Usually, we would laugh it off, but Mom often grew very frustrated.

After she received several stitches and then drove herself home about dinner time that day, Dad scolded her, "Where have you been? I couldn't find you and I had to eat crackers for lunch!"

Dad's new hip, advancing age and hearing problems never prevented him from enjoying life, however. In the final 25 years of his life, we traveled to such places as Puerto Rico, California, Mexico, Hawaii three times, as well as taking several cruises to the Caribbean, in addition to the trips I scheduled for him to see college football games.

As long as I could push him in his wheelchair, and Mom could look after him, he was willing to go anywhere.

The wives would go shopping or hang out at the pool or beach, while Dad and I would explore or find a quaint bar somewhere to throw back a few beers.

And we also always seemed to find some sort of mischief.

One time, when our cruise ship stopped in San Juan, Puerto Rico, Dad and I headed to the old part of town. After we found a few bars, and drank a beer or two in each, I started pushing him in his wheelchair back to the ship. Problem was, not all of the sidewalks in old San Juan are smooth, so I had to divert to the old cobblestone streets. That became way too bumpy for him.

"You are about to jar my teeth loose!" he told me.

When I went to steer him to the left, away from a pothole, the front left wheel of his chair became caught in a gap. The chair tilted left, throwing him out directly onto the street. He landed hard on his shoulder.

I picked him up and brushed him off, as he said, "Damn, Jeff, do I need to call a taxi just to get back to the ship in one piece?"

I told him, "Dad, remember when you almost ran over me with your company van when I was a kid, and you didn't want Mom to know? Well, you owe me one, so don't let her know what just happened here! Because she will never let us go anywhere together again."

I always wanted to show my father a great time, even when I had to literally push him to it.

Another time while he was in his early 90s we got off the ship in Playa del Carmen, Mexico, when he noticed a sign which read, "All you can drink margaritas, $5." He just looked up at me and pointed to it. For the next few hours, we sat on rope-supported swing-sets at that bar, downing several margaritas. Like Dad had said, we had to get our five dollars' worth.

The bartender soon had noticed his World War II hat.

"Thank you, sir," he said. "What was the war like?"

Oh no, here we go, I thought.

About two hours later, every patron sitting around the bar knew much more about the war than when they had walked into the place. Finally, something made me look at my watch, and I realized we were running late to catch the cruise ship's scheduled departure. I handed the bartender $20 and started sprinting as I pushed his wheelchair toward the port.

We were about 200 yards from the ship when I heard its departure horn blasting away. I could see the dock workers were about to pull up the gangplank, so I started waving with one hand while pushing Dad with the other. I learned it's hard to steer that way. In fact, I think I made a complete circle at one point, before they saw us. We came barreling up to that ramp, made a hard right turn, then sped up the ramp before I somehow brought his chair to a screeching stop just inside the ship. Dad almost came flying out of his chair headfirst. I think I had worn the tires off that wheelchair.

Me and Dad at a port in Costa Rica in 2004 before we cruised through the Panama Canal, something he always wanted to see.

A few minutes later, we found our way to our cabins.

"JEFF! WHERE HAVE YOU GUYS BEEN?" Mom demanded.

"Ah . . ." I stumbled around for an answer . . . "Dad was invited to give a history lesson on the war!"

"You both have had too much to drink!" she said. "Where were you?"

"Well, Dad saw a place that had all-you-can-drink margaritas, so I went along with him to make sure he made it back in time. It was *his* idea!" I told her.

That was a running joke between us. Whenever we were in trouble with Mom, we always took turns throwing each other under the proverbial bus.

"*My* idea!?" he said, acting innocent. "I can't steer or push my own wheelchair! Wherever we go is always *his* idea!"

He had me there.

I always knew these adventures with Dad would eventually come to a screeching halt, too. It was just a matter of time before his body gave out.

Shortly after he turned 94 in 2013, the doctors diagnosed him with chronic lymphocytic leukemia, the slow-growth kind. Dad never heard the doctor's diagnosis that day, and we all agreed never to tell him. After all, there is no effective treatment for someone of that advanced age and we knew there was no way he would want to endure chemo treatments.

He had beaten prostate cancer once in his 80s through radiation, but this time, it wasn't the appropriate thing to do, and the doctors agreed with our decision not to put him through it.

We all knew he wasn't beating leukemia.

By the month, he would grow more and more tired and often have trouble with simple tasks. And he would nap often.

On October 8, 2016, we celebrated Mom's 90th birthday with a party of about 75 friends and relatives, including all of their grandchildren and great-grandchildren. The picture below of Bill, me, Becky and Mom and Dad, then 97, was taken that day.

They continued to travel to Florida to spend the winters with us until 2018 when Dad became too frail to travel. Until then, I usually caught a one-way flight to Ohio in early January, then drove them back to Florida in Dad's beloved van. He always wanted a car for Mom to drive during those three or four months in Florida. Then I would drive them back to Ohio each April and fly back home.

Dad's daily routine likely was pretty normal for someone in his 90s. He would awaken around 9 a.m., drink some coffee, eat his cereal, play cards with Mom, then take a two-hour nap each afternoon. He would watch *Gunsmoke* and *Bonanza* and then around 5 p.m., he would give me that look.

I knew what the look meant.

"Beer, wine or a margarita?" I would ask him.

He would make his selection, then enjoy a drink or two. He always stopped at two, because he had been diagnosed with diabetes while in his 80s. Then he would eat dinner with us and watch the nightly news.

Grandfather and grandson, born 90 years apart, grabbing a nap together on the sofa one afternoon in 2013. Dad was 94 then, and my son, Dillon Jon, was four.

Over the final few years, after breakfast, he would talk into my tape recorder as I peppered him with questions for an hour or more, working on this project.

"You know, I used to know my army serial number by heart," he said one day. "I knew it better than my own name and my birthday. But over the years, I forget it sometimes. Then it will come back to me again. The guys I served with . . . I can still see their faces, but sometimes I even forget their names. You know, I never wanted to forget their names."

We all realized Dad's body and mind were slowly giving in to the leukemia's effects while he just chalked it up to his advancing age.

"Why am I so tired all the time?" he would complain.

Mom and I would just give each other a look. We knew, but we couldn't tell him.

"It took me 20 minutes to button my shirt today," he told me one winter morning in 2017. "My fingers just don't bend anymore. Damn it's frustrating!"

One day, he told me he wanted to go swimming in the ocean. Dad always loved to swim in saltwater because he claimed it cleared his clogged sinuses.

"Dad, are you sure?" I asked him.

"Yes, one last time . . . ," he said. "I have been having that sinus pressure, and I know a good swim in saltwater will relieve it."

I then drove him and Mom to the beach in nearby Manalapan, south of West Palm Beach, and I walked him down to the ocean.

"No sharks around, right Jeff?" he asked me.

"None, Dad!" I answered.

Hell, I knew better. There are always harmless sand sharks or other kinds swimming in the shallow waters off most beaches in Florida. It was something Dad had feared since he had read about the sinking of the USS *Indianapolis* in July of 1945.

FROM OHIO TO OKINAWA ...

After the ship delivered the atom bomb (which was later dropped from the *Enola Gay* on Hiroshima while Dad was on Okinawa) to the island of Tinian on July 26, it had started its return to Pearl Harbor when it was hit by two Japanese torpedoes, sinking in eight minutes.

Three hundred men of the 1,195 aboard went down with the ship. It was probably the most top-secret mission in World War II, so the ship had not been reported late or missing for the following three days. The remaining 890 or so went into the water, and only 316 were alive to be rescued three days later.

Most of the others died either by dehydration or shark attacks as they awaited rescue. As the years passed, most World War II veterans either read or heard about it. The event also led to actor Robert Shaw's famous scene speaking of the Indianapolis during the movie *Jaws*.

Dad knew his war history, too. He also had realized the Indianapolis had participated in the battle of Saipan a year earlier, pummeling the embedded Japanese soldiers with its shells before he ever stepped ashore for battle. He also knew it delivered the bomb that ultimately may have saved his life.

There wasn't much about World War II that Dad didn't know as the decades passed, because he was an avid reader, having read probably 10 to 15 non-fiction books every year. He never touched fiction, but he read dozens of books and watched almost every documentary made about the war.

Formally, he had only a high school education, but I like to believe he was very educated. He jammed a lot of knowledge into that head during his long life. And he knew enough about the USS *Indianapolis* to be frightened of sharks.

One time, in 2009, during a family trip to Sanibel Island, Dad and Becky and I were swimming in waist-deep water near the bridge which connected the island to Fort Myers. All of a sudden, a fisherman close to us reeled in a small hammerhead shark, which was no more than three feet long, and held it high in the air.

The next thing I saw was a blur to my right, something splashing from the water to the shore in a nano-second. It was Dad. I had never seen him move that fast since he was in his 50s playing basketball at the YMCA, as he did daily. He had taken one look at that tiny Hammerhead and made a mad dash toward the beach.

I looked at Becky to see her collapsing in laughter. So was I.

"When I go, it won't be by getting eaten by a damn shark," Dad quipped.

Anyway, he happily splashed about in the Atlantic that day, as I stayed close to him, and sure enough, it cleared up his sinus problems, just as he said it would.

Helping Dad to the Atlantic Ocean in 2017, for one final swim in saltwater, something he loved so much. Mom is watching anxiously to make sure nothing happened to the man she loved. And of course, he is wearing his beloved World War II hat.

The first time he tasted the ocean salt was on that motorcycle trip with his buddies to the Pacific in the summer of 1941.

Now here we were, 76 years later, in the Atlantic at the opposite end of the country, and he was taking his final swim in saltwater.

Throughout 2018, Becky continued to bring up whether to plan Dad's 100th birthday party on January 21, 2019. And I would usually say, "Let's wait. Let's not jinx it."

That hope faded quickly after one night when he sat up in bed and started talking gibberish, alerting Mom that something was seriously wrong. He was rushed to the hospital in Ashland, and doctors believed he had suffered a mild stroke. Mom then admitted him to the Brethren Care Nursing home on the edge of town.

It was October 21, 2018.

He was now 99 years and nine months old, and we all realized it was the beginning of the end.

He spent almost a full month there, resting for the most part without any pain. But his condition started to deteriorate rapidly once he was admitted. Within weeks, he eventually lost all of his hair. Dad always had a luscious head of hair and losing it really bothered him.

On November 7, he rubbed his now balding head, and asked me, "Can you bring me my hat?"

I didn't have to ask which one. Dad had a hat rack in their garage which contained about 20 baseball-style caps, from those of the Browns to the Indians to Ohio State to his three World War II hats. I knew which one he wanted to wear for his final days.

The next day I brought him his favorite World War II hat and placed it on his head. I then held his hand that afternoon and he asked once again, "Am I dying today?"

Then he fell asleep. Over that final month in the nursing home, Dad used one other phrase frequently: "Thank you."

Whenever the nurses tended to him, he gently grabbed them by the arm and whispered, "Thank you."

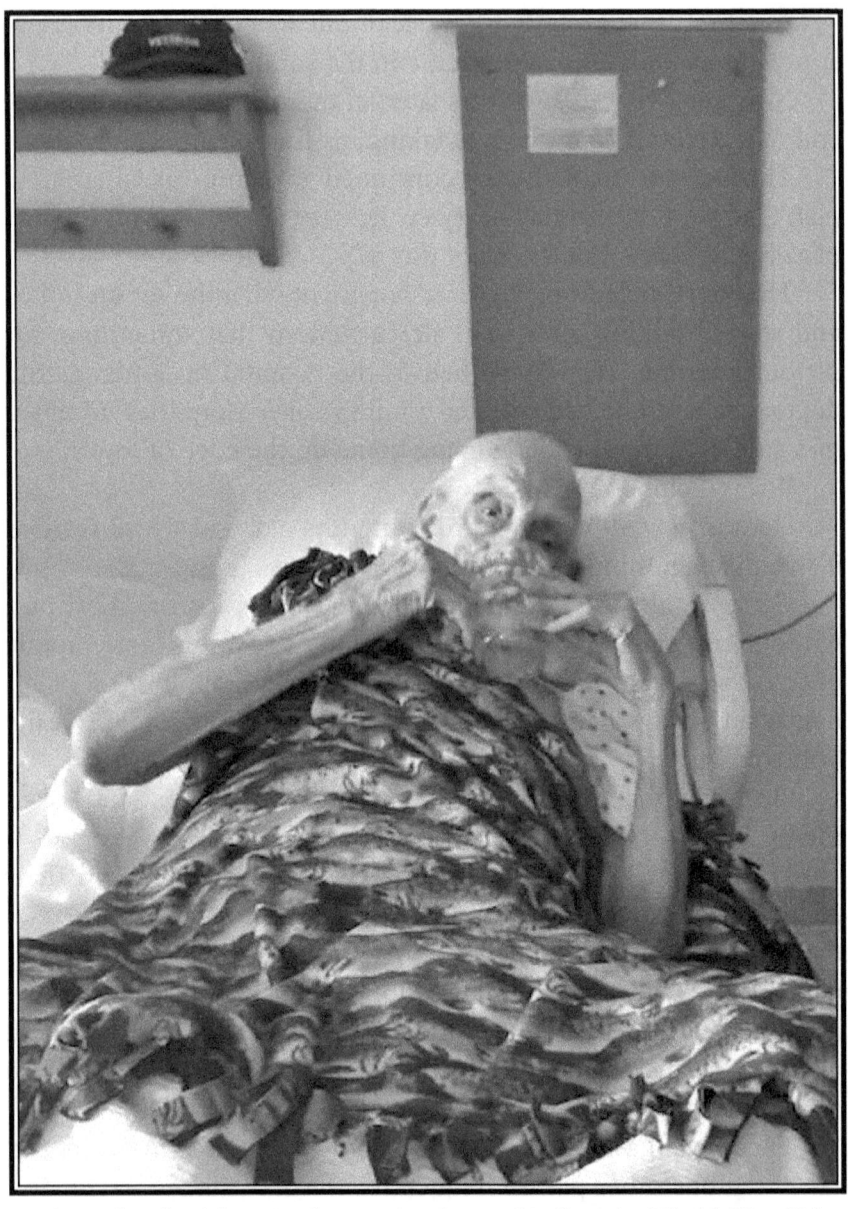

Dad sips his final beer in the nursing home, his favorite World War II hat resting on a shelf behind him.

Whenever they bathed him, he always said, "Thank you."

Whenever they brought his food, or took his tray, it was always the same: "Thank you."

One day, a nurse asked, "Has he always been this polite? I have been nursing for years, and I have never heard anybody thank us this much."

"Yes, pretty much," Mom said. "He always said the words 'Please' and 'Thank you.'"

On November 11, Becky's two daughters, Melissa and Michelle, visited and while they were in the room, Dad requested a cold beer. They bolted from the room, came back with two cold ones in their purses, cracked one open and one of them stuck a flexible straw in it. He sipped away and smiled.

"Thank you," he whispered. "Tastes so good!"

It was the final beer my father ever had.

Ironically, it was on Veteran's Day.

I like to think Dad knew what day it was, because he asked again on that day, "I am dying, right? *Today*?"

The other thing Dad said often in his later years was "I love you."

As I said, I never heard him say it when we were kids, but as he grew older, the phrase came out of his mouth almost every day.

On November 15, he received his final bath. I walked down to the bathing room with the nurses as they attended to him.

He was shivering terribly.

"COLD!" he said. "IT'S SO COLD!"

Afterwards, as they dried him off and bundled him in his pajamas, a bathrobe and a blanket, he thanked them again. I pushed him in his wheelchair back to his room. I didn't think of it at the moment but it would be the final time I ever pushed him.

At this point, he was almost unrecognizable from his previous self, even from just three weeks earlier, when he had been admitted. He was so frail and gaunt. His body was basically just skin and bones, as he said he was when the war ended, and he had lost all of his hair.

It was so sad for all of us to see.

He took just a few bites of his food that night when they brought him dinner.

"Thank you," he told the attendant who took his tray away.

He never ate again.

The following day, as the nurses tended to him, he pleaded loudly, "Help . . . help!" and I could tell he was lapsing. He was delusional and I am not sure he knew where he was or who was around him. He was disoriented that he no longer recognized the nurses who had been so good to him as he pleaded to them for help.

It also seemed he was in pain for the first time. He was moaning almost constantly, crying for someone to help him.

I looked at Mom, and she had tears in her eyes.

"I am sorry, Mom," I said. "I know it's hard to see."

I walked into his room the following morning, and there was Mom, sitting as always by his bedside, just staring at him. Not reading. Not watching TV. Just staring at the love of her life as he was dying.

That was their life together. Their favorite song as a couple was "Always," and whenever they heard it at whatever function or at a dance they attended, they just looked at each other, smiled, and headed to the dance floor . . .

> "I'll be lovin' you, always . . . when the things you planned need a helpin' hand,
> I will understand, always, always . . .
> Days may not be fair, always . . .
> That's when I'll be there, always . . .
> Not for just an hour, not for just a day . . .
> Not for just a year, but always."

Now that Dad was non-communicative, and Mom appeared worn out, Bill and I pleaded with her to go home so she could get some rest.

"Go on home Mom," I said. "You can't be getting much sleep here."

"I don't want to leave him," she said. "What if he wakes up and asks for me? I don't want him thinking I left him when he needed me here."

She had slept in a small bed next to Dad's bed every night for the month he was in the nursing home. She never wanted to leave, because when he was awake and alert, he noticed her and talked to her. They talked about big things like their life together and little things like the food and the weather.

But now he was unconscious and the nurses told us it was for good.

"I don't think it will be long now," one nurse whispered to me.

Mom still didn't want to leave, but we finally convinced her. I then left, too, while Bill stayed with Dad.

I drove back to my summer home at Charles Mill Lake at noon that Saturday, watched Ohio State survive a thrilling game to beat Maryland 52-51 in a miraculous finish in which the Buckeyes stopped a two-point conversion which would have won the game for Maryland.

An hour after the game ended, Bill called me.

"He's gone . . . he just died," he said. "He never woke up or had any final words."

Then he added, "The funeral home people are coming in to get him now. I cannot stay and watch them put him in one of those black body bags, so I am going to go home."

To think of that great man in one of those was beyond heartbreaking for both of us.

"Don't call Mom yet," I told him. "Let's let her get a good night's sleep and I will tell her in the morning."

Dad had died peacefully early that night of November 17, 2018, in a nursing home bed just three miles from his childhood home, and two miles down the road from the house in which our parents raised us.

His almost 100-year journey between the two places at the opposite ends of town was simply remarkable.

When Bill hung up, I turned off the TV and just stared at the wall for about an hour, thinking about what a great man and great father he had been. What a wonderful life he lived. I thought about some of the good times we shared together through all those years.

Strangely, I did not cry that night, having already done so almost every day during the previous week. It was as if I was cried out, if that is a thing, and now I was somewhat relieved he was gone. I told myself that he was no longer in pain and that he was ready.

He had spent a good portion of his 20s in several battles to survive, and now his final battle, the one against leukemia, was over. He could rest now. And if any man deserved to rest in Heaven, it was our father. He was a churchgoing, God-worshipping, good-hearted man who usually did things the right way during his 99 years and 10 months on this earth.

He had saved a life or two or perhaps many more on the battlefield, a number we will never know exactly. He had taken a few too, as was his ugly duty of war and in service to his country. He had laughed a lot, he had loved a lot, worked hard for more than 40 years, and he rarely ever had a cross word to say about anyone.

That night, I started to write his obituary, a story I knew I had to get exactly right. I wasn't leaving this up to the funeral home or to the local newspaper, which is routinely given to a young, inexperienced writer anyway. The number of simple and glaring mistakes I have noticed in obituaries over the years always was frustrating to me and surely so for those left behind.

The following morning, I knew I had to arrive at Mom and Dad's condo before she drove to the nursing home. I couldn't imagine how she would have reacted if she had walked into that empty room and heard the awful news from a nurse that the love of her life was finally gone.

I set an alarm, drove to town, then quietly opened the front door with my key at 7 a.m. I slept on the floor an hour or so before she awakened and walked into the kitchen. As soon as she noticed me, she started crying.

"He's *gone*, isn't he?" she asked.

"Yes," I answered.

I held her up as she started crying uncontrollably.

"I knew if I left him, he would die without me," she said. "I just knew it! I didn't want him to die alone!"

"Mom, Bill was with him," I said. "He didn't die alone."

"But I wanted to be there with him!" she said. "I knew I shouldn't have left him! He knew that I left him. Because that's the first night I left him . . . and he died."

She had stayed 25 consecutive nights in his room. And on the first night of what had to be only 30 or so nights apart during the 72 years they were married, he died.

Dad lived to reach only 65 days from his 100th birthday. His father had lived to the age of 98 and I can still see Grandpa Snook sitting in his favorite chair a year or two before he died. Remarkably, he looked exactly like Dad did in his final days.

"My Dad once said he wouldn't make it to his 100th birthday and he didn't," Dad once told me of Grandpa Snook. "And I may get close, but I don't think I will make it, either."

Somehow, he turned out to be prophetic. It's as if he knew years earlier when he would die.

The following week was Thanksgiving, so we could not hold a funeral on that Thursday or Friday. So, we decided to wait until the following Monday, November 26.

That Saturday, Ohio State scored the most points it ever has in the 128 years of its rivalry with Michigan, winning 62-39. I stood on the sideline that day at the game's conclusion, thinking how Dad would have enjoyed watching it. Truth is, I had to believe that he did, just from a different vantage point.

We had a private viewing for the family on the Monday morning before the funeral. We had picked out one of his favorite Hawaiian shirts, but as I looked at his body, something was missing to me. I went to the car and found it. I then handed the pastor Dad's favorite World War II hat. A funeral home worker slipped it on his head before we closed the casket.

The backside of Dad's headstone, honoring his service to the country, at the Ashland Cemetery. On this particular day, the sunlight made the details of his rank and dates of his life and death glow.

They then draped the U.S. flag he loved so much over it.

More than 100 friends then filed by over the next hour, as the screens above played a video montage of pictures from his life to the backdrop of Hawaiian music. There were so many pictures of all of us in Hawaii, with Dad usually wearing a Hawaiian shirt, or of us in Florida.

In all of them, he was smiling. Always smiling.

I had wondered for years how we all would handle this day and how it would feel. I felt somewhat numb, having a hard time believing he was finally gone. As I sat in the front row of the church pews that day, holding my sister Becky's hand as she sobbed, I know that I smiled as I watched the video.

The local American Legion post then conducted a 21-gun salute at the Ashland Cemetery before his burial. At the end, one of the honor guard members folded the flag from Dad's casket and handed it to Mom.

It was a common scene that has played out across America for more than a century, when a soldier returns from war and is buried with the grieving widow crying by his grave. However, this ex-soldier was 99 when he died, having lived a long and enjoyable life, and his grieving widow was 92 years old.

We had been so blessed by those numbers. They too had been blessed because they had 73 wonderful years together.

I like to believe Dad was one man who was destined to live a long life. Otherwise, why wouldn't he have been hit by a Japanese mortar or sniper fire on Saipan, as several men close to him were? Or from that artillery shell which barely missed him on Okinawa, the one that left him severely deaf? Or die one of the two times he went head-over-handlebars on his Harley back in the 1930s and '40s? Or succumb to prostate cancer in his 80s, or from that severe case of pneumonia I allowed to progress too far in his early 90s?

One other thing I want to emphasize is that during his retelling of the war in this book, at times it may have seemed as if he was boastful about his contributions.

He wasn't.

He just wanted to tell his story accurately and completely and the truth is, he was a hero. He was brave. He never backed down from gunfire or retreated from duty.

Consider this: In addition to his Bronze Star for Valor and his Sharpshooter Badge with Rifle Bar, two medals which Dad knew about by the time the war ended, he had no idea he also had been awarded the Good Conduct Medal, the Presidential Unit Citation, the American Defense Service Medal, the Asiatic-Pacific Campaign Medal with three bronze service stars, the World War II Victory Medal, the Army of Occupation Medal, the Combat Infantry Badge 1st Award and the Honorable Service Lapel Button for World War II.

Four days after his funeral, on November 30, I drove Mom to the bank when I noticed her tearing up again.

"You know what I was doing 73 years ago today?" she asked.

"I have no idea," I said.

"Dad and I were having our first date," she said. "We met on October 30th (1945), had our first date on November 30th, and got married the following June 30th . . . I already miss him so much."

We all did.

Dad's death would be the first snowball in an avalanche of heartache for our family.

I spent the month of December that year doing what I could to encourage her to live her life fully, to go on without him. As Dad would say, "Pep her up." He loved using that phrase when someone was feeling down.

"Pep up!" he would say. "Bad times won't last. Pep up and go on!"

One morning while we had coffee, I told her, "Mom, now that you don't have to take care of Dad every day, you can rest and take care of yourself. We can go to Vegas one more time. You can get out of the cold of Ohio and come stay with us again this winter. You need to have things to look forward to."

She just listened in silence, probably doubting she could ever smile or have fun again without my father around. Then she said, "I don't know how I am going to do it. I cannot even walk into that room . . ."

She pointed toward the den, where Dad had spent his days and nights, reading, napping and watching TV over the past 10 years or so.

That New Year's Eve, 44 days following his death, Mom and I and Becky and most of her family went out to dinner and then returned to my cabin for a small party. Sitting on the couch with a glass of wine in her hand, she had tears in her eyes as she turned to me.

"I am glad you gave me that pep talk . . . I am ready to go on and live some more, but I sure do miss him," she told me.

I flew back to Florida a few days later, with plans for Mom to fly down in mid-January after she tended to a few upcoming doctors' appointments. Two weeks later, a nurse from her heart doctor's office called me.

"Jeff, we are seeing a mass on your mother's pancreas, but this is not our area of expertise," she told me. "She needs a specialist to check this out. Do you want us to tell her?"

"No, don't say a thing," I told her. "Is this what it sounds like?"

"Probably," she said. "It's rather large."

They had taken Mom to Columbus Grant Hospital via ambulance to insert a stent to relieve a blockage of her bowel. My brother, sister-in-law and I then flew from Florida and headed directly to the hospital. We walked into her room to find her resting and in good spirits.

We surprised her.

"What are you guys doing here?" he asked, startled at seeing us.

I had waited to tell her the awful news until the following morning, and was just about to do so, when an oncologist walked into her room unannounced and blurted out the words: "You have about four to six weeks left. You have pancreatic cancer, stage four."

Mom looked at me, but she didn't fully comprehend what he told us.

"What did he say?" she asked.

I ordered him to leave the room.

"Mom, you have cancer," I said. "I am so sorry, but you don't have much time . . ."

Tears started streaming down her face.

". . . But I thought we were going to Vegas one more time?" she said.

It was the worst conversation I ever had with my mother, much worse than telling her that Dad had died, news I knew she was expecting. To deliver this terrible news, to see her hopes of a future crushed so soon after her heart had been broken . . . I started crying, too. I felt awful for making the promises I had.

Then she said, "I always knew we would die close together. Just like in *The Notebook*. I always said it. I just knew it in my heart we would die close together."

Two days later, we accompanied Mom on a flight to Florida. I wanted her to be able to say goodbye to my children in person. Every day, I managed her pain with first Percocet and when that didn't work effectively, drops of morphine.

Watching her do everything for the final time was heartbreaking.

One night in February, my Aunt Barb—Uncle George's wife—called to give us an update on their health. George wasn't doing well, either, at the age of 98, and now he was in a nursing home.

"Tell them I still will try to make it to 100!" he said from the background.

It was a milestone my grandpa and my father came so close to reaching, but didn't, while Uncle George seemed confident that he could become the first Snook to make it.

He wouldn't.

George Snook, the hero flight engineer/top gunner once under Jimmy Stewart's command, died on September 28, 2019, at a nursing home in Sylvania, Ohio—10 months after Dad had died.

Like Dad, he was buried with full military honors.

Anyway, I knew we faced a tight timeline to get the most out of Mom's final trip to Florida and yet to fly back to Ohio while the trip was still manageable for her. I picked the date March 7 and booked our return flights.

As she hugged my family and said her goodbyes that morning, I walked into the kitchen, unable to watch that scene and then I loaded her luggage into my car. As I drove to the airport, she looked out the window. I wondered what she must be thinking.

She told me without me asking.

"The last time I will ever be in Florida . . . ," she said. "That's hard to believe."

I spent the next day with her going through the details of what she wanted for her funeral.

What type of casket?

"Same as your father's," she said.

What dress?

"Becky just bought me a beautiful black dress with red trim," she said. "I never even got to wear it. It still has the tags on it."

Every afternoon I would drive to her condo, fix her dinner and make sure she was taking all her pills.

On Sunday, March 17, after we had dinner and shared a bottle of wine, Mom went to the bathroom, but she didn't return for some time. I had been watching TV but finally got up to walk into her bedroom where I saw her lying on the floor. She had fallen, and had been calling me, but I didn't hear her.

"Oh Mom, did you break anything?" I asked. "Your hip?"

"I don't think so," she said. "Can you get me up so I can get into bed?"

I lifted her, laid her on her side of the bed and covered her with blankets. Even after Dad was gone, she wouldn't move to the middle of that queen bed. She remained on her side of their bed, just as if he was still there. Then she closed her eyes and went to sleep.

Those were the final words she ever spoke. She lapsed into unconsciousness that night and did nothing but moan for the days to come. I would slip morphine under her tongue, but it was no longer effective by the second day. Hospice workers would come and go and change her as she moaned with every movement.

Finally, I couldn't take it any longer and called my sister.

"Ask them for the patch . . . the Fentanyl patch. She needs it," Becky told me.

"The what?" I asked.

"You can't listen to her moan in pain day after day," she added.

Now if anyone was a trained expert in how to comfort the dying, it was my sister. She had spent more than 20 years as the CEO and director of the Seneca County Hospice in Ohio.

The local hospice which took care of Mom, however, did not want to issue a patch laced with Fentanyl.

"Insist on it!" Becky instructed. "They have to give it to you if you ask for it."

So, I did. They finally delivered two patches, which I had to sign for. I read the instructions, along with my sister's oldest daughter, Melissa, who had worked as a volunteer for her in hospice. I put on rubber gloves, peeled the patch off of its base, then leaned over Mom, lifted the sleeve of her nightgown and rubbed it into her shoulder.

She stopped moaning within minutes.

Six hours later, she took her final breath.

Now she too was out of pain.

FROM OHIO TO OKINAWA...

It was Saturday, March 23, 2019—four months and six days after Dad had died.

We all have heard that well-known phrase about someone special: "They are as beautiful on the inside as on the outside..."

That was my mother in a nutshell. She was simply a beautiful person. She was very caring and sensitive, sometimes overly sensitive. But she also was the most unselfish person I have ever known. She had the biggest heart in the world. She was a born worrier, too. When one of us three children were hurting, she was hurting. All in all, we could never have asked for a more wonderful mother.

Now my parents were together again, just as they had been almost every day for the past 73 years.

In the days that followed, I tried telling myself maybe this was how it was meant to be. Maybe we were spared the pain of seeing Mom struggle to go on without the love of her life. And maybe she was spared the pain of trying.

I told myself Mom just wasn't cut out to be a widow for very long. She wasn't made to go on without my father.

Over time, I have learned as everyone eventually does, that death is just as much a part of life—and you get touched by it way more often than you would prefer when you grow older. Many of your relatives and loved ones will pass away while you go on living.

You can only hope that when it arrives, and takes someone important from you, that they had enough time on this earth and that they were ready for it. But sadly, however, you also learn that will not always be the case.

Today, the four couples of Mom's side of the family—Paul and Helen, Neil and Martha, Aunty and Dan and my parents—are buried on the west end of the Ashland Cemetery, side by side below four matching headstones.

At least once each summer, I visit them, pick a few weeds and talk to them. Sometimes I take a wet cloth with me just to wipe the bird droppings off of Mom and Dad's headstone.

"When I am gone, don't worry about keeping any flowers on my grave," Dad once told me. "And don't worry about the weeds, either. But if you get the chance, just keep the bird shit off of our stone . . . and make sure there's one of those tiny U.S. flags over our grave, too."

For some reason, Dad was almost obsessive about bird droppings. If he ever noticed a spot of it on his car, he would quickly grab a sponge and clean it off. He would hose it off his sidewalk daily.

At Mom's gravesite service after her funeral, I noticed a small white drop of it on their headstone, walked over and wiped it off. Becky noticed it and smiled at me. And yes, per his wish, there's a tiny American flag waving over their graves today.

In the ensuing days after Mom died, I was looking through a box of cards and letters she had saved over the years, when I found six or seven Christmas cards postmarked from Tallahassee. They were addressed to Dad. I opened them to see they were sent from Bobby Bowden, the famous football coach he grew so close to in just a few meetings. Each contained a short note, wishing Mom and Dad a Merry Christmas and Bobby always added a line to tell me hello.

He always signed them with that perfect Bobby Bowden signature—aligned with what I once heard him tell his players, "Men, now when you sign an autograph, take your time to write your name so people will always know exactly who signed it!"

That was pure Bobby Bowden. As it had turned out, Dad and Bobby had become pen pals in the last years of his life, through Mom's handwriting of course.

Those two great men—one an unknown ex-soldier and one a college football legend and part-time World War II historian—had forged a lasting friendship. I will always be happy and proud I brought them together to get to know each other.

And I will worship my memories of them until the day I die.

Bobby then died August 8, 2021, at the age of 91 of pancreatic cancer, the same awful and painful disease that took Mom's life. They were now all gone, but the worst was yet to come . . .

CHAPTER NINETEEN

MY SISTER BECKY

This is by far the most difficult chapter for me to write.

Because from my earliest memories, having to say goodbye to my one and only sister, Rebecca Sue, always seemed to bring me to tears.

From the time I was a toddler, we had a special bond despite our 12-year, 20-day age difference. I really believe that gap only brought us closer, because when I was young, Becky was more than just an older sister to me.

So much more.

From the time I arrived home from the hospital, she doted on me and took care of me just as a mother would. She watched out for me, fed and bathed me when I was a toddler, and helped me with my homework or quizzed me before a test whenever I needed it in grade school.

It seemed everywhere she went, she took me with her: To restaurants, to pep rallies or high school football and basketball games, or to her friends' houses. Wherever she went, I usually tagged along.

I cried when she graduated and went off to work as a registered nurse in Akron when I was seven. Then when she got married the following year, on July 13, 1968, I sat in the corner of the reception,

Becky, 12, holding me one week after our parents brought me home from the hospital, March of 1960.

wearing my tiny ring-bearer tuxedo and cried yet again, thinking she was leaving us for good now that she had a new man in her life.

Her husband, Jim Shank, had grown used to the idea of me tagging along just about everywhere they went when they started dating in high school.

Then when I went off to college in the fall of 1978, it was her turn: I still can see the tears running down her cheeks as I walked from the car to my dorm on the day she and Mom dropped me off at Ohio State.

Seven years later, in the summer of 1985, she and Jim and their three children moved from our hometown, 53 miles away to Tiffin. But as the years progressed and she raised her family, which led to six grandchildren, nothing would change for us. The geographical distance between us was no obstacle.

She wouldn't allow it.

And I wouldn't allow it.

As we grew older, she and I behaved almost like twins at times, albeit twins born half a generation apart. We had many identical likes and dislikes, the same biting sense of humor and sarcastic wit.

We both loved fine dining and often spent the day researching restaurants while we were on vacation. That drove each of our spouses crazy. We both loved to follow a great dinner with Crème Brûlée. We loved to lie in the sun all day in Las Vegas or Florida, seeing which one of us could become darker. We loved getting massages at nice resorts. We liked to watch the same sitcoms. She also became a huge sports fan over the years and loved everything Ohio State, just as I did.

Perhaps one of the only differences was that I drank alcohol, like Mom and Dad and my brother Bill did at times, and she never liked the taste of it. Becky loved Coke or a diet iced tea.

We traveled together about everywhere over the years when some of my favorite places became some of her favorite places. We went to Las Vegas several times, to Lake Tahoe, to Atlantic City, to the Florida Keys, to Laguna Beach, to Hawaii, to Carmel-by-the-Sea, to Big Sur, to Napa Valley, to Myrtle Beach, to Biloxi, Mississippi, and to Puerto Rico.

The one vacation she could never take was a cruise, because she was prone to seasickness.

During Valentine's Day 2018, three couples of us vacationed in Carmel. So, when the week was over, I told her I had a surprise for her upcoming 70th birthday, which was two weeks later.

But first it involved a long drive. I didn't tell anyone where we were headed. My wife Amy and I, Becky and Jim, then drove south to Los Angeles. I turned the rental car off the freeway to drive due west to Long Beach, where we pulled up to the dock holding the famous *Queen Mary*.

"That is our hotel for the next two nights," I told them.

"It's not leaving the dock, is it?" Becky asked.

"Nope," I told her. "You're safe."

I had figured if she couldn't do a cruise on the high seas, I would bring the cruise ship to her. With the *Queen Mary* resting at dock, there was no chance of seasickness. That first night aboard, we dined at the renowned Sir Winston's Steakhouse in the bow, one of the best meals any of us ever experienced.

"That was so much fun!" she said two days later. "I just wish I could take a cruise . . ."

Our holidays such as Thanksgiving and many Christmases were spent at her house, and her Florida vacations were spent at mine, and we would have it no other way.

Seeing her laugh and have fun on any given day was always a gift to me. Especially because at one point in her life, when she was 57, we never thought she would live long enough to see her 60s.

It was June 14, 2005, when our world changed.

That day, Jim called to tell me Becky had been diagnosed with stage-four ovarian cancer. I hung up the phone, sat on the edge of

With Becky, in 1986, at Mom and Dad's 40th Anniversary party, trying to muffle one of her wisecracks directed my way. This is my favorite photo of us.

my bed at my Florida home and cried all over again, praying to God to leave her with us for at least another five years.

I remember asking Him specifically for that amount of time.

"Please God, give her five years!" I prayed.

My nine-year-old daughter Savanna wrapped her arms around me and said, "Don't worry Dad . . . Aunt Becky will be okay . . . she will be okay."

That next day, she called me, saying her primary care doctor wanted her to start chemotherapy treatments immediately, but she didn't know if it was the right thing to do.

"Don't do anything yet," I told her.

That is when being a part of Ohio State's extended family pays dividends. My sister, like all of my family, just loved the Buckeyes. I called Jim Tressel, who was about to begin his fifth season as the head football coach and told him of her diagnosis. We had collaborated on the book *What it Means to be a Buckeye* two years earlier, and he knew all the right people at the university's James Cancer Hospital, for which he was the face of major fundraising events.

Coach Tressel had sent a few emails and wasted no time making sure that she would be seen by the best oncologists the James Center had to offer. Then he called me the following day.

"She has an appointment. There's only one thing you must know . . . ," he told me.

"What's that?" I asked.

"The doctor she will see is a Michigan grad."

If he could help my sister beat cancer, I didn't care if he went to medical school on the planet Mars. I flew to Columbus immediately and met her and Jim in the parking lot of Dr. David Cohn's office on Olentangy River Road. When we walked into his office, I noticed a picture on the wall behind his desk of that structure they call the "Big House," otherwise known as Michigan Stadium.

Becky noticed it immediately too. She elbowed me and pointed to it.

"Are we sure we want HIM to treat me?" she whispered, somewhat joking.

As much as I hated his choice of wall art, through the ensuing years, the good doctor from the school up north earned our trust by guiding her through the ups and downs of ovarian cancer. It seemed he pushed all the right buttons as far as her treatment was concerned. (Plus, it was much easier visiting his office during an era when Tressel's teams and then Urban Meyer's teams were beating his alma mater each November.)

After she underwent initial surgery to remove a tumor on her ovary, Dr. Cohn advised that she did not need any chemotherapy treatments. Not yet anyway. He would continue to monitor her white-cell blood count and delay any radiation.

He once told me, "Our cemeteries are full of women who had ovarian cancer and listened to their primary care doctor's recommendation to get chemo right away, when they never needed it in the first place. It killed them before the cancer would have."

For the first 10 years following her diagnosis, chemo was not needed. Then once the cancer started to advance, he recommended a series of chemo treatments. They seemed to be working until a large tumor emerged on her colon. She underwent surgery to remove it in 2018, which forced her to wear a colostomy bag, something she—just like Uncle Neil had—hated with a white-hot passion.

There were other times during treatment when she lost all of her hair and was forced to wear a wig, such as when we traveled to the see the Grand Canyon and then to a place where I always wanted to take her, Paradise Valley, Arizona.

But no matter what, she always battled on and looked to the future.

And at times, her cancer all but disappeared.

And at other times, it re-emerged and required treatment.

Through it all, we each worked to keep most of the details from Mom and Dad. They had enough to worry about with their own health issues that Becky never wanted them worrying about her.

In 2019, the year Mom died, her white cells were increasing, indicating the cancer was growing. Dr. Cohn had recommended that we consider an experimental drug called Mekinist, or Elahere, which had been used in the United Kingdom to effectively fight lung cancer. It also had been effective fighting ovarian, but he was not allowed to prescribe it. So, we had to find another method of obtaining it.

There were two problems: The drug was very expensive for a year's supply and would not be covered by insurance. I knew my sister, and there was no way Becky wanted to spend thousands of dollars each month on a drug that may or may not work, so I emailed the manufacturer to see if there was anything they could do.

With my sister, Becky Shank, 2007.

Surprisingly, a representative replied back that the company would ship the drug directly to her at no charge.

The other problem: It had one major side effect—it often weakened the patient's heart over time. Thus, a cardiologist had to be consulted to monitor her heart during treatment.

Within two years of treatment, the drug worked very effectively, reducing her cancer cells drastically until her cardiologist became alarmed. He recommended that she stop taking it or she would suffer heart failure.

Unfortunately, as soon as she stopped the drug, the cancer returned in full force and also spread to her lungs.

Then on the day she was to start chemo yet once again, in early May of 2021, she suffered a mild stroke in the hospital waiting room. She survived emergency surgery that night and then continued her fight. A month later, she was brave enough to travel with her family to Orlando for a planned vacation, even though she felt awful. Just two weeks after they returned home to Tiffin, my brother-in-law called me.

This one was the worst telephone call yet.

"I think you need to fly here now," Jim said. "She will not make it much longer."

The news left me stunned. For some reason, I had figured she still had three or more months left. I grabbed the first flight out of Portland, Maine, where I had accompanied my son Dillon to a summer camp, to Cleveland and then rented a car. But by the time I made it to Tiffin, she had lapsed into unconsciousness.

I never heard her speak again.

Jim, their three children, and my daughter Savanna and I spent the next few days and nights at her side, as she laid on her favorite sofa in their living room. Hospice workers came and went, tending to her needs.

Then she died.

It was early on a Saturday morning, July 3, 2021.

FROM OHIO TO OKINAWA...

She was only 73, the same age Aunty was when she passed away. I thought back to that day Becky called to inform me. And it was painfully ironic, since she and Aunty had been so close.

By the time she took her final breath, it hit me that He had delivered on my prayer from 2005. It had been answered three times over, plus another year. Give her five years, I prayed. We had her in our lives for another 16 years after her initial diagnosis—and I will forever be grateful for that.

But I would have given anything for even more.

I remember at her viewing the day before her funeral, dozens of her friends and colleagues told me their wonderful stories about her. They all adored her just as I had. They all loved her just as I had. She had served on several boards of directors in the healthcare field, as well as many other boards in the community. She was especially gifted at fundraising, organizing and leadership while inspiring others to give back to the community as well.

I always knew my sister was very popular, and successful in her field, but what I learned is that she had touched thousands of lives. She chose a career of helping others, first in hospital ERs, then as a registered nurse in doctors' offices, then by teaching Lamaze courses in her spare time, and finally, as the long-time executive director of the local hospice.

She had spent her lifetime treating the sick, helping deliver new life to the world and comforting the dying. But what she did most of all was make the people she loved, as well as so many others, feel special. She had that gift.

I was so proud of her for all the love she gave to so many others during her 73 years. Just like our mother, she was a giver, not a taker. She was a loving mother and doting grandmother. And she was the best sister a guy could ever ask for.

She was my only sister, my best friend, and frankly, she was the best human being I have ever known.

Her funeral was one of the hardest days of my life. I cried yet again, just as I had when she left for nursing school and the day she was married. This time, however, we all realized she was never coming back.

I had one moment of solace: I was so thankful Mom and Dad were not alive to experience losing their first-born child. Dad had passed away 31 months earlier and Mom only 27 months earlier. Seeing her gone would have been too much for either of them.

Dad had especially doted over Becky throughout her youth. She was so special to him. She was much more than a daughter to him. His eyes always lit up when Becky walked into the room.

And as I write this, she has been gone four years. That is hard to believe. There hasn't been a day in that span when I haven't thought about her, or of the giant hole she left in all of our lives.

Ever since that dreadful day she died, Thanksgivings haven't been the same. Christmases haven't been the same. March 1, her birthday, hasn't been the same. That day is a very tough day for me now, when it used to be one of my favorite days on which I couldn't wait to wake up and call to wish her a happy birthday.

And my life just hasn't been the same—because she's no longer in it.

CHAPTER TWENTY

LEGACIES: WHAT WE LEAVE BEHIND

Now that I have reached 65 years old, as I write these final pages as a tribute to my father, I have gained a new appreciation for his life and what he sacrificed for his country from 1941 to '45.

I have lost all of my aunts and uncles, both parents, one of my two siblings, as well as more than half of my hearing ability when I was hit with a severe case of labyrinthitis on January 3, 2015, when returning home from covering the Sugar Bowl in New Orleans.

Overnight, almost like Dad, I became completely deaf in my right ear, just as he had after the shelling on Okinawa in 1945 when he was only 26 years old. Worse yet, I have suffered from severe and constant tinnitus, a ringing in my useless ear—at least one condition Dad never experienced.

I do believe what we do while on this earth for such a short period of time matters somehow, some way. I try never to lose that perspective of what life, and eventually what death, is all about.

Perhaps we should try to do the best we can each and every day to create some sort of lifelong resume of good deeds done, good friends made, good children raised, and a good legacy to leave behind:

To try your best to make memories, not enemies.

To try to laugh more than you cry.

And to contribute, whatever that contribution may be.

I know my father certainly did.

As did my mother.

And so did my sister Becky.

As I once heard during a eulogy of a friend, the key to this thing they call life just may be to make that long dash, the one which extends from the year you were born to the year you die, count for something—and to fill it with meaningful and significant contributions as well as fond memories.

William E. Snook, 1919 – 2018.

Ferne D. Snook, 1926 – 2019.

Rebecca S. Shank, 1948 – 2021.

Those three dashes were filled with good deeds, good memories and good times. They were filled with fun and laughter and love. They meant something.

As you know, as was the impetus for writing this book, my father was a World War II hero. I do realize he was one of thousands during his time, most likely. But that wasn't his entire identity.

He did more than his part in the Pacific, almost died several times in battle, lost a good portion of his hearing, then came home to meet and marry the love of his life and start a family. He became a wonderful husband, grandfather and great-grandfather in a full century of living.

The woman he married, our mother, was a loving and giving homemaker and a community volunteer at the highest level. They distributed their love to each other, to their three children, seven grandchildren and 11 great-grandchildren in those 73 years together by the time they died within four months of each other.

As I said, my parents' devotion and love never stopped with us, their three children. When they were younger, it extended back to their parents. When they grew older, it extended down their large

FROM OHIO TO OKINAWA . . .

Dad dancing with my daughter Savanna in 1998 on his 79th birthday.

family tree which they created—and which lives on as one of their legacies.

They were wonderful grandparents, to my two children, to Becky's three and Bill's two. Mom and Dad loved them all equally, as they did their great-grandchildren.

One of my favorite singers, Frank Sinatra, once made the lyrics to "My Way" famous: "Regrets I've had a few, but then again, too few to mention . . ."

I do know Dad had a few, too, like not going to Japan at the end of World War II with other members of the 27th Infantry when he was given the choice. It was more than understandable—he wanted to come home after spending four years overseas. He later made it to Normandy on a senior tour to Europe, largely because he had read so much about it after the war, but he always regretted never visiting Saipan in the years after the war as well.

As I said at the beginning, I will always regret not finishing this book in time for him to read it. It was personal to me. It is my father's book, and I owed him the effort to take the time to tell his story as best I could.

I hope I did that.

In talking to him about his service for dozens of hours while he was in his 90s, and then in putting his words into this book, I came to understand him much better—as a child growing up in the Great Depression, as a soldier, as a veteran and then as a father and a grandfather.

Hell, I don't blame him one bit for wanting only two children after he married in 1946. Times still were tough. Dad didn't have a college degree, realizing he would be limited in how much money he made over the course of his working career.

I have a much clearer picture of what he was all about and stood for, although the horror of battle and what he faced her for four years in the 1940s will be nothing anyone in my generation can fully comprehend—having a constant fear that his future even existed beyond the next enemy bullet or artillery shell fired his way. It had to be overwhelming at times during battle.

Through his words and memories, I have tried to envision it, to put myself in his army boots if you will, but I will never fully comprehend what it was like for him, or for Uncle George, and millions of others who served the country in the European or Pacific Theaters.

Someone once said war is hell.

It is, but it's often a necessity to stop evil, which has existed in this world for centuries, or to guarantee freedom.

As far as regrets, I will always be angry at myself for not reaching my sister's bedside in time to talk to her one final time and to tell her how much I loved her, before she passed in 2021.

I learned a valuable lesson from her death, and I do not want to repeat it. I have tried to tell my children that I love them almost every day I am with them. Dad told us that almost every time he saw us in his last decade or more, something I never remember him saying when we were growing up.

It was obvious to all of us he had gained that perspective over time.

I regret getting into a few scrapes along the way. I think I got that from Dad. When he was younger, he didn't walk away from anyone who started trouble, just as he had whipped the kid who had beaten up his younger brother George's butt, yet he had a smile on his face 99 percent of the time. He was never an angry person, looking for a fight.

After one fight, which earned me a three-day suspension in high school, he asked me, "Did you start it?"

Of course, I hadn't. So, he was fine with me defending myself. When it came to fighting, I knew Dad's philosophy well because he once told me: "Don't you ever start one, but don't allow anyone to take your dignity—or attack your family or your country for that matter."

He came out on the winning side of that last one. I know Japan's attack on Pearl Harbor really had lasting effects on my father, as it did with most Americans at the time. Then what happened on September 11, 2001, when he was 82 years old, did as well.

I remember him watching TV coverage of that horrible event, and muttering, "I would go back to war over this one if I was younger . . ."

While writing this book, a recurring theme continued to surface and really make me think—about the many times my father could have died, and yet he lived. Maybe that was divine intervention, so Dad would be there to save John Lewis' life and other lives next to him during the war.

And what if he had been killed in battle?

We three children never would have existed. It was something John Lewis first brought to my mind in 1974—that his return home, marriage and eventual children were made possible by Dad's heroic actions.

And I sometimes think about all the times I could have died, and yet I was spared. My life had been spared often, too, first by a neighbor who pulled me back from being hit by a speeding car around a school bus when I was in grade school, then when I dived out of the way of Dad's work van on a snowy day, later by just a foot or two when two cars crashed into store fronts five years apart in South Florida, just missing me by a few feet, as well as two serious car crashes, and even by a tiny ledge that had no business being there in the first place when I foolishly fell off a cliff in Big Sur, California, in 1995.

I had saved a few lives along the way, such as Mike McCuen's when his hand got caught in a corn-picker when I was 15, and the drowning kid I pulled from the pool while lifeguarding when I was 24.

I always wanted to reconnect with Mike, so in June of 2025 I looked up Mike's address and drove out into the cornfields of

FROM OHIO TO OKINAWA...

Butler, Ohio, to find him. I did not have his phone number, or I would have called ahead. I pulled down a long driveway to see an elderly man was sitting atop a John Deere tractor.

I knew it had to be Mike, who now was 84 years old, but still an active farmer.

"Is your name Mike?" I asked.

"It is," he responded. "Who are you?"

"Well, I last saw you when your hand was stuck in your corn picker," I told him.

His next words touched me deeply.

"JEFF SNOOK!" he exclaimed. "I was just talking about you the other day when I showed somebody where that happened. *You saved my life!*"

Mike then revealed some things I never knew about the incident.

He pulled out a large pocketknife and told me, "I always carry one of these and I was about five minutes from making the decision to cut off my left hand that day . . . I really had no choice . . . then I noticed you playing basketball."

He also told me the first two doctors who examined him in the hospital's emergency room wanted to amputate his hand that night. He talked them out of it.

He then held his hand up and flexed his fingers.

"It was never perfect again, but it was usable," he said.

We talked for more than an hour that afternoon, catching up on our lives.

"Fifty years goes by pretty fast, doesn't it?" he said. "Maybe you were meant to be there playing basketball in order to help me. I am a man of faith and I really believe that . . ."

Was that all meant to be?

I like to think so, because I have that faith, too. I do believe in God, as Dad did. And Mike does. I believe in Heaven. I believe in Jesus Christ, and that God gave Him to us as his only son. And as a Christian, we are taught that if we believe in Him, we too will experience a heavenly afterlife.

It is there, at that mystical, magical place in which I hope to be reunited with those precious family members and good friends who have left before me, those I have seen buried and those I grieved.

I hope to be reunited again with my parents and grandparents. I want to thank my mother for all she did for us, to have a draft beer one more time with my father, maybe listen to yet another of his war stories, and to tightly hug my sister.

As I described earlier, while he was pinned down one night in a foxhole in Okinawa in the final months of the war, Dad had prayed to God to spare him when the shells were falling all around him. It was, as he said, the most frightening part of the war for him.

When he survived to return home, he was very consistent in his faith and made sure we attended church as a family when we were growing up—the same church in which he and Mom were married.

Now that they are all gone, I also often pray for the future of this country, the one Dad fought for and almost gave his life for.

These days, I see national polls revealing the younger generation generally doesn't possess as much pride in the country as we did while growing up. That saddens me. I know it would anger Dad. He just wouldn't understand it. And I can confidently state that I believe a large percentage of those born after 2000 probably never heard much about the Greatest Generation—or what it accomplished in the 1940s to provide the freedom they enjoy in order to voice their opinions today.

I do know that one thing Dad passed on to all of us, or maybe we just picked it up naturally, was an unbridled patriotism and love of our country from our childhoods. Our house always had a U.S. flag flying on the front porch each Memorial Day, July 4, Veteran's Day and Labor Day. Loving the United States and living in a free country was never taken for granted or shunned in the Snook household.

Dad saw to that, just through example.

He never had to tell us to love our country. We just saw him, as well as most of our neighbors, and those in our hometown, display their patriotism, too.

When I drive by my childhood home about once each summer, I can still picture that U.S. flag flying from the front porch.

A few summers ago, I went a step further and pulled into our old driveway. It didn't appear the new owners were home, so I walked across our front yard which I mowed each week during the summers of my childhood. All the pine and oak trees Dad had planted in 1959 are very much alive and are more than 80 to 100 feet tall now. I envisioned where Dad and I played one-on-one on the stone gravel driveway or played catch with a baseball by Mom's vegetable garden. I envisioned the snowman which Becky and I once built in the front yard.

I walked around the house to the backyard where in the summer of 1974 John Lewis happened to tell me the story of Saipan and how Dad had saved his life.

The house's current owners had left an old, rusted table and chairs on that very spot where John had approached me.

The house appeared unkept and past its prime. It had seen its better days.

The great memories of it, however, were still fresh in my mind.

It is where Mom and Dad raised us, their three children, and where we each began our pursuit of happiness.

I guess that is maybe the longest journey of the lives we live. Seeking it, finding it, and then maintaining it.

I know Mom and Dad accomplished it: They were very happy people.

Of my accomplishments, none have made me prouder than being a father—to my daughter, Savanna, and my son, Dillon. They are amazing people, with big hearts, big dreams and bright futures. I love them dearly. And ironically, they share the same age distance, a bit more than 12 years, I had shared with Becky.

My children, Dillon and Savanna Snook, in 2022, at Mirror Lake on The Ohio State University campus.

When I am gone, they will be the most important part of my legacy.

I know that I, my brother Bill and sister Becky were blessed that way: We had wonderful parents, and they always did their best and put our well-being first. They were selfless that way.

As I wrote frequently in this book, I believe we had a saint for a mother. We had an ex-soldier for a father, a man strict in his principles. As I said over and over again, Dad was a man who stood for all the good things in life.

Maybe I am proud of that the most . . .

I was the youngest son of a genuine World War II hero.

And I know my brother Bill—William E. Snook Jr.—feels the same way about our father. He also has a deep faith and has contributed a lot of good to this world during his life as well. He has raised two great children and now has five grandchildren. His legacy is solid and everlasting and he worships Dad's memory and legacy, as I do.

I hope my son and daughter always remember their heritage—and that they are grandchildren of a very courageous man who did his part during the most important war in world history. Fortunately, they got to know him well before he died in 2018.

And that just like me, my brother and my sister, they never would have graced this earth if he had not returned home from the war.

Dad left us all with great memories when he passed.

He also left behind a large case of his many war medals, which my brother has and will be passed down for generations I hope.

The fact is, Dad never realized all the medals he had earned during the war until he was in his 80s—some 60 years after he had come home, when our cousin Dennis Biddinger, a career military man, obtained Dad's service record, went through the appropriate channels and surprised him with the case full of his medals.

The newspaper photo Dad said he regretted posing for.

They hung on the wall of his den for the last 15 or so years of his life. For a December 7 story one year, a reporter for the local newspaper interviewed him about his recollections of what Pearl Harbor looked like when he and the rest of the 27th arrived in Hawaii in early 1942. And he and a photographer talked him into holding his war medals in front of the American flag that flew on the front of their condo.

Dad later told me he regretted posing for that photo, because it came off as he was boasting about medals or honors he was given while other comrades of his never made it home.

"That wasn't very smart of me," he said. "That picture appeared on the front of the newspaper, as if I was showing off my war medals. The photographer saw them hanging on the wall in the den and asked if I would hold them outside so he could take a picture of me and I just followed his instructions, not thinking how it would look."

Personally, I loved the photo. But it went against my father's character and his modesty. I know he was proud of what his Bronze Star for Valor represented, because it came from saving John Lewis' life. And he was proud of his rifleman's sharpshooter badge because he had put so much work on the firing range in Mineral Wells, Texas, in the late fall of 1941. And of course, the victory medal, since he was proud his country won the war.

Today, the flag which draped his casket rests on one of my bookshelves, along with one of his two bronze stars. I also have, as morbid as it sounds, the blood-stained yen he once handed me from the first life he ever took in the war.

I always wondered about that first Japanese soldier whose life was ended from Dad's M-1 on Saipan. What was his name? How old was he? What city in Japan did he come from?

That's one thing about a war like World War II. So many questions will never be answered. The answers will remain unknown forever.

Years, decades and centuries after we are all gone, the events of World War II and its lasting impact on the world still will exist in history books.

We all want to believe that the fight for freedom and righteousness will always thrive in this world. And unfortunately, evil will exist somewhere and have to be confronted or stopped.

My father William E. Snook Sr. sacrificed and contributed to the righteous side, to the winning team when it mattered most in the most important war ever waged. He was courageous and brave most of the time and understandably frightened to die at others. He was normal that way, I am sure.

I know one thing for certain: He was a patriotic American. He served honorably, survived against all odds and then came back to his hometown to live a well-deserved long and good life.

What's more, I was with him to hear his war stories in great detail over the years.

Then I was given the privilege to write about them on these pages.

And that's not a bad legacy to have . . . for all of us.

AFTERWORD

I will always owe John Lewis a debt of gratitude.

From the day when I was 14 and he told me what a hero my father was, I was on a quest to find out more, to pry every detail and story about World War II, and his part in it, from my father's mouth.

Fortunately, he gladly told me over his final years.

And that resulted in this book being written.

John Lewis passed away on December 14, 1994, in Endicott, New York, at the age of 77. His wife Cora died less than two years later, March 28, 1996, at the age of 69.

They left behind four adult children, eight grandchildren and many great-grandchildren.

As John once told me, none of those people would have been possible without my father there to save him when he became seriously wounded on Saipan in June of 1944.

I recently located his oldest son, Greg Lewis, and we have since spoken often over the telephone. I told him of our fathers' story of the fox hole they shared in Saipan, with his dad critically wounded, and the aftermath of it. I also recounted to him what his father told me in our backyard in 1974 and how emotional he was that day. And also, how he had reacted when he saw that Japanese knee mortar in our basement.

It was the first time he had heard any of the details of his father almost dying in Saipan.

"Dad just didn't talk about the war much," Greg told me. "I knew he was wounded and he had a Purple Heart, but I always thought it was from sniper fire. We all saw the scar on his body, but I never knew exactly what happened to him. I am so glad you have told me all of this.

"I had heard your last name before . . . Dad called your father 'Snooky.' So, I guess we can say that we each had great fathers."

Yes, we can certainly say that.

They grew up two years and about 425 miles apart, not knowing each other until meeting in Mineral Wells, Texas, shortly before Pearl Harbor was attacked.

They bonded forever three years later in a fox hole under the most terrifying of situations, in the heat of battle, under attack.

And they each escaped from that fox hole, eventually made it back home, linked forever by what happened there—and reunited decades later to celebrate their survival.

Greg Lewis, along with his siblings, and I along with mine, are each very proud to claim we are the children of genuine World War II heroes.

Today, they are gone, but they will never be forgotten by the extended families they left behind—and their legacies will live forever.

■ JEFF SNOOK

FROM OHIO TO OKINAWA...

John G. Lewis, on Saipan, June, 1944, just days before he was critically wounded, an event which created a lifelong bond between two great men of the U.S. Army's 27th Infantry Division.

www.ingramcontent.com/pod-product-compliance
Lightning Source LLC
Chambersburg PA
CBHW070532160426
43199CB00014B/2247